FLAMINGOS IN THE DESERT

Exploring Almería

Kevin Borman

Kevin Borman

Published in 2014 by FeedARead.com Publishing

A CIP catalogue record for this title is available from the British
Library.

Contents

Introduction

Andalucía occupies the whole of southern Spain and is made up of eight provinces: Huelva, Cádiz, Sevilla, Córdoba, Málaga, Jaén, Granada and Almería. Of these, Almería is the most easterly and one of the least known. This far south-eastern wedge of Andalucía is something of a hidden corner. It's well-enough known by some of those who live here but I think it's nowhere near as celebrated as it deserves to be.

Almería province covers just 8,774 square kilometres, well under a tenth of Andalucía's area, and has never been heavily populated. Even by 2008 the province had only 667,000 people, of whom 187,000 lived in Almería city, leaving fewer than half a million people scattered over the rest of the province.

By Spanish standards the Almerían coast is quite undeveloped and this is one of its greatest attractions. One reason for the lack of development is the protection afforded to parts of the area, most notably the Cabo de Gata-Níjar Natural Park. Michael Jacobs, in his book *Andalucía,* refers to 'the lunar-like volcanic peninsula of the Cabo de Gata' as 'one of the least spoilt and most haunting sections of Spain's southern coast.'

There are several conventional guidebooks to Almería, particularly to the Cabo de Gata-Níjar Natural Park and Almería city, and there are plenty of 'we came to Spain and these are the amusing things that happened to us' narratives. I appreciate both genres and I include occasional aspects of both, but I am trying to do something different here: to get under the skin of Almería province for an English-speaking readership.

There is no single chronological narrative running through the book, although there are elements of that, for instance in the early chapters that describe a walk along the Cabo de Gata coast. I have played around for ages, sequencing the chapters to see how they might work best but to compartmentalise things is not what I want and is impossible anyway, so in the coastal chapters there are films, in the film chapter there are landscapes, in the landscape chapters there is history and so on.

You could read this book right through in one go but equally well you can simply dip in to see how land and people meet here. Social history and personal reflections mingle with a fair bit about birds and plants, some art, films, meteorology, musings about maps, suggestions for walks both short and long, and even the odd recipe. I hope the tone is conversational and accessible. That said, I have deliberately included a lot of factual material, much of which comes from Spanish sources that are not otherwise accessible in English: see the acknowledgements and bibliography sections for more detail. If you find some parts of the book a little heavy on the history or the geology, skip these and move on; you'll soon find something lighter.

H V Morton, in the preface to his book *In Search of England*, wrote something that mirrors my intention, although in the following quotation I have replaced his 'England' with 'Almería': 'I have gone round Almería like a magpie picking up any bright thing that pleased me. A glance at the contents will expose me to the scorn of local patriots who will see, with incredulous rage, that on many an occasion I have passed silently through their favourite village. That is inevitable. I followed the roads; some of them led me aright and some astray. The first were the most useful; the others were the most interesting.' Consequently, the residents of certain places will find here less than they might expect about their towns. Much of the book concerns itself with the rural rather than the urban. That is where my leads have taken me and where I think many of the most intriguing aspects of Almería are to be found.

I live in the municipality of Sorbas, about 15 kilometres distant from the town. W G Hoskins, one of the great interpreters of landscape, said: 'You should walk around and describe the boundaries... of whatever is your chosen territory... at least you will get the feeling of it in a way that nothing else can give.' The English nature writer Richard Mabey calls a parish, which we might equate to a '*municipio*' here in Spain, 'that 'indefinable' territory to which we feel we belong, which we have the measure of'. And so, some of what follows focuses on the Sorbas area, whilst feeling free at times to stray way beyond it.

A number of chapters are based on specific geographical areas or features. Where appropriate I have indicated which Spanish maps link to these chapters. Most of the maps in question, the closest approximation to the OS maps with which British readers may be familiar, are from the series called Mapa Topográfico Nacional de

España, at a scale of 1:25,000. For more detail see the chapter 'Exploring the maps'.

Spain is a delightful country but it has its frustrations, one of which concerns road numbers. Even quite minor roads tend to have numbers but the ones indicated on the road signs themselves don't always match the ones given on maps and road atlases. To an extent this is understandable as road systems evolve, but it can be a cause of confusion for those of us trying to navigate around the place. As far as possible in the text I have given road numbers as they appear on the signs by the roads themselves but do bear in mind that these don't always match the maps.

The economics of book publishing mean it is unrealistic to include photos in this book. However, I encourage readers to email me at kevindborman@googlemail.com and I will reply with a link to a web album where I have put many photos relating to *Flamingos In The Desert*.

And one final point. Spain is less 'health and safety' conscious than some other countries, certainly than the UK. Ruins, precipitous drops, old mines: they are not uncommon and on occasion this book explores such places. They should be treated with respect and a large dose of common sense. Always take care if you go there, accept that you need to look out for yourself, and other members of your party, if appropriate, and have a fully-charged mobile phone with you in case of emergency (when the number to ring would be 112). That said, there is much to see so don't be put off.

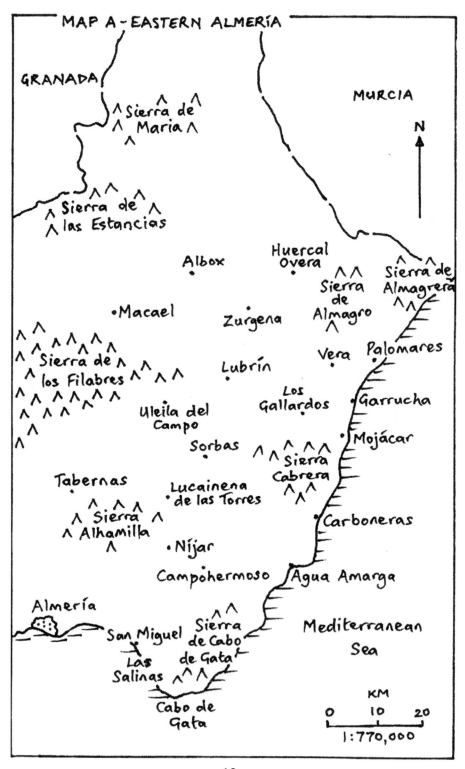

MAP A - EASTERN ALMERÍA

GRANADA

MURCIA

N

Sierra de María

Sierra de las Estancias

Albox

Huercal Overa

Sierra de Almagrera

Sierra de Almagro

Macael

Zurgena

Vera

Palomares

Sierra de los Filabres

Lubrín

Los Gallardos

Garrucha

Uleila del Campo

Sorbas

Mojácar

Sierra Cabrera

Tabernas

Lucainena de las Torres

Carboneras

Sierra Alhamilla

Níjar

Campohermoso

Agua Amarga

Almería

San Miguel

Sierra de Cabo de Gata

Mediterranean Sea

Las Salinas

KM

0   10   20

1:770,000

Cabo de Gata

1. Coasting: Flatlands

'Caminar es atesorar'
('To walk is to gather treasure': a Spanish proverb)

The Virgin from the sea

It seems appropriate to start with a walk to get some fresh air, and where better than a natural park and the coast, all in one? A long-distance walking route, the GR 92, follows the coastline of Almería province, though much of it can be explored by car too. The notion of walking not the entire Almerían coastline but the coast of the Parque Natural (Natural Park) Cabo de Gata-Níjar in a single journey had been intermittently occupying my thoughts for some time. Let me say now though, that if a four-day, seven-chapter walk along the coast is not how you wish to start this book, please jump ahead to Chapter 8 and come back to the coast later.

The Natural Park's western boundary lies immediately south-east of Retamar, a large modern urbanisation not far from Almería city. Retamar's redeeming features, other than its beach, are not immediately apparent. Apologies to any residents who like its ambience and realise that its attractions are too subtle for me to appreciate.

So it was that I began my walk at the edge of Retamar. In the great scheme of things the current line of the coast here is recent. In the blink of a geological eye, five million years ago, the coastline was much further inland. Retamar and the entire city of Almería and its airport would have been many fathoms deep at that time.

The first fifteen kilometres of the walk from Retamar follow the beach until it finally reaches the cliffs where the Sierra de Cabo de Gata tilts down to the sea. Although this is essentially a single beach it has seven different names. In those fifteen kilometres, although it's all flat, there is an astonishing range of natural features. To the right lies the Golfo de Almería and, to the left, what might be considered unspoilt land in a low-key kind of way. The map which best shows all of this is the finely-detailed 1:45,000 scale map produced by the Junta de Andalucía's *Consejería de Medio Ambiente* (Ministry of the Environment). Its symbols show *matorral* (scrubland), *arenales* (sandy areas), *dunas* (dunes) and much more but it is only on the ground that the sheer variety of detail, the natural background and the human overlay, become apparent. Another very good map of the same area is the 1:50,000 scale Cabo de Gata-Níjar Parque Natural map from Editorial Alpina. Having said that, it is perfectly possible to explore the coast without a map; simply set off and keep the sea on your right, assuming you are heading the same way as I was. But for me at least, having a map enhances the experience.

Finally, late one January, after a two-day postponement caused by torrential rain, I shoulder a pack weighing ten kilos on a bright Thursday morning and set off from where a few small boats lie upturned on the dark sand of Retamar's seafront to walk towards the sun.

This is not wilderness. A broad unsurfaced track lies more or less parallel to the shore. It is bounded by low wooden barriers, beyond which notices advise *'Prohibida la circulación de vehiculos a motor no autorizadas'* in a bid to protect the steppe dunes, a mixture of gravel, pebbles and sand broken by low grey and brown shrubs. A pale yellow hermitage looms ahead, circular and with eight buttress-like pillars and a white cupola. This building was made in 1951 to house a statue during the annual *romería* (pilgrimage) of Torregarcía on the first Sunday of each January. Nearby, a rectangular cream building with six portholes in one side and a hole smashed gratuitously through the wall at one end proves to be a toilet block, now in need of some attention. Another building, bigger and in better repair, has the look of an accommodation block about it, a base used perhaps by the Royal and Military Brotherhood of Our Lady of the Sea, the organisation behind the pilgrimage.

In December 1502, Andrés Jaén, who was a tower keeper and fisherman, discovered a statue washed up on the beach. Carved from walnut wood in Catalan gothic style, it was apparently from a shipwreck. At some point the image was taken to the church of Santo Domingo in Almería and from 1806, named *Virgen del Mar* (Our Lady of the Sea), it became the patron saint of the city. The January *romería*, involving thousands of Almeríans who arrive in the early hours of the pilgrimage day, marks the culmination of the Christmas celebrations and is a mixture of devotion and fun. A place deserted for most of the year becomes, after a solemn mass for the pilgrims, a scene of dancing and singing and the sharing of food and drink until, at dusk, the statue of the *Virgen del Mar* is taken back to Santo

Domingo in Almería city centre. The crowds trail away; the surroundings of the hermitage fall quiet for another year. The broad track leading here with its huge parking areas looks strangely out of scale once the crowds have gone.

Close to the domed hermitage but far older is Torre García, one of a network of centuries-old watchtowers. A precise date of origin seems not to have been recorded but there is mention of Torre García at the beginning of the sixteenth century, shortly after the expulsion of the Moors. When danger from the sea threatened: Berbers like Al-Dogaili and El Joraique, pirates such as Gálvez and later, warships from England and the Netherlands, the watchers on the towers signalled to each other with fire and smoke. A chain of ten of these towers protected the coast of what is now the Natural Park.

The towers were built of masonry to a standard cylindrical design, slightly tapered, with the lower section solid and the only access an entrance two-thirds of the way up, a distance I estimated at seven metres. An iron ladder, fixed to the wall and protected by a cylindrical iron cage, appears to be the most recent form of access but even this only starts three metres above the ground. The tower-keepers were clearly drawn from the ranks of champion high-jumpers. Okay, so maybe they brought their own ladder and pulled it up into the fort behind them.

The zenith of the watchtowers' significance came in the middle of the 18th century, when Carlos III enacted the Regulations for the Defence of the Coast. Torre García was rebuilt at this time. In the late 1980s it was restored but it still retains a plaque from the 1940s relating the details of the finding of the *Virgen del Mar* statue. Old towers like this are still a living part of the local ecosystem: one spring day we watched a pair of hoopoes with a nest high in a chink in the tower's stonework, making forays like huge pink, white and black butterflies to find food for their young.

The garrisons assigned to these towers, presumably just a couple of men, must have had a grim and tedious existence, basic in the extreme. The entrance gave on to the main room, three metres in diameter at most and with a couple of slit windows. Above that was the signal platform with a low parapet. Below the main room was a small storeroom, presumably accessed via a hatch in the main room's floor as there would be no other way of getting into it. Below the storeroom the whole bottom third of the tower was, and is, solid masonry. What did the lookouts do all day? One at least peered out to sea, no doubt, scanning for corsairs. And maybe the other did the same on the night shift.

A hundred metres away from the tower, and less than that from the waves, a series of masonry walls and enclosures no more than thigh-high marks the site of a Roman fish-salting factory dating from the first century AD. The ancient Romans were particularly partial to *garum*, a sauce made from pickled fish produced in just such a place as this. A crude and crumbling cement capping on some of the walls looks like a ham-fisted twentieth century attempt at preservation, and the chain-link fence surrounding the site, whilst its existence is understandable, similarly does nothing to enhance the evocative nature of the site. The fence at least provides a handy perch for a black redstart as I stand making my notes.

Ancient beaches

Various sources, including the 1:45,000 map, show the GR 92 along here, stretching from one end of the Natural Park, via the coast as far as is practicable, to the other. Overlaid on this concept, or possibly separate, but certainly with no reference to the GR 92, are various shorter *senderos* (footpaths) that use the same route. Notice boards announce these *senderos,* such as the one I come to now: 'Sendero El Pocico – Las Marinas. 6.5 km. 3 horas. Dificultad: Baja'. Low difficulty, yes, well of course it would be; it's a flat track just in from the beach. But the information boards, with a map and a house-style, make no connection to the long-distance walk of which the *senderos* form a part. Of course, it wouldn't be the first time that different tiers of government laid themselves open to the charge of a lack of joined-up thinking.

The *sendero* soon dips into the Rambla de las Amoladeras (which might mean Riverbed of the Grindstones? I'm not sure and I'm happy to be corrected), a broad dry riverbed. When I crossed it a couple of days after phenomenally heavy rains, it had standing pools among its grey sand and a fringing scrag of debris: smashed *caña* (giant cane), plastic bottles, nondescript vegetable mulch and broken branches that proved witness to the height of the recent floodwaters.

A short way inland along the *rambla* a slender stone tower marks the site of a well that is also thought to date from the Roman period.

A *rambla* is a normally dry watercourse. In the south-east of Spain they are everywhere. Roads cross them, and in many places they borrow them for a while and run, unsurfaced of course, along them. If the access to your house involves a *rambla*, you have to accept that for those few days each year when the heavens open, the riverbed will fill and you won't be able to leave the house. Soon after we bought a house here, I read a newspaper piece about a German resident who was caught in his car in a *rambla* after heavy rain. Unaware of the danger until it was too late, he and the car were washed out to sea. The flash-flood came howling down the riverbed and away he went. Sad but true. This is a semi-desert; when it rains, it sometimes simply drizzles but equally often it hammers down and, anytime from a few minutes to a day later, the *ramblas* are suddenly and dangerously bank-full.

You wouldn't realise, unless you were an observant geologist, that the Rambla de las Amoladeras area has classic fossil Quaternary beaches. During the Quaternary period, which began 1.8 million years ago, repeated climatic changes meant that the world's ice-caps grew and shrank, taking up and then releasing sea water so that the sea level varied vertically by as much as 130 metres. Uranium-thorium dating has given ages of 250,000 years, 180,000 years, 128,000 years and 95,000 years to the four successive beach levels at the mouth of the Rambla de las Amoladeras. The latter three beach levels contain fossils of Strombus bubionus, a marine mollusc that still lives along modern tropical coasts such as the Gulf of Guinea, indicating that tropical conditions reached as far north as Cabo de Gata at times.

Steppe specialists

Beyond Las Amoladeras a fuzz of spiky poles fringed with short branches appears inland. These are the flower spikes of sisal, a type of agave, that was planted and exploited in the past to provide fibres for ropes and sacking and that took a great liking to the conditions when introduced to the area.

The track becomes stony, still heading relentlessly for the Cabo de Gata range where the mountains fall sharply into the sea, a little less silver now the sun has shifted southwards. The walking is easy. Somewhere a wader I can't identify pipes a mournful note. An old concrete bunker looms quietly from the sand, almost hidden by wiry grasses. Larks preen and pose, apparently untroubled by my presence.

The vegetation of these coastal steppes bears investigation. For example, there's an initially undistinguished-looking scrubby plant with whitish zigzag branches and a thorn at each change of angle on the branch. As far as I can work out, this is Ziziphus lotus, a shrub with the English name jujube. In Castillian Spanish it's called *azufaifo*. Before we knew its correct name we called it the barbed-wire plant. Its particular adaptation to allow it to survive in arid conditions is long roots that can find water deep in the ground.

Other plants are ephemeral. The sea daffodil appears after rains, producing large, scented white flowers, then disappears in times of drought. Mastic, an evergreen shrub or small tree, favours a squat form and leathery leaves to minimise evaporation. It's found widely, it has an unpleasant aroma and its bark is the source of mastic gum or resin. Another adaptation, employed by purple phlomis, which has attractive pale pastel flowers, is to have leaves covered with hairs to limit water loss. Its new stems are covered with loose white fluff for the same purpose.

Inland from here the steppe landscape stretches past the Las Amoladeras Visitor Centre up to the *aerofaro*, literally a lighthouse for aircraft, which perches on a low hill just 70 metres above sea level. Specialised birds of this steppe environment can be seen, though usually only by the fortunate. Perhaps the greatest prize for birdwatchers here, and I've yet to see one, is Dupont's lark. The book *Bird* says of it: '...a strange and elusive lark, found in quite isolated areas of Spain and North Africa, mostly in dry places that are searingly hot in summer.' *Birds of Iberia* adds: 'The Dupont's lark is possibly the most overlooked of all Spanish breeding birds,' and goes on to say: 'It is an extremely difficult bird to observe, with disturbed birds running away from the intruder to disappear in cover.'

In *Espacios Natural Almerienses*, José Manuel Miralles, as part of a narrative of a walk through the steppe area, has this: 'At a certain point we hear a bird that we hadn't detected during the morning. We look around and there's no trace. One moment, there, there! It was only a second but it was enough for us: Dupont's larks, the small jewels of the thyme steppes, easier to hear than see and, because of their rarity, we decide to study them next year. *(My translation)'* Jesús Contreras, who earns his living by showing people the wildlife of Almería province, told me that even he has never seen a Dupont's lark, though he knows where to hear them singing for a minute or two at a time between seven and eight in the morning during March.

Other specialist steppe birds are black-bellied sandgrouse (I've never seen one here), little bustard (nor one of these) and stone curlew (yes, these I have seen). The stone curlew, evocatively called *alcaraván* in Spanish, is another quirky avian character. One of its old English country names is goggle-eyed plover, referring to its large yellow eyes. Although a large bird, its cryptic colouring proves to be superb camouflage in its usual standing or crouching positions on the ground, and only when it flies, with large areas of black and white revealed on its wings, does it become strikingly obvious.

Lawrence of Arabia

By now, the Playa de Torre García lies behind. Its continuation ahead is the Playa de las Amoladeras. This stretch of beach was the location for the shooting of the most spectacular scene in David Lean's classic film *Lawrence of Arabia*. 2.5 kilometres of rail track was laid, 60 labourers having prepared the ground beforehand, for the scene in which a train of eleven carriages and a locomotive is blown up. Two complete trains no longer required by Renfe, the Spanish national rail company, were acquired by the producer. The engine driver got the locomotive up to full speed and jumped clear seconds before the explosion.

In Almería province, as well as the filming along the Cabo de Gata beaches, scenes were shot in the Parque de José Antonio (now called the Parque Nicolas Salmerón) in Almería city, in Carboneras and in the Rambla El Cautivo near Tabernas. Parts of the film were also shot in Jordan, Morocco and at St Paul's Cathedral in London, where T.E. Lawrence is buried. Filming of the Spanish parts of the production took place between 21st March and 7th July 1962, with a budget of 40 million pesetas. The finished film won seven Oscars, including Best Film and Best Director.

Three kilometres on from the Rambla de las Amoladeras and just before the Rambla Morales, pedestrians can go through a gap in the seaward side of the wooden barrier. This area is known as the Dunas de Las Marinas-Mazarrulleque. The dunes in question are semi-circular barchans or half-moons (spelled either barchan or barkhan, take your pick: the word is from Turkestan). Wind, from the west in this case, picks up beach sand and carries particles inland just above ground level. When they hit an obstruction such as a plant the particles' journey is halted and a dune begins to form. If the obstacle is high and the sand does not overwhelm it, the dune is fixed. But if the dune overtops the obstruction, the end result is a mobile dune.

The barchans at Las Marinas are arranged transversely to the wind direction. At either side the dune is elongated into 'horns', which are created because the wind speed is greater at the sides than in the centre of the dune, hence the half-moon shape. Sand particles are blown by the wind up the convex windward side of the dune and over the top to roll down the concave leeward side. In this way the barchan gradually migrates inland. As the migration continues, continuous dune-lines called parabolic dunes form. Such dunes began to bury the small settlement of La Mazarrulleque, one and a half kilometres inland. Then in the 1970s and 1980s, before the declaration of the natural park, which happened in 1987, the four major lines of existing dunes were destroyed by the extraction of sand which was used for soil improvement in the burgeoning intensive cultivation of early vegetables. A photo on an information board at Las Marinas records the outcome of this environmental vandalism with the poignant caption: '*Antiguos cordones de dunas parabólicas (1984), hoy desaparecidos.*'.... 'Old lines of parabolic dunes (1984), now gone'.

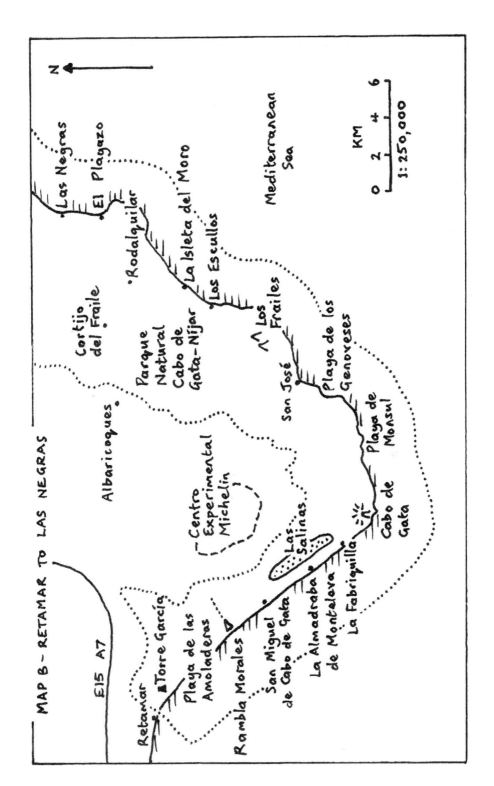

21

2. Coasting: Turtles and salt

'But the farther I walk and sleep beneath the stars the quicker I'm coming to the conclusion that a man who doesn't spend enough time thinking about how precious and intricate life is has no wisdom at all.'
(Jerry Ellis)

Reintroducing loggerheads

The Playa de las Amoladeras is also playing its part in a more modern drama. In July 2010, 80 one-year old loggerhead turtles were released there as part of an ongoing reintroduction programme. When fully adult, loggerheads are the largest of all hard-shelled turtles. They can typically be up to a metre long, their carapace having a central ridge with five plates down either side. Their heads have a segmented, rather giraffe-like pattern. They are impressive creatures although rarely seen because, apart from when they are breeding, they remain out at sea.

Eggs for the current project come from Cabo Verde (the Cape Verde Islands, in the Atlantic Ocean off the coast of Senegal). This initiative began in 2004, with the first eggs coming from Cabo Verde in 2006. Between then and 2010 approximately 1,300 eggs were transferred to Andalucía, of which 700 went to beaches in the Parque Natural Cabo de Gata-Níjar and 600 to the incubators at the Estación Biológica de Doñana. Additionally, many turtles born during the project so far have been liberated on various beaches along the Mediterranean coast. When eggs hatch on the beaches the young are collected and taken to the Centro de Gestión del Medio Marino de Algeciras, where they are nurtured before being returned at the age of one year to the beaches where they were born. Hatchlings are only 4.6 cm long at birth and weigh only 20 grams, so they are very vulnerable to predators such as gulls. By protecting the hatchlings for a year they can reach an adequate size and their shells can harden, giving them a higher survival rate in the face of threats from their natural predators.

The long-term objective is that, when they reach sexual maturity at 15-20 years of age, the turtles will return to breed on the beaches where they were born and re-establish a stable population. It will only be possible to assess the success of this project many years into the future. At that stage, if all goes well, females will come up the beaches under cover of darkness to scrape a pit in the sand and lay clutches of, on average, 110 eggs.

The reintroduction project is hedged with uncertainties, however. Rising temperatures, both in the air and in the sea, may affect the outcome. Rising sea levels may threaten breeding beaches. And crucially, the sex of loggerhead turtles depends on the incubation temperature of the eggs which is obviously dependent on the temperature of the surrounding sand. Those kept at a constant 28°C become male; at 32°C they become female, and only at a constant 30°C will there be an equal balance between the sexes.

During 2010 alone a total of 386 young turtles were planned for release at Playa de las Amoladeras and a further 500 eggs were coming from Cabo Verde, 400 to the Parque Natural Cabo de Gata-Níjar and 100 to the Estación Biológica de Doñana. In the summer of 2011 a further 273 small turtles were released. So we may hopefully be in the early stages of having these mysterious creatures using the Cabo de Gata beaches to rebuild a sustainable population.

Among the prey of loggerhead turtles, especially when they are migrating in the open sea, are jellyfish. On 30th April 2009 the *Diario de Almería* newspaper reported an increased incidence over recent years of Portuguese men-of-war, the sting of which can be fatal and is certainly far worse than that of the jellyfish normally found along the coast. The increased numbers are thought to be a result of the changing climate, with the sea water gradually warming. A further factor which has been suggested is that the drier climate is allowing the waters of the open sea to mix more easily with the waters closer to the coast, presumably because less fresh water is being discharged from the rivers. So, one eventual by-product of the turtle reintroduction scheme, from the perspective of bathers on the Cabo de Gata beaches, may be a reduced risk of jellyfish stings.

The white-headed duck saga

As we follow the route along the coast, the map shows the thin blue line that runs along the Rambla Morales widening out into a funnel-shaped lake prominently labelled El Charco (The Pool), right behind the beach. Troy and I had first come across this site by chance, strolling to it one evening when we were staying at Camping Cabo de Gata a few years ago and finding a gem of a wetland with tall reeds, fringing shrubs, open water and muddy edges; a rich mosaic of bird habitats.

The open water that evening, edged with thick vegetation, held a good number of white-headed ducks. We've been back many times since and almost always seen this quirky species. A Spanish ornithologist familiar with the site has told me that white-headed ducks like eutrophic conditions, that is, when the water is over-rich in organic nutrients. Such conditions occur at Rambla Morales when there is a lot of treated waste water being pumped there from the nearby village, San Miguel de Cabo de Gata. This happens in summer, for example, when there are more people staying on the coast and therefore more waste water. In contrast, after heavy rain the water in The Pool is 'cleaner' and there is less chance of seeing the ducks.

The species is distinctive, with a sky-blue bulging bill, white head, brown body and erect black tail, and has become a symbol of Spanish conservation success. In 1977 the population of white-headed ducks in Spain, following hunting pressure and habitat loss, was down to 22 individuals. And then in the late 1980s, the similar-looking ruddy duck, a close relative of the white-headed duck, began to appear in Spain and consort with the white-headeds. The source of these ruddy ducks was their rapidly and assertively expanding population in the UK. By 1991 the aggressive ruddy duck males in Spain, characterised as 'feathered lager louts', were breeding with female white-headed ducks and producing hybrid young, raising concerns that the pure white-headeds would be genetically swamped and bred out of existence. The image of ruddy ducks was probably not helped by the facts that their penis is half as long as their body and that they abandon their partner after mating.

In an attempt to protect the pure white-headed ducks, by the turn of the century Spanish environmentalists had shot 98 ruddy ducks and 58 hybrids. The focus of the issue meanwhile moved to the UK, the source of the invasive ruddy ducks. (Actually, the full story is even more convoluted, as the ruddy duck had only been introduced to England in 1948 by Sir Peter Scott, when three pairs were taken from North America to the Wildfowl and Wetlands Trust at Slimbridge, from where escapes soon occurred and a feral population established itself. By the year 2000 the UK population was about 5,000 birds.)

Initially, £800,000 was spent in the UK on assessing the feasibility of eliminating the entire British ruddy duck population. Under a pilot scheme a total of 2,500 ruddy ducks had been shot by 2002. The issue was the source of intense controversy, with discussion of the ethics of introducing alien species and of 'ethnic cleansing', despite which the go-ahead was given in July 2002 for the culling of all UK ruddy ducks. By early 2011, 6,200 ruddy ducks had been killed in the UK at a cost of £4.6million, some £740 per bird. Only 120 remained and the policy was to pursue them until they had all been culled. Opponents of the scheme, such as Lee Evans, founder of the British Birding Association, continue to suggest that this expensive scheme is pointless, given that other European countries, including France, are not culling their ruddy duck populations.

Now, although its global status remains a matter of concern, the Spanish population of the white-headed species exceeds 4,500; a 'good news' story, unless you happen to be a British ruddy duck. So at the moment, white-headed ducks, and many other species, can almost always be seen floating in and out of the reeds that fringe the *charco* at the Rambla Morales.

One October afternoon of heavy grey skies after a spell of high winds and intensive rain, we had walked again from the neglected, littered area beyond the campsite, out along the sandy track leading to the south-east side of the pool. It became apparent that the water level was way down. There were very few birds. Even before we had reached the beach we could see that the usual natural sand barrier that maintains a good depth of water in the pool had been breached, allowing most of the contents of the pool to drain out to sea. Temporarily deserted by my geographical understanding, I was distraught at the fate of this prime wildlife site and immediately thought of going to the natural park authorities to find out whether they knew of the disaster and to see if they intended to do something about it.

Walking back, we met a Spanish guy emerging from the reeds with a camera. I expressed my shock at the breach of the beach-bar. He said, equally, words to the effect that in four months or so it would have re-formed and the water level in the *charco* would gradually be replenished by rain. Only then did it hit me that this is a natural cycle. Geomorphologists call the occasional times when the beach is breached a 'high energy phase' and the much longer periods when the pool is sealed off at its seaward end a 'low energy phase', the 'energy' referring to the erosive potential of the water coming down the *rambla*. As in most specialised disciplines, the jargon is a formalised way of saying something very simple. It could just as well be 'lots of water with a huge amount of power' and 'not much water with almost no power' but that doesn't sound very scientific.

On my January backpacking trip, the pool is still emptying out to sea and I have to dance through the outflow to try to keep my feet dry. (Six weeks later, in mid-March, I was back again at the Rambla Morales, the breach had healed and the water in the pool was higher than I'd ever seen it.)

Along the beach beyond the Rambla Morales my eyes are glued to the tideline of what is now the Playa del Charco, its name having changed again, where gentle waves wash vibrant colour into the pebbles. And what colours: yellow, red, ochre, grey, white, everything, it seems, except green. Cockleshells are here in bewildering array: small and orange, large and purple, ridged, banded, wonderful. A village is visible ahead as the sand saps strength from my feet and a buoyant tern squeals by, looking down from its flight-path ten metres above the shallows. An onshore breeze springs up as the land heats up and the air above it rises, leaving a void to be filled by air sucked in from the cooler sea.

San Miguel de Cabo de Gata is a substantial low-rise village, quiet for most of the year but always able to offer sustenance to the traveller; in my case a delicious €10 *menu del día* (a set menu of the day) at a bar on the seafront. As I eat, two cutters with red superstructures, which I imagine to be coastguard vessels, patrol the Bay of Almería. Expecting a night where I will be fending for myself, I stock up with bread, cheese, *chorizo* and juice from a nearby shop and continue south-east.

At the edge of the village the remaining fishing fleet is pulled up above the high-tide line. Three fishermen are busying themselves among the ropes, buoys, small boats, floats, timber, nets, winches and huts. Adjacent is a tower within a square walled enclosure. A sign announces 'Guardia Civil' and 'Torreon de Cabo de Gata'. The former legend is outdated as the *guardia civil* now have a modern base in the village. The tower itself was built in 1756, during the reign of

Ferdinand VI. It was defended by two small calibre cannons and had quarters for troops, a powder store and a stone staircase leading to a drawbridge. The surrounding adobe wall was put up only during the 1980s. As at so many other places along this coast, the sense of ongoing history and the evidence of interaction between inhabitants and place such as the fishermen and the watchtower enriches the experience of passing through.

Salt and flamingos

A fine though exposed beach stretches ahead for several kilometres, the Playa de Cabo de Gata. During *Semana Santa*, Easter week, and through high summer, this is busy, with cars parked all along the verges. For the rest of the year it's pretty much deserted. On the seaward side of the road low vegetated dunes are protected by squat wooden railings whilst inland, beyond more scrubby dunes, lie the salt pans, Las Salinas.

Five metres ahead of me the sun appears to be shining through the short red beaks of a couple of small birds on the wooden rails. Only one small bird found in this area has a red beak, the trumpeter finch, another local speciality. The trumpeter finch is a nondescript LBJ, a 'little brown job', nothing to write home about but for the fact that it is a bird of the Middle Eastern and African deserts, its only European toehold being in the south-east corner of Spain, where a population estimated at about two hundred pairs has found a niche among the dry gullies, rocky slopes and arid steppes.

Delighted by this chance encounter, only my second sighting ever of trumpeter finches, albeit a fleeting one, I cross to the sandy path leading to the first hide overlooking the salt lagoons. As sometimes happens, further avian riches follow in quick succession: a large bird with a striking wing pattern flying west, a stone curlew; then something with a long black and white tail and a rosy wash on its front, a southern grey shrike; and a small bird with a fading orange breast and a suggestion of a paler collar, a female stonechat.

All this even before I reach the hide from where distorted pink shapes resolve themselves into sleeping flamingos balanced on one leg. These are greater flamingos, with a length up to 1.4 metres and a wingspan up to 1.7 metres. A wedge of vivid red sticking out behind each bird proves to be the raised leg, mostly hidden, as are the heads,

27

with the sinuous necks twisted back as the birds rest. A few are awake and actively feeding, heads in the water, swaying from side to side. They draw their tongue back to suck in the water, which contains minute invertebrates such as brine shrimps (Artemia salina), midge larvae (Chironomidae) and various species of Hydrobia, a very small crustacean. The tongue is then flicked forwards like a piston to expel the water and as this happens the tiny organisms are filtered out by a mesh of fringed plates in the birds' mandibles. From somewhere across the shallows come their calls, a cacophonous, clanging, honking racket. The biggest treat is to see them in flight, necks straight out, legs trailing elegantly behind and, in the breeding season, the wings a blaze of black and crimson.

The modern commercial saltpans between San Miguel de Cabo de Gata and La Fabriquilla are based on a natural *albufera*, a backshore lagoon system; in other words, a series of shallow pools behind a beach barrier. Material is washed down to the coast via the *ramblas* that I've crossed earlier in the day and is moved, in this case south-east, by the process of longshore drift. It is this material that maintains the beach.

Longshore drift is a common and simple process. Waves come in at an angle to the beach, driven by the prevailing wind. As they do so, the swash, the dying water of the wave, washes sand grains up the beach at that same angle. As the water loses impetus, it returns down the beach as backwash, dragging some of the sand grains with it. This second movement is perpendicular to the slope of the beach. Thus, an indeterminate number of sand grains will have moved a small distance along the beach. This process is repeated endlessly, moving trillions of sand grains a centimetre or two at a time, many times an hour, with each wave, day and night, month after month. This is the process that mends the occasional breaches affecting the Los Morales pool, as described earlier.

Evaporation by sun and wind brings about the natural concentration of the salts in the shallow lagoons behind the beach. The Phoenicians, in the first millennium BC, were reputedly the first to appreciate the potential of this situation and began to extract the salt. For many centuries though, the saltworks were used only intermittently. In 1762 the area was described as 'an impassable swamp'. However, by the early 20th century things had been put on a commercial footing. Since 1925 the salt pans have been operated by Unión Salinera de España, S.A. This company still produces common salt for industrial purposes, as well as bromine, bromide and magnesium sulphate, with a total production of some 70,000 tonnes per year.

To ensure a commercially viable continuous supply to the 300 hectares of pools seawater, with a salinity of 36 grams per litre, is led via a narrow channel into a series of shallow lagoons, each of a slightly different colour, a range of pale blues and greys and ultimately almost pink, as the water becomes increasingly saturated with salt. Eventually, at 325 – 370 grams per litre, the salt crystals precipitate and are extracted for storage in gleaming piles.

Salt production follows the seasons. The lagoons are topped up during the early months of the year, ready for the scorching summer temperatures which accelerate the rate of evaporation. Harvesting of the salt then occurs mainly between August and October.

Adjacent to the saltworks are short rows of squat white houses in the village of Almadraba de Monteleva, originally the saltworkers' cottages. In the mid-twentieth century Juan Goytisolo, visiting the area, wrote: 'The houses are rectangular, white, almost resembling bunkers.' His comment does a disservice to this somehow attractive and appropriate vernacular architecture. Alongside the houses is a disused church, the Iglesia de las Salinas, dating from 1907. Its tall tower forms a striking vertical alongside the pallid horizontals of the lagoons. For several years a sizeable hoarding announced that work on renovating the church was imminent but nothing happened. Finally, in 2011, the church was clad in scaffolding and during 2012 the restoration project was finally completed.

A few metres away, a tilted pebble beach stretches away in both directions. The remnants of a masonry pier crumble into the sea. Formerly, portable rails linked this to the storage yard at the saltworks. Snorkelling here once, I discovered lengths of the old rails on the sea bed just off the pier. The salt was brought here in hopper wagons hauled by humans or animals and tipped into barges that took it out to bigger ships moored two or three hundred metres offshore, for export. The pier was able to process 700 tonnes of salt per day. Now, inevitably, the salt is all taken away by road.

As I pass, the seaward side of the road is blocked by a high chain-link fence, behind which workmen are filling sturdy wooden shuttering with beach material. In a couple of places well-specified wooden ramps with strong handrails have been made to allow disabled access down what is in effect a low cliff to the beach; an example of the modern, all-inclusive Spain, though sadly achieved at the price of clearing away some of the paraphernalia and old huts of the fishermen which gave the place a lot of its character.

Also part of the scene are upturned weather-beaten boats; capstans patterned in white and rust; locked and bolted ice-cream kiosks, their red plastic curves awaiting summer; and a small hotel hoping for the occasional January customer. It's an evocative place, with something of the mystery and allure of parts of England's flat eastern counties – Lincolnshire, north Norfolk, Essex. There's a touch of the obscure out-of-season resort, big lost skies, a constant sea where gannets occasionally beat westwards, gulls wheel and shriek and, far out, hazy shapes of huge ships pass like drifting cities. Over it all a sense of otherness, a strangely pleasant desolation, prevails.

3. Coasting: Cliffs and coves
'No journey starts until the last prearranged pillow is left behi
(Nicholas Crane)

To the lighthouse

At this south-eastern end the lagoons look pinkly saline, with crusty fringes and floating layers of scummy halite. Just beyond where they taper to a salty conclusion lies the quiet village of La Fabriquilla. Almost always when I've been to La Fabriquilla, neither of its bars has been open. And then in 2012 I read that the permanent population of the village is just six, so it's unsurprising that there are usually few signs of life there, out of season at least.

The modern road veers inland just before the village and immediately begins to climb across the seaward slopes of Cerro de la Testa. The ancient road continues between the few white houses and the sea, its nameplate appropriately enough showing that it is the Carretera Antigua del Faro, the Old Road to the Lighthouse. In the 1974 film *The Wind and the Lion*, directed by John Milius and starring Sean Connery and Candice Bergen, La Fabriquilla was used as a North African look-alike village.

Pedestrians can take the old road through the village, a stroll of only a few minutes because just past the houses it climbs, pitted and neglected, to join the new road. Below, the Playa de La Fabriquilla, the seventh and final incarnation of the beach that has been with us all the way from Retamar, is at last squeezed out of existence by the mountain slopes. Bulky rocks, tan and dark grey, rear above the road. A sign tells motorists that the road is about to get narrower. The view back is wonderful: the slim strip of land holding the small settlements of La Fabriquilla and Almadraba de Monteleva between the sea and the multiple pastels of the *salinas* then, further, the coast curving away, the Golfo de Almería somewhere between blue and silver and a far suggestion of the Sierra de Gádor rising into a fading haze.

Suddenly, at a bend in the narrow and sinuous road the lighthouse, the Faro de Cabo de Gata, comes into view. A few metres on two guys are brushing the road clean at the conclusion of their task of clearing a rockfall, no doubt a regular deployment after heavy rain. To my greeting they offer back a cheerful: "Hola, amigo!" A few

31

metres further on I pause to take in the now wider view and my attention catches on a black wheatear, an iconic bird of these parts. Ever alert, all black but for a sharply contrasting white rump, and a specialist of steep Iberian rock and cliff faces, flicking from one rocky perch to the next, it's a regular companion if you walk the upland part of this coast.

Immediately below, with the lighthouse beyond it, is La Corralete, a valley carved by the eponymous *rambla* with a beach called La Calatilla. From the road you can look down (but only as a pedestrian; it's too steep to do this from a car) and have a bird's eye view onto a group of six villas, definitely luxurious but also out-of-place. Here in this rocky coastscape, one even has a tennis court. Money talks even in a natural park or, to be charitable, perhaps these were built before the natural park was designated. As I'm pondering the incongruity of these six fine but questionably-sited houses, five Porsches glide past me, each a different colour; a convoy of red-white-blue-black-silver.

The road, and there's no alternative for the walker here, veers inland and begins to dip into the valley of La Corralete. This is a stronghold of the dwarf fan palm (Chamaerops humilis), Europe's only endemic palm. They are compact, shrubs rather than trees, in effect a clump of fan-like leaves at all angles, the whole being up to 3m tall and in favoured sheltered places forming clumps as much as 5m in diameter.

After crossing the *rambla* the road climbs to the lighthouse on its prominent headland. It is this headland which is Cabo de Gata itself. To the Phoenicians the rocky prominence pushing into the Mediterranean was the 'promontory of cornelians and agates' which, under the Moors, became Cabpta Gata and subsequently Cabo de Gata. A fort with a semi-circular artillery platform was built here in 1738, though the guns were removed in the early nineteenth century. In 1863 the first signalling station began to operate here. Juan Goytisolo was moved to say of it: 'The mountains shelter it completely from the land and, beaten day and night by the sea, it rises up, solitary and rustic, overlooking the Moorish coast, today a faithful watchtower of storms and shipwrecks, yesterday, of Berber disembarcations'.

From the parking area and viewpoint just below the lighthouse there's a good view of the Arrecife de las Sirenas, the Reef of the Mermaids, a dramatic offshore stack. It's a famous feature of this coast even though it's no more than one detail among many in a spectacular array.

To continue along the coast it's necessary to go back a couple of hundred metres to a junction where a road leads east, past the Aula del Mar, substantially enlarged in 2009, a 'Classroom of the Sea' for visiting students. The drama of the coast here is a result of its structure, a series of volcanic domes, of which the two most important are one below the lighthouse and another a short hop east at Punta Baja. The domes were formed 12 million years ago when thick slow-moving lava accumulated around each vent. The most visible feature today is columnar jointing, caused when slow cooling of the lava resulted in its slight contraction, whereupon it split into tessellating hexagonal columns of basalt. Like a miniature Giant's Causeway, these distinctive features can be seen to good effect if you take the short path that leads towards the pointed cone of Punta Baja. Now protected, these intriguing hexagonal columns were in the past taken away for use as paving slabs.

A kilometre or so further along the road, a track leads down to Cala Rajá. There's a small parking area by the road and the rough track has been improved of late so that motorists can access a further parking area nearer, but still high above, the beach. The final access to the cove can only be negotiated on foot by one of two paths, either down a steep slope with loose pebbles in places or via a gully partly choked with vegetation and boulders. Both ways are passable but require care. It's worth the effort and, presumably because of the awkward access, Cala Rajá is favoured by skinny-dippers. The beach is delightful, the snorkelling is excellent and the geology is dramatic. Most obvious are the striking white rocks known as tuff, consolidated volcanic ash produced by highly explosive eruptions, which are the oldest rocks in the area.

One October day we were here with friends who were out from England for a week when a *guardia civil* helicopter, after quartering the skies, landed on the cliff-top above us. A few minutes later one of the policemen had scrambled down to the beach and asked us whether we'd seen a boatload of illegal immigrants. I said we hadn't and the police left. Our friend Rob, when I explained what they'd been asking about, said: "Oh yeah, I saw a small boat full of people out there." An hour later, as we drove back past the saltpans towards San Miguel de Cabo de Gata, we saw a group of Africans, marshalled by *guardia civil* personnel, trudging along the sand, their body language suggesting they were bemused by their welcome to this strange land.

Just offshore from Cala Rajá is the Arrecife del Dedo, the Reef of the Finger. One fanciful notion is that this is Neptune signalling to heaven from his kingdom. In an eighteenth century document this sea-stack was known as Frailecico, the Little Monk. The cormorants and yellow-legged gulls that use it as a perch, oblivious to its changing names over the centuries, have crowned it, prosaically, with a white cap of guano.

Beyond the White Sail

Back at the road, the gradient increases as the tarmac, potholed in many places, zigzags up to Vela Blanca (White Sail, named after a prominent outcrop of white tuff). Here a watchtower occupies a spectacular site right at the edge of a vertiginous cliff with the sea 200 metres below. Climbing steadily with my 11 kilo backpack, not a great burden but heavy enough on a sharp gradient late in the day, I reach Vela Blanca at 6.30 pm.

There was mention of a tower at Vela Blanca as long ago as the 12th century but the current structure was built much later, under the supervision of Francisco Pepín González in 1767. It was passed to the police in 1850 though it's so remote that this would only make sense if the police role at that date included coastguard duties. In the 1960s it was bought from the State and passed into private hands, reputedly with the intention of turning it into a distinctive home. However, soon afterwards the telecommunications company Telefónica put up a mast and associated paraphernalia, literally right beside the old tower, so the notion of living there no doubt instantly lost its attraction. Nowadays the Telefónica enclosure, a scrappy site littered with an old bath among other things, totally blocks access to the watchtower unless you are prepared to scale walls and fences. And the tower, like its companions along the coast, can't be entered anyway unless you are a magician, its only door being three-quarters of the way up and presumably locked.

At the highest point of the tarmac road is a barrier. The tarmac surface ends here. Beyond it a vehicle-width track continues. The barrier was installed a few years ago by the Natural Park authorities to cut the vehicular route along the coast. A masterstroke! With such brave decisions this part of the Spanish coast has been largely spared the desecration visited on huge stretches of the Costa Blanca and Costa Brava.

There's a cool breeze and, as this is towards the end of January, it is sunset. In less than a minute the horizon melts from egg-yolk through gold to burnished red. Crag martins swoop under the heavy brown overhangs of the outlying ridges that fall from the highest peak in these parts, Bujo, 373 m. Night seems to fall almost instantly. The crag martins become invisible, or maybe they don't fly after dusk. A full moon is already high, its pallid cream disc a suitable companion to the continuing wind that blows much colder now.

It's too early to stop for the night and, having walked this stretch several times before, I know the track is obvious. Also I'm not worried that I'll miss crucial wayside gems. Some years ago, when we first came here, my partner Troy had tracked down the endemic Cabo de Gata snapdragon (Antirrhinum charidemi), nestling under the rocky outcrops alongside the roughly-surfaced track. In fact, we brought friends here a couple of months later, on a rare rainy day, and found many clumps of this superb delicate pink flower shimmering against the wet gleam of the dark red cliffs that they colonise.

By moonlight I walk on, my heart stopping only once when a couple of unseen red-legged partridges take off from under my feet with an explosion of noise. At the base of the steep drop from Vela Blanca is a further barrier with, just beyond it, a turning circle. This is as far as vehicles can come if they have approached from the east. I continue further, past the turn to the lovely cove of Media Luna (Half-moon). In our early days in the area we spent many nights here in our campervan until, one morning, a polite uniformed man from the environment agency knocked on our van door, took the details of our number plate and my passport, and explained that we couldn't park there overnight. It's fine to overnight at places with houses or development, he explained, but at the more remote beaches it's not allowed.

On foot, I find a sheltered spot for the night not far from the Ensenada (Inlet or Cove) de Mónsul, tucked out of the wind but in the moon's light so I can see my sparse picnic. The truism about food tasting better outdoors still holds, even on a cold night. Soon enough I spread my foam mat, feed my sleeping bag into its protective bivouac bag, take my boots off and ease myself into my makeshift bed. Orion hangs prominently above in a sky pin-cushioned with stars. I look for a while, resolving yet again to learn more about the constellations, then pull the sleeping bag over my head against the night air. It's only 9 p.m., the earliest I've been to bed in years.

Indiana Jones

When I wake at dawn, invisible red-legged partridges are chuntering close by. The unspoilt and deserted beach of the Ensenada de Mónsul, with fine sand and shallow water, is only a minute's walk away but early on a January day, even a bright one, it's much too cold for a dip to appeal.

These beaches also have attracted many film-makers. Back in 1964 Sidney Lumet directed *The Hill* here. Part of Terry Gilliam's *The Adventures of Baron Munchausen* was shot on Mónsul beach in 1988 and likewise Steven Spielberg's *Indiana Jones and the Last Crusade* the following year. Trivia, of course, but of interest if you're walking through the area. There's well-presented information about this in the Los Amoladeras Visitor Centre, back beyond Cabo de Gata village.

One side of the beach at Monsúl is fringed by La Peinata, a remnant outcrop of volcanic activity that took place between 10 and 12 million years ago. Sea level was higher then and the volcanoes were erupting underwater, with the erupted material being deposited in stacked layers on the seabed.

I climb across the fringes of a huge sand dune, another of the distinctive features at Mónsul, the sand largely stabilised by sisal agaves and fan palms. The sand deposits are much more recent than the volcanic features and partly overlay them. Footprints lead through the sand, the only access to a relatively hidden cove, the Cala de Barronal. I'm heading up the adjacent small hill called Cerro del Barronal. Suddenly I reach a point where the sand dunes stop, butting up against the hexagonal columns of volcanic rock. The sisal stops here too. It grows only in the sand and can't get a foothold on the andesitic lava.

The blocky rock, patterned with grey and orange lichens, makes for easy climbing to the summit, a mere 163 metres above sea level but a great viewpoint. Back, way beyond the beach of Mónsul, the tower at Vela Blanca is obvious with ridges reaching inland and higher up to the bulk of Bujo. To the east a neck of high land reaches out into the sea, ending at the Morrón de los Genoveses. A few white buildings hint at the settlement of San José, most of which is hidden behind the intervening hills, and further again rises the cone of El Fraile, at 493 m the highest point in the Cabo de Gata-Níjar Natural Park.

Right by the cairn as I reach the summit of Cerro de Barronal, the tall spikes of white asphodel are flowering. Blocks of stone with a scattering of loose pebbles make for a sometimes awkward descent on the continuation of my high-level traverse. The next minor summit, unnamed, has a spot height of 141 m on the map. The grey and cream volcanic rocks I'm sitting on are splashed with vivid orange lichens and small red succulents. It's an ideal place for a second breakfast. This is the same as my brief first breakfast and indeed identical to last night's supper: bread, *chorizo* and cheese, dried fruit and nuts, and grapefruit juice. Repetitive but still delicious and, eaten on a peerless morning and with this view, close to perfect.

Below, to the north, is the broad low swathe of the Campillo de Genoveses, beautiful because unspoilt, and used in the past for the production of cereals, wine and firewood. In the late 18th century the area was used for grazing horses and it was then that the larger farmhouses were built. The estate was long protected by the landowner, José González Montoya, especially during the decades of the Francoist government that always favoured economic development over environmental considerations. The heirs of José González have continued to spurn the financial rewards of development.

I heft up my now marginally lighter backpack and pick my way between the tufts of low vegetation, enjoying unexpected moments of encounter: the tan flash as a kestrel flies below, a toad intent on hauling its way between the ground-level plants, the tiny flowers of

37

wild stock flagging into the breeze. A stony path leads up to the trig point on Morrón de los Genoveses, its modest 73 metre altitude providing a fine panorama down across the long gentle curve of Genoveses beach and round the bay to the Cerro de Ave María.

Local tradition, widely believed, is that the name of the bay dates from 1147, when the Genoese fleet, with a force including Pisans, Catalans and Navarrese, used it as a refuge during an attack on Almería. The bay's strategic value and the agricultural riches of its hinterland meant that plans were drawn up in 1570, 1584 and 1733 to protect it with fortifications but nothing significant was ever built.

The beach on this bright winter day is deserted but for a handful of saucer-sized jellyfish, a few cockles, the finely-patterned shell of a sea urchin and a tiny flock of waders that skitter off before I can identify them. At the northern end of the beach, among a grove of eucalyptus trees, an old concrete bunker has had a psychedelic spray job, giving it the look of an art installation. The view out from the slit in the bunker would have allowed its defenders to scan the whole beach, well over a kilometre in length.

From immediately behind the bunker a narrow path leads up through a sisal plantation to meet a broader, more level track on the seaward slope of Cerro de Ave María and this in turn leads to the tarmac streets of San José. Both of the immediate choices, Calle Cerro Gordo or Calle La Mora, lead into the small town, the latter maybe slightly more quickly.

4. Coasting: Central

'Oh, it's enough to be on your way, it's enough just to cover ground.'
(James Taylor)

The way from San José

San José grew up as a fishing and mining town during the 19th century but fell on hard times as the latter industry foundered, so that when Juan Goytisolo passed through in the 1950s he saw: 'A sad town, lashed by the wind, with half of the houses leaking and the other half with cracked walls.' The then mayor of Níjar (in which municipality San José lies), who was trying to develop the area, publicly expressed his wish to string up Goytisolo 'by the balls'. Nowadays San José, the largest settlement in the Cabo de Gata-Níjar Natural Park by some margin, relies on tourism for its economic survival. It has hotels, a camp site, banks, restaurants, a marina and a range of shops catering for visitors.

For the past several years a summer weekend bus service has linked San José and the beaches to the south. In conjunction with this car access along the unsealed road to the beaches has been controlled. During the summer of 2010 a dispute broke out between business owners and residents from San José on the one hand and the Junta de Andalucía on the other. The Junta made a decision to allow only 150 cars per day to access the beaches, a scheme that can be enforced by means of a barrier just outside San José. Locals demanded a better road (presumably they wanted a tarmac surface) and a limit of 450 cars per day. On one occasion in late July, amongst angry scenes, locals forced up the barrier to allow free passage for vehicles. After this a compromise was reached at 250 cars per day, with San José businesses muttering that this was not enough.

A fortnight later though, the Junta de Andalucía changed its mind and announced that it would allow unrestricted access to the beaches before 11 a.m. and after 7 p.m. Between those times the barrier would be closed. However, if the car parking areas at the two main beaches, Genoveses and Monsúl, which between them could accommodate about 470 cars, were full before 11 a.m. the barrier would be closed early. Until August 31st buses would run between San José and the beaches at half-hourly intervals every day from 9 a.m. to 9 p.m. The mayor of Níjar, Antonio Jesús Rodríguez, who some

Spanish newspapers suggested was behind the protests, said he was happy that the situation had been resolved. In contrast, environmentalists were dismayed by this change in the Junta's position. Juan Pedro González, speaking for the pressure group Condor, said that people had got used to using the buses to reach the beaches in summer and the Junta's climb-down would undo years of good work. He added: "If they want to allow unrestricted access, it should be in the off-peak season when there won't be hundreds of visitors." The precise details are a tiny slice of history but the saga is a typical illustration of the stresses that crop up when local government is caught between environmental and economic concerns. By the time you read this, the scheme may well be different again.

San José lacks distinctive architecture but is attractively situated, particularly where its buildings clothe the lower slopes of Cerro de Ave María on the south side of the bay. The marina, or *puerto deportivo*, is tucked under the conical hump of Cerro de Enmedio which rises to 136 m just north-east of the town. Those who value the restrictions placed on development by natural park status might wonder at the substantial recent expansion of San José and hope that the labyrinthine and snail-paced workings of Spanish planning law will not allow it to continue.

I've always liked the feel of San José and, despite the fact that much of the town (it's a January weekday after all) is closed, I have a good if simple lunch of *tostada* with tuna and a couple of coffees in surprisingly strong sun outside a café on the main street, followed by a pastry from the *pastelería* next door. Stocking up with more bread, *salchichón* and another litre of grapefruit juice, I shoulder my pack and head out of town, past Camping Tau which, like much else in San José, is silent and locked because it makes its killing in the months from March to September.

In one of his novels, Ian McEwan has this: 'There is a simple pleasure in entering and leaving a village on foot. Temporarily, the illusion can be sustained that while others have lives that are fixed round houses, relationships and work, you are self-sufficient and free, unencumbered by possessions and obligations. It is a privileged sensation of lightness that cannot be had by passing through in a car.'

A broad track leads to Cala Higuera, the quiet Cove of the Fig Tree, where I've read that some evidence, though I'm not sure what, of prehistoric settlement has been found. Before reaching the cove a further track leads off left, steadily gaining height across the flanks of one of the outliers of the El Fraile volcano. High above, 227 m above sea level, looms another of the ancient coastal watchtowers, the Torre Vigilancia de Cala Higuera. The view from there must be spectacular. One day I will climb up to it.

There's a sharp rise in the track to a well-maintained shooting butt, a hollow circular dry-stone structure, camouflaged with the thick wiry grass esparto – watch out, you red-legged partridges and rabbits. A brief drop follows then a final short steep pull with a trillion sparkles from the rock dust underfoot delivers me to a superb view out over the sea.

I negotiate a major rock-fall from the pale strata above that has dumped many tonnes of boulders on the track. A long coastal walk here can be guaranteed to deliver surprises: such a one comes now, with a group of half a dozen trumpeter finches. They pass, flitting and calling, and in a matter of seconds are gone. I'm astonished and feel privileged to have seen this species on two consecutive days.

A woman approaches, unplugs her headphones, and asks me if this is the way to San José. I have a flashback to the song those of a certain age may recall; it was Dionne Warwick, wasn't it? A different San José, of course. I tell her it's no more than half an hour away, she thanks me and plugs back in to her music. I love music but when you're walking somewhere like this, with a chance to hear trumpeter finches, why would you want an entirely different and alien stimulus coming into your ears?

The Little Monk and the House of the Tomato

I pass more columnar rock, evidence of vulcanicity. This feels like the wildest stretch of the walk so far. It's all relative as I'm less than an hour from the nearest village, but there's a good unspoilt feel to this twisting track high above the sea. Talking of vulcanicity, the evidence is close enough. I'm contouring below the twin peaks of Los Frailes. To be more specific, they are El Fraile, The Monk (393 m) and the more recent El Fraile Chico, The Young Monk (345 m). Trainee Monk? Apprentice Monk? Novice? Monklet? The mind runs away with ideas. It can do this when you're not plugged into an iPod.

41

The lower parts of these two summits represent the remains of an incredibly complex series of events. Technically, they are described as amphibolitic andesites. I don't know what that means either, but I'll try to interpret the situation. It went something like this. As a result of massive explosions, huge amounts of lava were ejected from a magma chamber that then collapsed. The result was a chaotic mix of rock fragments which included remains of the volcano's dome and bits of lava flows. Particularly explosive episodes added tuffs (compacted volcanic fragments and dust) of various types to the brew. Add to this a series of fossil-rich intercalations of sedimentary rocks which are the remnants of beach and shallow marine episodes. The experts differ in their opinions as to exactly when this happened but agree that it was somewhere between 10 and 15 million years ago. That there is some dispute is heartening for an interested amateur who struggles to comprehend even the basics of what went on here in the geological past and wonders at the skill of anyone who can read ancient rocks in such a magical way.

The upper part of Los Frailes dates more precisely from about 8.5 million years ago. Associated marine sediments indicate that it was a volcanic island during its formation. There were two vents emitting lava at a temperature of about 1000°C, and it was only during the final phase of volcanic activity that the two cones developed. These mark the sites where the two eruption vents were finally sealed. The present cones have extensive columnar jointing, indicating the slow cooling and shrinkage of the lava, and which made them the victim of quarrying for paving stones in the past.

Just after 3 p.m. I round a bend in the track to be confronted by a large ruined building that has clearly gone up in flames at some point. Even stranger, the map tells me this is the Casa del Tomate. House of the Tomato? Then, when I look up 'tomate' in the dictionary later, just in case, I find it can also mean 'hole' and there by the house is a big disused quarry. I guess this was the quarry manager's house/office and jot down a reminder to try to track down more detail.

I find a way in to the building. Most of the walls, two storeys high, are still standing. A flight of stairs is covered in rubble. The odd roof timber is still visible but the roof itself has gone. The walls are charred, with the usual cargo of messages announcing who was here and when, scratched white into the black soot. Old washbasins, chimney hoods, an upturned pan: there's debris everywhere but enough remains to show that this was once an impressive building, and it's in a truly spectacular location with a wide view out over the Mediterranean.

From the track I'm on a side-track tilts down into the vast white hollow of the quarry, the bottom of which holds a lake, though this may be temporary flooding from the recent rains. At times like this I wish I was a geologist. The quarry itself, although well below the Casa del Tomate, is still high above sea level. What were they quarrying here? All my enquiries come to nothing. No-one seems to have any idea and even the internet is silent on the matter. It's only three years later, by chance, when I'm researching bentonite that I discover this is what they were after. (For more on bentonite, see the chapter 'Exploring the maps.')

Ravens and fossil dunes

Another trumpeter finch passes. Its song is often likened to a tiny toy trumpet, hence its name, and although I can't say I hear the toy trumpet, it's certainly a unique song, drawn-out in a peculiarly nasal way. Black wheatears flit down the rocks. Crag martins are flickering along the rock faces. It's a fairly nondescript bird, the crag martin, brownish, pale-ish, but its skill in the air is a delight. Rob Hume in *Bird* describes its flight perfectly: 'Most elegant of all the swallows and martins, it has a swooping, free-flowing action…".

Two ravens pass overhead, calling loudly: *Cronk, cronk…* There is something about ravens that makes me smile, maybe that chance of seeing them flipping onto their backs in flight, sometimes even following through to do a full revolution, seemingly just because they can. The collective noun is 'an unkindness of ravens' which, according to the OED, is recorded as far back as the 15th century. It seems rather unfair. Ravens have been seen sledging repeatedly on their backs down a snowy Welsh mountainside. That also makes me smile. They have a world distribution and are closely linked to humankind, having featured in the Book of Genesis and any number of literary works and place-names. Despite this they are not particularly common. Along this part of the Spanish coast though, you have a good chance of seeing them in the more remote parts. It never occurred to me until

43

now but I wonder whether my having lived for a couple of years on Raven Road in Sheffield in the early 1970s was just a coincidence.

The track passes an information board about the Reserva Marina de Cabo de Gata-Níjar. Different sections of the coast have varying levels of protection but in those with the highest status, that of Reserva Integral/No Touch Area, all marine activities, including fishing, snorkelling and diving, are prohibited. These areas are so critical for the health of the marine ecosystem that it's instructive to realise that, as I write this, the enormous pressure exerted by conservation bodies in the UK has only recently and partially borne fruit. It was only in November 2009 that the Marine and Coastal Access Act paved the way for some protection of marine habitats off the coasts of England and Wales.

The track dips as it leaves the volcanic slopes of Los Frailes. Alongside the track a shrine surrounded by cacti holds a picture of a pretty teenage girl who died aged sixteen in 1997, all the more poignant for the fact that we are left to wonder what happened to her.

I'm at sea level again now. There's a broad area with a few scattered campervans, mostly northern Europeans down for the winter, by the look of the registration plates. Offshore are a few bare rocky islets. This is Cala del Embarcadero, Cove of the Jetty or Wharf. Could this have been where the bentonite from the quarry alongside the Casa del Tomate was brought to be taken away by sea?

The obvious square mass of the Batería de San Felipe at Los Escullos lies ahead, with the glaringly white splash of La Isleta del Moro a couple of kilometres beyond and, further still, dark cliffs falling to the sea. The *batería* or fort was constructed in 1765 in the reign of Carlos III. It had an artillery platform with four cannons, a chapel, living quarters and barracks. After many years of neglect, the fort was restored at the beginning of the 1990s at the prompting of the Natural Park authorities.

The San Felipe fort stands on a dramatic outcrop of fossilised oolitic dunes. This strangely contorted white rock is the best example of such a feature in the Natural Park. The dunes in question were formed during the last interglacial period, between 128,000 and 100,000 years ago. The oolites consisted of a nucleus, a quartz grain or the faecal pellet of some sea creature, say, around which concentric layers of aragonite accumulated. This took place in very shallow warm seawater that was saturated with carbonate and highly agitated by waves. Subsequently, after the oolitic sediments were raised above sea level, the wind created dunes from them.

It's no good peering closely at the fossil dunes in the hope of seeing oolites though. You would need a microscope to be able to see that amount of detail. What are obvious to the naked eye are the layers of the fossil sediments, with their slightly varying angles showing the different phases of dune formation, depending on the precise nature of the prevailing winds. The place-name Los Escullos comes from the Spanish 'escollos' meaning a reef and referring to the collapse of large blocks from the fossil dunes.

To La Isleta del Moro

An official footpath, a sendero, links Los Escullos with La Isleta del Moro though I suspect it is recent as it doesn't appear on the maps. Initially, it's simple enough as it follows the beach, the Playa del Arco. There's a wonderful array of colourful pebbles then a hint of sand but when I pass it's largely hidden under a great drift of wave-piled seaweed. In the shallows, three anglers stand like statues, waterproofed by their waders. The route then becomes a little more complex and I'm not always sure I'm on it. There's an occasional low wooden post with an arrow to offer some reassurance but it's an up-and-down affair, dropping into cobbled coves and teetering across the odd problematic slope. There's no chance of actually getting lost though because it's just a matter of following the coast and La Isleta is only a kilometre away.

There's a lovely profile view ahead to La Isleta. The village is perfectly in tune with its landscape, tumbling briefly down a slope and occupying the neck of land leading out to a small headland whose pleasing dome ends in low but sheer cliffs. And just seaward of this is an island, the neatly appropriate shape of which makes me think that maybe there *is* a higher power with an eye for landscape. This is called Isleta del Moro Arraéz, taking its name from a Berber leader called Mohamed Arraéz.

Either side of the path I'm on there's been an attempt at replanting, shrubs rather than trees, I think, but having peered into many of the protective plastic tubes, even though it's too small a

45

sample to be considered scientific, I deduce that the project has had limited success. With the tide lapping at my feet I reach a series of steps that leads up to a *mirador* (viewpoint) at the southern edge of La Isleta del Moro. There's a distinctive panorama back, beyond Los Escullos, to the twin cones of the Frailes volcanoes.

La Isleta is a very attractive place that hasn't outgrown its natural site, so although it now relies largely on tourism it still has the feel of a small fishing village that has only recently been touched by the outside world. And so it proves: it didn't have electricity until 1969 or a paved road until 1979 or telephones until 1982. It has two coves, a sandy one facing north, the Playa del Peñón Blanco, and a smaller cobbly one facing south. The village has places to stay and eat, a shop or two, and a diving school.

At one side of the small square is a public washing place sporting a smart new information plaque. It tells us that these *lavaderos* were a focus of the community where the women and the young used to meet to chat and gossip and that the coming of washing machines has made these features redundant. Now they serve to remind visitors of life in a different age, it says, a time when clothes were rubbed clean in the communal stone sinks. As I'm reading this and noting that the washing place was renovated as a feature of great ethnological interest in October 2009, one of the village women is busily scrubbing her family's clothes in one of the basins. Not everyone here has a washing machine.

I've texted Troy to let her know I'll be able to make it to here for the second night of my coastal walk and she has come down with the campervan, arriving soon after I do. I'm waiting on a strategic bench to intercept her and we find a suitable overnight spot. Seeing her and having the chance to chat about some of my experiences over a shared bottle of red in relative luxury makes for a very welcome evening.

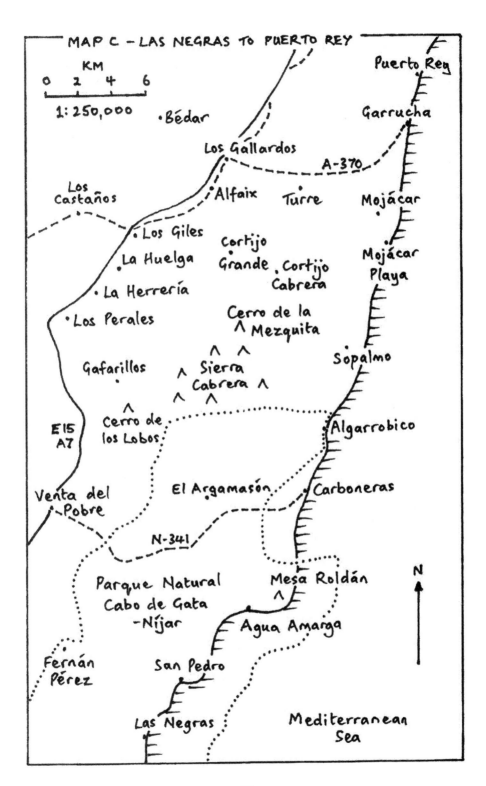

MAP C – LAS NEGRAS TO PUERTO REY

5. Coasting: Beyond the Amethyst

'...an intense scrutiny of minute particulars....'
(William Blake)

Viewpoint of the Amethyst

For the next stretch of the walk there is no real alternative to following the road. Fortunately it's not normally busy. A mountain barrier separates La Isleta and Rodalquilar, my next objective. In well under an hour I've climbed to the Mirador de la Amatista, the Viewpoint of the Amethyst. Below the ornate ironwork of the balustrades, spectacular cliffs stretch away and again, just west of south and now about ten kilometres distant, the Frailes twin peaks pierce the sky.

Just after the viewpoint the road's convexity finally crests to its summit and the broad Valle de Rodalquilar lies sprawling ahead. Having driven this road many times, it's only now I'm walking that I notice the small details: a couple of hazel trees, for example, normally lost in the tall eucalypts that fringe the road. They're aliens, the eucalyptus trees, but they have adapted well to this corner of Spain, especially along the *ramblas* where there's more accessible water. They do have the habit though of unpredictably shedding large branches, so watch out if you decide to have a picnic underneath one.

The modern village of Rodalquilar stands just inland from a sharp right-hand bend in the main road. At the junction where a road leads off left into the village a tall metal statue of a miner symbolises the village's former gold industry. (For more on this see the chapter 'Gold and murder'.) Much of the village was abandoned after gold mining ceased in 1966 and there is still widespread evidence of this. Unsurfaced streets lead away on the left, lined with ruined houses and fenced off because of the crumbling state of the buildings.

Beyond the *rambla*, the character of the village is quite different. It's fully functioning, with houses, the occasional bar, and a whole series of developments led by the Andalucian Government's Environment Ministry. It's still early in my day's walk though and I want to push on so I head past the Botanical Garden back to the main road.

Alongside a couple of houses a sign announces Los Méndez, though the name does not appear on the maps. A low, terracotta

48

complex on the opposite side of the road is the Hotel de la Naturaleza with, just behind it, the Hotel Rural El Ajillo. A hundred metres further on is a turning on the right to the Torre de los Lobos and Cala del Carnaje (the ferociously-named Carnage Cove). This is a fairly long out-and-back diversion, the best part of 10 kilometres, so I decide to save it for another day.

That other day finally arrives in early 2012. The turning to the Torre de los Lobos is a metalled road, though with some spectacular potholes. It is driveable for a while, maybe a kilometre or so, until a huge metal gate blocks the way, beyond which access is only on foot. From here it's a 40-minute walk via the tarmac up a series of zigzags to the tower. Built in 1764, the watchtower is now used by the Almería Port Authority as a lighthouse, the Faro de la Polacra.

The tower and the hill it is on are named not after wolves *(lobos)*, as it might appear, but after the monk seals that formerly lived on this coast. Now a seriously endangered species, monk seals were also known in Spanish, because of the sounds they emitted, as *'lobos marinos'* or sea wolves, hence the name.

So, belatedly, some time after my long coastal walk, I discover that this is one of the great viewpoints of the whole coast, despite the somewhat intrusive masts by the lighthouse. South-west, past La Isleta del Moro, rise the twin peaks of Los Frailes. In the opposite direction, if you walk the forty metres or so to the trig point and look north-east along the coast, the *castillo* at San Pedro is obvious. Beyond that the high, strategically prominent table of Mesa Roldán, with its ancient watchtower and more modern lighthouse, seems to stick far out to sea. In fact, as the map confirms, it juts out only a couple of kilometres, a mere blip of the coast, but it makes for a great feature in the view. Inland, between these two extremes, lies Rodalquilar and the silent remnants of the defunct gold processing plant. This is a beautiful place to be looking out from and, as always when you have to make the physical effort to reach a viewpoint, the reward is all the greater.

The walk back down is much easier than the walk up, not just because gravity is in your favour but also because of a number of strategically placed short-cuts down the zigzags. These are much easier to see from above than from below. You just need to look out for the cairns, the neatly balanced piles of rocks. In one case, a zigzag jinks off to the right and then veers left, gradually downhill, more or less parallel to the road but far more interesting, weaving its way through the tall grasses to bring you back ultimately to the road close to the barrier gate.

Back down again at the main road, turn right, and very soon another road goes off to the right. This is the route back to the coast. The junction is festooned with a rash of signs including three to the Hotel Los Patios and two to the Playa del Playazo. The concrete-surfaced road meanders across the flat Valle de Rodalquilar. Low masonry walls protruding from the vegetation are the remains of an ancient aqueduct and water storage tank. This area is where the original village of Rodalquilar used to be and some of the older buildings, or modified versions of them, still remain. By the *rambla* is La Noria, now a private house with the waterwheel its name alludes to sticking rather oddly out of its top. There's a circular tower adjacent, then the hamlet of La Ermita, the site of the original church, with another tower, as well as a mix of ruins, modern houses and the understated, low-rise Hotel La Ermita.

The pièce de resistance though is the Torre Fuerte or the Castillo de los Alumbres (it has two names). Stranded in a field just off the present road, this 16th century stronghold, although a tumbledown shadow of its original self, is still mighty impressive. A solid square tower sits inside an outer wall which is set with bulbous projections at each corner. It's possible to find a way in where the outer wall is broken down and then through a small doorway in the thick inner wall. I peer up at the remnants of a stone spiral stairway and down through a large hole in the floor, something you definitely wouldn't want to fall down, at what was presumably a dungeon (for more on this, again see the chapter 'Gold and murder'.) I was reminded of this when a chance purchase of the newspaper *La Voz de Almería* one day in May 2013 alerted me that Níjar local council is intending to put *rejas* (metal grilles) on the entrances and fence the whole ruin off to prevent accidents.

Snowbirds and disappointing food

The sea is only a kilometre away, past a large plantation of irrigated knee-high fan palms to the right of the road. At the north side of the Playa del Playazo, a sweep of unspoilt sand, the Castillo de

San Ramón, which is now a private house, squats defiantly on a plinth of solidified ancient dunes. As I explore these, fascinated by the numerous imprints and fragments of scallop shells, two Alsatians bark a warning from their stance on the castle roof.

A couple of hundred metres back from the *castillo* there's an information board giving details of the footpath ahead, the Sendero La Molata. It's two kilometres and an hour to Cala del Cuervo, Raven's Cove. There it is again, that iconic bird. The path veers left along the foot of an obvious slope then climbs and narrows as it passes high above the sea. Suddenly the ground falls away and, like some kind of alien plantation, a long narrow regimented campsite appears below alongside the Rambla del Cuervo, the Watercourse of the Raven. This is Camping Nautico La Caleta. 'Snowbirds', as North Americans would say, have come here for the winter from northern Europe. Twenty or so campervans have staked out their territory on the pitches and under the awnings.

A steep descent, finishing via a rocky gully, brings me to the *rambla* and up to a ribbon of tarmac that leads in, across the seaward flank of a low hill called La Molatilla, to Las Negras. It's not a big village but it has of late sprawled inland. Las Negras follows the usual pattern of such villages, tourism having taken over from fishing as the main economic activity. Half a century ago, tourists were not expected, if Juan Goytisolo's observations are anything to go by: 'In the only laid out street there is a bar and a tobacconists, inside their sties the pigs grunt and the sea rumbles and lurches on the beach.'

It's lunchtime when I arrive and I assume there'll be a few restaurants with a good value *menu del día*. This is despite disappointing experiences on a couple of previous visits. I do a couple of turns round the few places that are open and there's very little choice. I end up at a place with a €15 menu on the sea-front. It turns out to be a rip-off, with very average food which is little more than a single course and service that is slow and indifferent. The only option for *postre* (dessert) is an apple.

As I'm eating a small fishing boat comes in, so small it's easily pulled up onto the beach, and the catch, in several buckets and baskets, is unloaded. People appear, seemingly from nowhere, and cluster around. A few sales are made but the two guys from the boat carry most of the catch up the beach and off into the village. The best aspect of my lunch is being able to watch a cormorant swimming and diving after fish no more than three metres from the shore.

To the hidden village

In Calle Las Aguillas there is a green sign on a house wall indicating the way to Playa de San Pedro. On the road out of the village are a couple of further signs then a *rambla* after the buildings thin out. Just beyond this a *'Sendero'* noticeboard shows a map of the walk to El Plomo and Agua Amarga, giving the distance as 12 kilometres with an estimated time of four and a half hours.

An obvious track angles up a broad shelf on the hillside, emerging above the sea with a wide view back over Las Negras to the hills beyond. As the track veers north-east the dark rocks of Punta del Cerro Negro, Point of the Black Hill, rear out of the Mediterranean directly ahead. Two ravens fly over it, calling darkly.

The track cuts inland of the main summit of Cerro Negro (172 m) and within a few minutes a narrow path can be seen leading off left to the Cortijo de Ricardillo. Hopeful fans of early rock 'n' roll might undertake the brief 'out and back' to explore this Farmhouse of Little Richard, but will find only a ruin with the slopes of the eponymous hill (Ricardillo, 309 m) rising nearby. The main track bears right at this point and contours along the seaward slopes of the Sierra de la Higuera (Range of the Fig-tree). Two Dartford warblers flit across the path. With a bright red eye and burgundy under-parts contrasting with a blue-grey back, this tiny bird is not often or easily seen, but is all the more memorable when it is.

In less than an hour from Las Negras the Cala de San Pedro comes into view, backed by a deeply-scooped valley. The *castillo* (castle) is obvious below, with a smudge of aquamarine water offshore. Even today this valley has no road into it and a relief map makes it clear why this would be an expensive undertaking. Nevertheless, in late 2011 two groups, Friends of the Cabo de Gata-Níjar Park and Ecologists In Action, expressed their opposition to plans from Níjar Town Hall to open an access road into San Pedro, claiming that there had been 'speculative interest' in the area for many years, with plans to develop it for tourism. The pressure groups consider the San Pedro cove to be 'one of the most emblematic places in Cabo de Gata-Níjar' and say that the Junta de Andalucía and Níjar Town Hall should not give in to 'blackmail and speculative plans'.

The feature that made San Pedro a historically attractive base was a permanent spring. An atlas of harbours made by the Mallorcans Yafuda and Abraham Cresques in 1375 called it Santo and in a map drawn before the end of the fifteenth century it appears as San Pero. After various proposals a tower was built here in 1583, with a garrison of twelve soldiers. It almost immediately came under bombardment from five Muslim ships, though they inflicted only minor damage.

Worse was to follow. On New Year's Eve 1658, the defensive tower was partially destroyed by an earthquake. The Governor was killed as his own fort collapsed. The tower was rebuilt by its new Governor, Baltasar de Almansa and in the late 17th century it was reinforced with an adjoining artillery platform. Subsequently the fortification came under bombardment on several occasions, one of which was in 1743, during the reign of Philip V, when an English ship with 60 cannons pounded the *castillo* from dawn until dusk, inflicting damage despite the 50 artillery rounds fired in return.

San Pedro, once abandoned, has for several decades had a fluctuating population of hippies and idealists living in a variety of tents, shelters and converted ruins. This fact is strangely omitted from guidebooks to the Cabo de Gata-Níjar Natural Park, which would have us believe that this idyllic valley is deserted, with sentences such as: 'There are some surprising buildings in the valley which until relatively recently still housed various families,' and: 'A small village sprang up, now long abandoned.'

The current population, no doubt fluctuating but apparently permanent, gives every indication of commitment. Imagination and hard work have gone into making the old ruins habitable, including the ancient circular dovecote, full of interior ceramic niches which are no longer visible to the visitor as it's now someone's home. Crops are being grown on some of the old terraces. Idiosyncratic notices ask visitors to respect the beauty of the local environment. However, at the time of writing it seems Níjar council is intent on taking action against those perceived as squatters in San Pedro.

One hand-painted notice, alongside the old dovecote, indicates the onward path, suggesting 'Agua Amarga 12 kms'.

Something's amiss here, as this was also the distance quoted several kilometres back at Las Negras. It's a long and hard zigzag climb out of the valley, as I discover as the afternoon wears on and my legs register the effort already made today. I can vouch for the fact that, if you do this climb at 4 p.m., the sun will be beating relentlessly on your back.

Beyond the top of the steep climb the path weaves on amongst unruly clumps of esparto, gaining a little more height. A Spanish couple who clearly have at least thirty years on me are climbing the path behind me and finally come past as I have a breather when the path reaches a point overlooking the coast. From here the distant clustered buildings of Agua Amarga gleam at sea level and, immediately beyond, the tabular profile of Mesa Roldán, with the squat tapered Torre de Mesa Roldán and the slimmer white lighthouse perched on its seaward rim, are all apparent.

After following the edge of the plateau for a short while, the path dips down to the right, across the seaward face of the slope. I've walked this stretch three times and on each occasion have seen ravens: a good omen, I always believe. Soon Cala del Plomo (Cove of Lead, as in metal) comes into view below and at just this moment my sunglasses come askew. One of the tiny screws has worked loose and, with no chance of finding it, I discover it's perfectly possible, if mildly eccentric, to wear sunglasses, these at least, with just one side-arm. The path descends into the afternoon's shade, skirting behind the small settlement of about four houses and emerging alongside the beach. Throughout the sixteenth century Cala del Plomo had its own lookout force to protect the local crops and watch for hostile landings. Now things are more peaceful.

6. Coasting: A coral reef in the sky

'The great affair is to move; to feel the needs and hitches of our life more nearly; to come down off this feather-bed of civilisation, and find the globe granite underfoot and strewn with cutting flints.'
(Robert Louis Stevenson)

To Agua Amarga

From Cala del Plomo I follow an unsurfaced vehicle track, which is the only landward access to the cove, as far as a low wooden post on the right indicating the onward path. This initially rises over bedrock and climbs steadily before descending gently towards an unfinished and seemingly abandoned building that lies inland from the lovely beach at Cala de Enmedio (Middle Cove). This unspoilt place is well worth a visit, easily achieved by following the track round to the right. Its fine sandy beach is flanked by pale fluted cliffs and abrasion ledges, rock platforms eroded by marine action at the base of the cliffs. On this occasion, with my left ankle increasingly painful from rubbing on my boot, I give it a miss.

I know the way to Agua Amarga (which translates as Bitter Water, though I haven't been able to pinpoint the significance of this) from previous ventures along here. It follows a narrow path that bears off to the left alongside a further wooden marker post. Again the path climbs, initially over bare rock and later with views south-east back to Cala de Enmedio. The rocky path steepens and briefly reaches a flat area, the Cerro del Cuartel (Hill of the Barracks) at about 100 m above sea level. My back and my rucksack are still sweaty from the big climb out of San Pedro earlier so I take the chance to prop my 'sack up and offer my soggy tee-shirt to the last of the sun in a vain attempt to dry it. Estimate of success in this venture: about 5%. Not really worth the bother. Within a few minutes I'm beginning the descent into Agua Amarga. Part way down, the track becomes a tarmac road that emerges alongside the *rambla* that splits the village.

Sheltered between Mesa Roldán and the Cerro del Cuartel, Agua Amarga was the base for a tuna-fishing enterprise in the eighteenth century. Old caves carved into the soft stone on the west side of the beach, and still accessible today, are thought to have been used formerly by some of the local population. An economic boost arrived for Agua Amarga in 1896 when a 32 km long railway was built from the iron mines at Lucainena to terminals just to the east of Agua Amarga. The whole enterprise (see the chapter 'The lost railway' for much more detail) operated until 1942.

More recently, tourism has been the lifeline of the place, plus the occasional film. A swish villa on the slopes above the village provided the set for the violent movie *Sexy Beast*, featuring Ben Kingsley, Ray Winstone and Amanda Redman in 2000.

My hoped-for re-supply point, the general store, is closed. I've been thinking I'll head for the beach and sleep the night in one of the caves but it's still relatively early, given that I have nothing to do but eat cold food, think and sleep. The upshot is that I have a coke and a coffee in the rapidly cooling air outside a bar, watching a couple of locals tossing back early evening brandies with abandon, before heading out of town.

Finding a bivouac

My new intention is to find a spot to bivouac for the night among the remains of the mineral loading facilities on the Meseta Alta, the High Plateau, above and immediately east of Agua Amarga. I ponder the idea of clambering up alongside the old industrial incline that strikes directly up the hillside from the beach. I've done this once before and remember it as quite steep and awkward. As I stand on the beach now, in an icy wind, eyeing up the prospect, a guy with a small yapping dog looks at my rucksack and says: "It's cold. You should find a cave to sleep in!" It's dark and the moon's not yet up so I think better of going up by the incline and walk back to the main Carboneras road.

A few minutes later I'm up at the Meseta Alta on a track that leads to a cluster of houses. Security lights come on. This isn't what I'm looking for. My memory of the layout up here is rusty and, after blundering about for a while longer on rough tracks in the scrub and finding nowhere suitable, I decide to head on to Mesa Roldán. The only way is via the main road again. It's a Saturday evening about 7.30, and fortunately there's very little traffic as it's necessary to go way past the towering rock table of Mesa Roldán to reach the turn-off for the road that climbs up to it.

A couple of kilometres along the main road, there's a parking area and information point for the Playa de los Muertos, the Beach of the Dead. It's one of the most popular beaches in the area and can only be reached by a significant downhill walk. But from this same point a narrow road leads up to Mesa Roldán. A short way along it, I come to the noticeboard for the Sendero de Mesa Roldán, beyond which the path shows up, taking a rising traverse across the slope.

The moon's up by now and throwing plenty of light so I decide to take the path, which is nicely graded and makes for easy walking. In the moonlight this is a spectacular line of ascent. Rearing up to my left are the glinting pale cliffs of a five and a half million year old coral reef. A surreal touch is added by the lighthouse beam, sweeping regularly across the skyline. Below, to the north, Carboneras is a mass of lights, the poor man's Las Vegas. Rings of red lights on the 240 m high power station chimney pierce the night sky.

Slow on the uptake, it's only when I'm at least halfway to the summit of the plateau, having come across some patches of tarmac and concrete safety blocks on the outer rim of the path, that I suddenly realise this is the original road that must have served the summit lighthouse, hence the regular gradient. The path curves round the southern side of the plateau and finally pops out near the ancient watchtower.

Its height, 222 m above sea level, made Mesa Roldán an ideal location for coastal defences. By 1501 two guards were posted there to keep watch on the coast but not until 1765-66 was any structure built. The artillery tower, the Torre de Mesa Roldán, had two cannons staffed by a garrison of two privates and a corporal. It was built to the plans of military engineer José Crame but it proved too far from the sea and too high above it for its artillery to be effective. The effect of this on Crame's reputation is not recorded. It nevertheless continued to be used as a lookout point. In the mid-19th century the present lighthouse was built.

I'm casting around for a suitable place to sleep. I need to be out of the icy wind, out of the direct beam from the lighthouse, away from the glare of Carboneras and away from the present road that climbs up the *mesa* from the north, as I imagine there's a good chance of Saturday night lovers driving up here to find a quiet spot. I settle on a small, almost level area near the top of the *sendero,* tucked behind a few large rocks and with a superb view away to the south. Agua Amarga is visible below, and far to the west are what I guess to be lights on the windfarm above Lucainena. As the raven flies they are over 30 kilometres away. It's a fine place for a brief, sparse evening picnic. The tiny thermometer permanently clipped to my rucksack shows 4°C and by ten past nine I've bedded down, hunkered right into my sleeping bag, woolly hat and all.

A coral reef in the sky

I emerge to an entirely different scene. Daylight has stripped away the mystery but not the superb views from this wonderful spot. The sun is firing on all cylinders behind the watchtower. A cool wind is still blowing and a pale cold moon hovers almost unnoticed over the Sierra de Gádor. I fuel up on bread, cheese, *salchichón*, a sesame bar, raisins, peanuts, chocolate and water. It tastes fantastic: maybe the view gives it extra flavour.

Having stashed everything in my rucksack, I head over to the trig point, the notional summit of Mesa Roldán, at 222 m. It's right by a telecommunications mast but it's also at the very edge of the plateau and there's a long view over to Carboneras and, more immediately, down the sheer cliffs of the coral reef to the *sendero* I came up last night.

Mesa Roldán is a volcanic dome 8.7 million years old, with sedimentary deposits including coral reefs on top of the remnants of the volcano. About 6 million years ago the dome of the volcano, which was underwater at that stage, created a seafloor that allowed corals to form a reef, exactly of the kind forming in tropical seas today. The skeletons of the corals accumulated as calcareous sediment. This was subject to erosion, then around 5.5 million years ago a further sedimentary deposit constructed from coral reefs began to form. In this phase the coral layers, only a metre or two high, were surrounded by oolitic sediments, further evidence that five and a half million years ago a tropical climate existed here. Oolitic, incidentally, means composed of tiny grains like the eggs or roe of a fish.

Half a kilometre north-east there's a smaller plateau which has a point that is actually a few metres higher than the trig point on the main plateau. As I'm walking over towards it I pass a friendly guy who has just parked and opened the rear door of his car. His furry dog leaps out, programmed for its morning walk. It has more energy than its owner by a factor of at least twenty.

The structure of the smaller plateau, which has no individual name as far as I can ascertain, is amazingly clear, with the volcanic rocks topped by reefs that show up as a striking, vertical-sided craggy outcrop. I have a penchant for getting to the tops of hills so I leave my rucksack and work my way up to the base of the reef through thigh-high vegetation which masks awkward boulders. There are ways up that would definitely 'go' with some easy climbing but although I've done a bit I'm not really a climber. I'm wary of trying this when I'm on my own. Maybe further round to the left there's an easier way. But my left boot has been rubbing for two days, the outside of my ankle is now very sore and, in truth, I have the end of the walk in my sights. No, I'll come back sometime with Troy and we'll do it together. I backtrack and head down to the main road.

I've driven this road down into Carboneras many times and I'm not looking forward to walking it, but actually it's fine, painful ankle notwithstanding. The downhill gradient helps. In less than an hour I've reached a blue-painted walkway and the industrial part of Carboneras. En route I've also passed out of the Cabo de Gata-Níjar Natural Park. Carboneras was excluded from the park because of its industries. The park boundary, which because of its marine component is normally two kilometres offshore, suddenly veers inland south of Carboneras, indeed just south of the Holcim cement works and its associated limestone quarries. It then tracks north, parallel to the coast and about three kilometres inland, to meet the *rambla* of the Río Alías, which it follows back to the coast north of Carboneras.

The biggest polluter in Spain

In rapid succession I pass the Holcim cement works, a new cooking oil reclamation facility, a desalination plant and then the Central Térmica, a coal-fired power station owned by the energy company Endesa. This power station, opened in 1985 and employing 250 people, is the biggest supplier of electricity in Andalucía. However, I read later of a lengthy report published by the European Environment Agency towards the end of 2011, in which this plant is identified as the biggest source of environmental pollution in Spain and the 57th worst polluter in Europe. Pressure groups such as Greenpeace have been criticising Endesa's failure to clean up the plant for years. According to the EEA report, after emitting an average of 6.2 million tonnes of CO_2 into the atmosphere each year, modifications now mean that the annual levels of CO_2 emissions are down, slightly, to 5.09 million tonnes. In terms of public health and environmental damage, says the report, industrial contamination costs the Spanish government between €6.4 billion and €10.1 billion annually.

Storage tanks and chimneys dominate the scene. Long stone and concrete breakwaters and jetties enclose sheltered waters. On this evidence there was no choice but to exclude this chunk of the coast from the natural park. The *Navios Luman*, red-painted and Panama-registered, is in port. I hazard a guess that it's unloading coal, as covered conveyors come high across the road at this point.

It's Sunday morning. The road along here is flat for several kilometres, a rarity on this coast. Cyclists, runners, joggers and mountain-bikers are out in force. A brief digression: the difference between joggers and runners is that joggers are slower than runners and don't cover as much mileage per week. The difference was explained to me by my friend Fil Tebbutt, indisputably a runner, who gets very irate if referred to as a jogger. Rather as do serious ornithologists or even ordinary birdwatchers who find uninformed people calling them twitchers. I'm also aware that I used to be a runner but am now inexorably slowing through 'jogger' to 'walker'.

At the end of the walkway that comes all the way here from the main part of Carboneras town I pause. Within five minutes three people, walking in a determined fashion, for exercise and not merely as a stroll, have come to this point and turned to go back. Oh, and as I make my notes, here's a fourth. Recreational walking is alive and well in Spain. Its rural equivalent takes place in the hour or two before dusk when the women of a village, rarely the men, will be out walking and talking their way for a kilometre or two along the road, out and back from the village. Exercise and gossip: two birds with one stone.

Tucked in amongst all the large-scale industry and towered over by the power station chimney is the Casa del Laberinto, the House of the Labyrinth, all curves and sinuous organic shapes. It was designed by the French architect, sculptor and editor André Bloc in

1964 as a reaction to the rationalism that dominated European architecture at the time. Bloc was born in Algiers in 1896 and died in New Delhi in 1966, only two years after the Casa del Laberinto was built. There are no sharp edges, few external windows ('apertures' would be a better word on the basis of those that can be seen) and it looks to have two storeys or maybe three in places. It's just a few yards off the road, its short access drive barred by a very large, no-messing-about metal gate. As this might indicate, it's not open to visitors, which is a great pity as it would be fascinating to see how such an unusual external shape translates into a liveable internal structure. Unable to investigate further, I head on into Carboneras.

7. Coasting: Carboneras and Algarrobico

'The dilemma is this: each individual development may be justifiable in terms of the welfare of some community as against the preservation of the environment, but the sum total of such developments is the death by a thousand cuts of the natural world, and the thinning of the human spirit.'
(Tim Robinson)

Carboneras

Carboneras translates as 'Coal Bunkers', which could be misleading as mineral coal was never found in the area. The place appeared as Carbonayrola in the Cresques' atlas of ports in 1375. It prospered as a fishing village and also as a source of charcoal (which is carbon too, of course) made in the woodlands behind the town. The definitive guidebook to *'El Litoral, The Coast'* explains the origin of the town's name and the fate of the woodlands: 'It owes its name to the pristine oakwoods, cut down on a massive scale and mercilessly converted into charcoal, with scant commercial return but huge ecological costs, between the 18th and 19th centuries.' A short way offshore lies the Isla de San Andrés which, although only small, provided some shelter to ships taking refuge in times of hard weather.

All this was enough to make Carboneras a strategic location so, given the risks of incursions this coast always faced, it was almost inevitable that fortifications would be built here. In 1587 Phillip II gave permission to a man with a mouthful of a name, Diego López de Haro y Sotomayor, to build such a fort. The result was the Castillo de San Andrés, square and very imposing, with a keep on one corner. In the mid-18th century it had a garrison of 35 soldiers.

It's still here and when I reach it it's fenced off for renovation. I ponder this outside an excellent bar over a couple of coffees and half a *tostada*. The proprietor explains his low prices (and excellent value) as a response to *'la crisis'*, the economic downturn. I look over to the *castillo* and note that right by its main door, which is arched by massive stones and above which is a stone coat of arms now eroded beyond recognition, there's a multiple electricity plug point, a litter bin and a bright yellow post-box. Who, I wonder, is responsible for this surreal juxtaposition?

I head for the sea-front and stroll north. I like Carboneras. It has no pretensions. Yes, there's industry here, mostly south of the town, but the place also welcomes visitors and does so without pretending to be a top resort. It feels like a working town and maybe because of this, a good place to be. On the way into town I pass billboards advertising apartments: 'This is your opportunity!' they say. One of the companies involved is called Indalgestión. This name is made up of two elements. The Indalo is the lucky symbol round here, a figure originally found on prehistoric paintings in the Cueva de los Letreros, Cave of the Signs, near Velez Rubio, and now found on mugs, tee-shirts, tea-towels and many other things the souvenir shops stock. And *gestión* means management, negotiations or the running of a business. Thus it's a perfectly logical name for an estate agency, but to a native English speaker it brings only the suggestion of not being able to assimilate the food one has recently eaten. So I probably won't buy a flat from them.

I'm back in Carboneras in November 2013 and am impressed by what's happened. The walkway mentioned towards the end of the previous chapter now has a vivid blue parallel cycleway attached and, back in the town, there's a fine white statue paying homage to the town's fishermen, with a powerfully evocative quotation from the poet Antonio Machado below it. And in the town square, commemorating the fiftieth anniversary of the filming of *Lawrence of Arabia* in the area, there's a striking new sculpture by Carmen Mudarra of Lawrence himself in flowing robes. The face is a very close likeness of Peter O'Toole, inevitably I suppose, rather than the original character he played so effectively.

Another enormous billboard announces a 'Plan de Recuperación del Atún Rojo', 'for our fish today and tomorrow' but without giving any clue as to how stocks of red tuna will be helped to recover. Slim metal bins, well-designed, are spaced regularly along the front. A small outline of a dog on them, together with the legend 'KiosPap' makes their function clear. A stroll through Carboneras involves constant entertainment.

Further along the front is a 'Parque Saludable para los Mayores', an exercise area for old folk. Set amongst mature palm trees on the beach is an assortment of mysterious instruments, cheerily painted red and yellow, with instructions for their correct use. The notice advises that you consult your doctor before undertaking the exercises. In the UK people spend a fortune to go to gyms to do this and here it is, all for free, on a wonderful beach in a stunningly fine climate. Mind you, no-one's actually using the equipment but close-by there are eight people of somewhat advanced years having a fine time on the pétanque court.

Lawrence of Arabia again

At the northern end of Carboneras the road begins to climb. A small wonky sign announces 'Mojácar 28 kms'. On its seaward side, white cubic developments are stacked up the hillside. 'From €130,000', blares a billboard, 'A paradise facing the Mediterranean…visit the show flat…guaranteed finance…'

I'm following the Mojácar road. Unfortunately there's no alternative. It rises past the new developments: Residencial Tortugas and the four-star Valhalla Hotel Spa and then passes inland of the Torre del Rayo, Tower of the Thunderbolt. On a hill with a strategic view back over the town, this is yet another in the coastal string of ancient watchtowers. The road now heads steadily downhill to the Playa de Algarrobico, (an *algarrobo* is a carob tree) the beach where the *rambla* of the Río Alías reaches the sea and where the boundary of the natural park, having skirted Carboneras, also comes back to the coast.

In 1962 scenes from David Lean's *Lawrence of Arabia* were filmed here. It was the first major film shot in Almería. This pre-dated the modern road, so it was perfectly possible to recreate, in precise detail, the Jordanian town of Aqaba. 200 people worked for three months to put up 300 buildings. Further inland was a Turkish military camp with over 70 tents. The construction work and the need for extras involved almost all the available population of Carboneras. 460 horses and 159 camels participated in the conquest of 'Aqaba'. Subsequently, Omar Sharif, one of the film's stars, said he thought David Lean was "mad" and described the film as: "Arabs on camels wandering round a desert for four hours." It used 1,000 extras, 400 technical staff, of whom 250 were Spanish, and was the forerunner of many further films, not least Sergio Leone's spaghetti westerns (see the chapter 'Behind the silver screen'). Opinions change though and, back in Carboneras for a civic reception to mark the fiftieth anniversary of the film in late 2012, Sharif said: "David Lean was brilliant. I now know he never did anything wrong, really. He had an extraordinary imagination."

Only 20 years ago, the Carboneras to Mojácar road journey was something of a minor epic. Where it came to Algarrobico, as many rural roads still do in Spain, the tarmac ended, vehicles crossed the grit and stones in the *rambla*, the bed of the Río Alías, as best they could and on the far side of the *rambla* the tarmac began again. Why tarmac the hundred metres or so across a *rambla* when it would be ripped up by the churning river-flow after the next prolonged downpour? So after heavy rain it would be impossible, sometimes for a few hours, sometimes for a couple of days, to drive between Carboneras and Mojácar. The road, single-track in places, went on, twisting upwards in perilous fashion across the slopes where the Sierra Cabrera tumbles into the sea. Eventually, the Carboneras-Mojácar road was closed for two years while the more primitive sections over the mountains were upgraded and a sturdy but unimaginative bridge was built over the *rambla* at Algarrobico.

The Algarrobico hotel affair

However, it is not the state of the road that has been the issue at Algarrobico these last few years. Carboneras has a dilemma. It doesn't know how to manage its situation. It wants people to live here and others to buy its burgeoning stock of holiday apartments. It turns its face to the beach and makes much of its climate. But it doesn't seem too bothered about the Cabo de Gata-Níjar Natural Park that entirely surrounds it, a place of astonishing riches.

At the northern edge of Algarrobico Beach is an enormous, incomplete hotel. It's a complex and sorry saga but the brief version goes something like this. Permission was originally given for a hotel to be built here in 1988 but it was not acted upon. Subsequently, in 1997 the Cabo de Gata-Níjar Parque Natural was established. Only in May 2003 did the developers, Azata del Sol, finally decide to take advantage of their planning permission and go ahead with their project, regardless of the fact that the site now lay within the Natural Park.

A monolithic structure resulted, a kind of ziggurat sloping back from the tideline, 22 storeys high and containing 411 rooms. Many of the residents of Carboneras supported the development on the basis of the jobs it would bring. Protest marches from Carboneras to the site of the hotel organised by opponents of the development attracted support, though not generally from residents of the town, and arguments flew to and fro. Then on February 22nd 2006 construction was stopped by a court decision. Greenpeace asked questions about the situation in the Spanish parliament and this brought the Algarrobico affair to national and international attention. Over subsequent years more legal judgements have been made and the development has been definitively declared illegal. The federal Ministry for the Environment and the Junta de Andalucía have agreed on how the matter should proceed. The Ministry will pay to demolish the hotel and the Junta will pay for clearing the site and restoring it to its former state but neither appears to have any money in their budgets to do this.

One point that appears not to have been voiced is simply this: given the ongoing economic downturn with the bottom having dropped out of the tourist market, even were the building completed, where would a 411-room hotel on an obscure, albeit stunning, part of the Spanish coast find enough visitors to be economically viable? Many other Almerían coastal hotels are already suffering low occupancy rates and opening for only limited periods each year. In February 2013 the huge Vera Hotel, 20 kilometres up the coast, suddenly closed without warning.

At Algarrobico, there is still litigation outstanding, not least the matter of possible compensation for the developers if the demolition goes ahead. And such demolition will only happen when all outstanding court cases have been settled. In a bizarre intervention in March 2013 the government's minister for the environment, Arias Cañete, said he "hopes to hire a large firm with explosives" to blow up the hotel once all the judicial cases have ended. Meanwhile, seven years after construction was halted, the Algarrobico white elephant still broods over a formerly unspoilt beach. I've taken the off-road route to approach Algarrobico, walking along the beach and across the *rambla* so, as the stagger-stepped white colossus hoves into view, it rears way above me.

After all this consideration of the Algarrobico situation, my walk ends with a whimper. By now my left ankle is sore enough to make walking a real trial. The final boundary of the Cabo de Gata-Níjar Parque Natural is a couple of kilometres further on. And the only way onward from Algarrobico is along the Mojácar road as it winds up towards Sopalmo. I want to go there to follow up more geological detail: one kilometre down the Rambla Granatilla that leads from the tiny settlement of Sopalmo to the sea, there are multicoloured badlands where the steeply dipping rocks of the Colorados Fault Zone, one of the three subdivisions of the complex Carboneras Fault Zone, can be seen outcropping. Here, tectonic plates are in conflict. I feel that I'm chickening out somewhat but I commit myself to doing it another time and anyway, I think I'd better take a geologist with me to interpret what I'm seeing.

I pull out my mobile to text Troy and let her know I've finished the walk. She's already said she will come and collect me. No signal. The only solution is to start hobbling back towards Carboneras. I try the phone at intervals but only once I'm back at the fringes of the town can I get through. It seems ironic that I'm identifying where I'm waiting to be picked up with reference to the blue and yellow flag atop the sales office of a gleaming new development. While Troy drives here to fetch me I have a further hour to reflect, in more than one sense, on the ups and downs of the Spanish coast.

8. A sense of place

'We can work at making sense of the colour-patches we see in an effort to discover where we so incontrovertibly are. It's common sense: when you move in, you try to learn the neighbourhood.'
(Annie Dillard)

The old terraces

After that prolonged stroll along the coast it's time to go back inland, have a break from the walking and focus more closely on one of the local mountain ranges, the Sierra Cabrera. Much of what can be learnt there will be applicable to various other hilly parts of Almería too.

Look from the terrace outside our kitchen and, beyond the valley, the slopes of the Sierra Cabrera, dappled with shrubs, rise to a ridge with the twin summits of Cerro de los Lobos beyond, forming the next layer in the steep undulations of the rucked land. It is a beautiful sight and eight years after we bought a house here we still stare at this landscape, delighted by the chance and the decisions that brought us to this place. Wherever there is a hint of a valley, a suggestion of where thousands of years of rain have just slightly eroded a line down the slope, there are the remains of terraces of varying sizes. The cumulative work to which these attest is staggering.

At first I fondly believed that we were looking directly across at the legacy of fifteenth century Moorish agriculture but I now know that in many cases the terraces date only from the time when this area had its maximum population, the late 19th and early 20th centuries. This coincided with the peak activity of the various mining enterprises in the region. Transport of basic foodstuffs was still very limited, so growing food locally had a real importance.

As to cultivation now, looking out across the valley, there are olive trees and almond trees and the occasional carob. Apart from a few *huertas* (vegetable gardens) with lettuces, broad beans and peppers, that's pretty much all. The olive and almond trees are almost always perched at the outer edge of each terrace. This must relate to the understanding of drainage, that this would be the optimum position for the trees. Many of these terraces and trees are now abandoned but with olives in particular being long-lived, they remain; quiet, living monuments to another time. Carobs too seem to be permanent features of the landscape, their hard dark brown pods a treat for the local goats and mules.

The cliff and the ridge

Our house is tucked into the top of a ridge. The people we bought it from had had an area behind the house excavated with a view to extending, as we have now done. The excavation they had had done created 'the cliff', an exposed rock-face up to 10 m high, which tilts down at both ends, more or less wrapping itself around one and a half sides of the house. The exposure is bewildering to a non-geologist so when an opportunity came to ask the experts, we took our chance.

In late 2009 a team of geophysicists from the University of Liverpool was looking for 24 sites in eastern Almería at which to locate seismic recording equipment for a research project, part of a global push to increase understanding of the Earth's internal structure. One of their key contacts was Lindy Walsh at the Urrá Field Centre. Lindy sifted through her address book and made speculative phone calls to some of her friends on behalf of the researchers, fairly sure she would get positive responses, which of course she did.

So when the Liverpool University geophysicists made their preliminary visit, we were not only curious about their work but we also quizzed them about our cliff. The Sierra Cabrera, where we are, emerged from the sea only about 5.5 million years ago but, as they explained, its constituent rocks are far older. We have extremely crumbly siltstones, formed of very fine particles deposited in low-energy conditions far out to sea. Some of the siltstone exposure is purple, indicating that it has been oxidised; other areas, similarly crumbly but beige rather than purple, have been reduced, which means they have had oxygen removed. The stresses of uplift are clearly shown in the cliff, with some of the strata tilted at 60°.

Some of the tilted strata are blockier. These layers are sandstone, predictably sandy in colour and made of bigger particles than the siltstone, indicating that deposition would have occurred in conditions of higher energy; in other words there was more water in the rivers and therefore more power to sweep the larger particles out to sea. The tallest part of the cliff is different again; this is dolomite, a magnesium-rich type of limestone, also originally deposited on the sea-bed, creamy-rose in colour and very strong. This dates from the Triassic, about 220 million years ago.

Because the cliff was only fairly recently exposed, parts of it are unstable and we have had some quite dramatic rock-falls, described elsewhere. The dolomite forming the tallest sections is fortunately very solid. Within the cliff a number of holes and pockets provide ideal nest sites for enterprising birds. The first spring after we bought the house, a pair of black-eared wheatears, beautifully patterned and elegant, raised a brood in a niche about three metres up. The following year the ground below the cliff was a building site and they didn't return. By the time the building was finished the house, two storeys high now, was only a couple of metres from the cliff; much too intrusive for black-eared wheatears. Not so for house sparrows though. Several pairs nest in the cliff, treating us to the endless raucous racket they mistakenly consider to be singing. Another pair nests immediately above one of our bedroom windows, where a small hole under a tile was an open invitation into the roof-space. A further pair happily occupies a nest-box on our front ground-level terrace.

This latter pair gave me an idea to try to tempt the others away from our bedroom and lower the decibel count. A three-storey nest-box was duly made and fixed to the house wall opposite the cliff, away from direct sun and more importantly, well away from where we try to sleep. So far the sparrows have shown no interest in it apart from crapping on its roof. The five or so pairs we appear to have are sticking resolutely to their traditional carefully-selected nest sites.

From the top of the cliff a rocky slope tilts down to the north and in 20 metres or so meets a narrow road. This leads, very soon, to the houses of two of our neighbours where it peters out. Just above those houses is the *deposito* (covered tank) that supplies the few scattered houses of our village with water. Recently this has been repainted in gleaming white and has had stencilled neatly onto its side: DEPOSITO DE AGUA PARA CONSUMO HUMANO. From the *deposito*, back to the point where 'the ridge' narrows as the road curves down to our gate, the distance is maybe 40 metres. In terms of disturbance, this small patch of land sees relatively little, with Paco the goat-man's animals the only occasional visitors. It is not our land but no one, other than Paco and his goats, uses it and certainly to us it seems to have quite a rich flora.

Some of the plants are fairly easy to identify, at least as far as working out their family, such as the gladioli that produce reddish-purple spikes of flowers in April. I think this particular one is Byzantine gladiolus. Then there's common asphodel, distinctive with its elegant tall spear-like shape. And there's purple phlomis, a shrub with pale evergreen leaves and grey-felted calyxes, very common in this area and another we had already managed to pin down. Rue too, there's plenty of that, but others, generally yellowish and rather nondescript to the untutored eye, are trickier. Again we were lucky enough to have the help of an expert when Lindy persuaded Roy 'Alex' Alexander of Chester University, a botanist who regularly stays at her field centre, to come over for a couple of hours and give us a master class.

As with all enthusiasts, it was a delight to spend some time in Alex's company. Without being exhaustive, or exhausting, he spent nearly three hours teaching us about some of the plants of the forty metres or so along the ridge top. Among others, he identified Thapsia, a bristly perennial with large yellow umbels; Sideritis, a shaggily hairy annual with pale yellow flowers; Coronilla juncea, the rush-like scorpion vetch (that's its English name), another yellow specialist of open rocky habitats; Anthyllis/kidney vetch, yet another yellow one. Not everything was yellow; there was Atractylis cancellata, an annual pinkish carline thistle, for example. And then there's Atriplex, called locally *salao*, saltbush, more officially known as shrubby orache in English. This is a tough shrub that the books about gardening in southern Spain speak very highly of. It's tolerant of full sun and drought, it's fire-resistant, a key plus here, and it can be shaped into a hedge. It's fine in the wild, up on the ridge, but it seeds easily and can be a pain in the garden. Once it develops a root system it's ferociously tenacious. But I digress into matters of gardening and my ambivalent relationship with saltbush.

Teucrium, the germander family, is up on the ridge too, as is Ononis natrix, described in one of the definitive plant guides as a 'much-branched dwarf subshrub'. It's right up by the *deposito*. In English it's called large yellow rest-harrow so, yes, it's yellow. Then there's Erodium, stork's bill, a geranium-like plant, and Phagnalon

71

rupestre, or possibly Phagnalon saxatile; they are so similar that even dry-land botanists can't always tell them apart. Oh, and they're yellow. Bupleurum fruticosum, an aromatic evergreen shrub known as shrubby hare's ear, has also found a home on the rocky ridge. And there's Chrysanthemum coronarium, crown daisy. I won't even tell you what colour these last two are. This is certainly the place to be if you are a plant-lover of the *amarillo* persuasion. Alex's visit was in May, so it may of course be the case that some of the plants that flower at other times of year do show a wider range of colours.

The most intriguing snippet we gleaned from Alex was about the strikingly prominent patches of vivid orange lichen on the tops of most of the rocks which project up from ground level on the ridge. Where the rocks stick up, those extra fifty centimetres or so of height supply the perfect perch for birds whose droppings provide ideal nitrogen enrichment to spur the growth of the lichen.

Mezquita dusk

Just before dusk I look across towards Cerro de la Mezquita, the Hill of the Mosque, the highest summit in the Sierra Cabrera. The air is crisp and the atmosphere sharp. The sun's embers light a tiny white beacon, the trig point at about 960 m, what they call here a *vértice geodésico*, perched on the bulk of the massif. The mountain shows hints of its rocky skin, usually more or less brown, just now somewhere in the spectrum between pink and peach at this captured moment before day's end, from among the shrubby greens of its tight pelt. Beyond the summit a single cumulo-stratus cloud, tinted peach but with just the faintest hint of salmon, drifts southwards. A minute later I look up from the compost heap to which I'm adding shredded hottentot fig and the cloud has gone, the mountain has reverted to a dull darkening shape, the day has closed.

Cerro de los Lobos

One March I walk with Alec, a friend who's staying with us, up to the col between the two tops of Cerro de los Lobos. We hang about nattering, appreciating the view to the sea that is revealed only when you reach this point and watching the goats that are just a few metres away on the slope leading up to one of the summits. The local goat-man, Paco, is sitting some way up the opposite slope, leaving his small tribe of scraggy, eccentric dogs to marshal the flock. I shout to him and he makes his way down towards us, calling: "Aren't you going to the top? (He's used to seeing me in my running gear doing just that.) Don't worry about the goats, you won't disturb them." "No," I say: "We're waiting for the women. They're coming up on the quad-bike." He nods and grins. "How many goats have you got?" I ask. "A hundred and twenty eight. Not many really, especially when there's so much for them to eat." Just then a throaty noise registers, grows louder, and Troy and Margaret come sweeping into sight right on cue.

The four of us go up on foot, maybe 40 metres of vertical height gain, to the trig point at the summit of what I call 601; that's its height in metres. The other top of Cerro de los Lobos is 603 in shorthand but is arguably not such a good viewpoint. We potter around the top, checking the ancient carob tree a few metres down the north slope for new pods, then train the binoculars on the twin grey trails of the motorway. It snakes off, silent at this distance, past Venta del Pobre, threading through the shimmering sea of *plasticos* (industrial greenhouses) on the Campo de Níjar and so towards Almería.

We look in the direction of our valley: a complex, crumpled landscape of hills and ravines, a scattering of white buildings, occasionally in clusters and there, not far down the slope, is Paco again. His charges are grazing, as always, and he's directing the dogs with a range of quirky grunts and shouts but he is sitting back, lounging, you'd have to say. I remember Enrique González demonstrating to a group of us, one time when we were walking together near Urrá, how goatherds would just sit back into a big clump of esparto grass, settling into its wiry 'give'.

Goat-men and shepherds seem to be referred to without distinction as *pastores*. Despite goats hugely outnumbering sheep here, the specific *cabrero* for the man or boy who herds the goats seems not to be used. I had thought the goatherds were always male until a friend mentioned a woman (would she be a *cabrera?*) tending a flock. The local mountain range though, is the straightforward Sierra Cabrera.

In 1953 the historian Clemente Flores first visited the Sierra Cabrera, staying in various hamlets and seeing at first-hand how the mountain people used the goats to keep the countryside clean, meaning they kept the vegetation down. But as emigration intensified in the 1950s there were fewer people to look after the goats and especially to keep them fixed to particular areas of ground.

Flores says obliquely: 'Alguien de la Administración introdujo el jabalí…' , 'Someone from the Administration introduced wild boar…'. Wild boar increasingly found the Sierra an ideal habitat, with plenty of cover due to the lack of 'cleaning' by goats. Flores goes on to make the claim that the boar didn't cause any bother for 'the Administration' but they did destroy trees and terraces, which leads to soil erosion through run-off.

Nowadays there are definitely plenty of wild boars about. They are nocturnal and rarely spotted but I've seen evidence of their digging in many places, some as close as fifty metres from our house, on the lower slopes of the ridge opposite. In several years of walking in the area I've twice seen boar during the day, albeit both times on late afternoons in December, just before dusk. On each occasion the encounter took place high on the slopes of Cerro de los Lobos. Once, in the gully leading up to the col between the two main summits, two adults and two young were making their way upwards. I'm sure they knew I was there, twenty metres higher up the slope, but they seemed unconcerned. The second incident was just before Christmas 2011. A rustling in the undergrowth stopped me and I was treated to the sight of a huge adult boar, front-heavy, close enough for the bristly nature of its coat to be clearly visible, moving away along one of the narrow contouring paths they have worn across the mountainside. Every few seconds it stopped, sniffed the air, snuffled and moved unhurriedly on. Neither time did I feel under the slightest threat.

Some time ago we heard that Chris, the son of an acquaintance who was then living in Mizala, five miles away, and his girlfriend Charlie, were knocked off his motorbike late one night by a wild boar. Chris heard Charlie cry out and turned to see the beast almost upon them, charging at full speed, presumably attracted or annoyed by the headlight. The story was that the boar 'ran through the bike'. Apart from bruising and shock, Chris and Charlie were both okay. As for the bike, amazingly it was none the worse. The boar ran off, hopefully also uninjured.

Summit sleep

Saturday 14th October 2006. Troy's gone back to the UK to spend some time with her mum who is very ill. I decide to sleep at the summit of Cerro de los Lobos. I leave the house at 7 p.m. with a full pack and, walking briskly, reach the summit of 601 m in forty minutes. I set about putting the tent up a few metres from the trig point. A green plastic garden sheet serves as an extra groundsheet to protect the tent floor against stones and whatever else might be lurking. It's a while since I've put this tent up; in the dusk there is some confusion as to which poles slide through which sleeves. Eventually it's done, after a fashion.

Using the trig point and an adjacent fallen concrete column as a shelter, a seat and a shelf, I stay out until nearly 9.30 pm. The stars are superb, the Milky Way a pale banner right above me. Small clusters of lights dot the darkness, some below me, some much further away. From their relative positions I can work out which villages they mark: La Rondeña, Gafarillos, Gacía Alto, Mizala, Peñas Negras, Venta del Pobre. At first cicadas provide a soundtrack but as the evening cools they gradually fall quiet.

I haven't brought a stove with me so it's a cold meal but I have made an effort nevertheless: almonds; red wine; pasta with sausage, aubergine and pesto; grapes; oatcakes and cheese; chocolate and brandy. It's a rough life, camping. A cool breeze springs up and drives me into my fleece top. The navigation lights of planes pass over the Sierra de los Filabres to the north-west. Lights flicker along the motorway a few kilometres away but no sound comes from that direction. A rhythmic four-flash pattern from the lighthouse on Mesa Roldán swirls a beam across the sky. As I sip red wine The Plough seems like a celestial wheelbarrow. Or maybe that's just the wine taking effect. It's silent and cool and beautiful here, a great spot for a wild camp. I text Troy in London and discover she's having a meal with her ex father-in-law. The wind is getting stronger and colder. Time for an early night and where better than in a good tent, secure from the weather but right in the midst of it, able to hear each sigh and gust of the pure air on this mountain top.

Kathleen Dean Moore devotes a chapter in her book *Riverwalking* to considering the reasons we spend time in wild places. She suggests that one of the greatest pleasures people get from travelling into a wild place is the feeling of security and safety the experience provides. That feeling comes from knowing that no matter what happens you can be safe and cosy with only what you are carrying on your back. Domesticity, she feels, is the central pleasure of the wilderness experience. Going into wild places, she suggests that the question: 'How little can I bring along...' ends in a phrase that is usually unstated but always understood: '...and still be safe and warm?'

9. Talking with Pedro

'Something feels right about sustaining and developing over many years markers to certain places and qualities.'
(Andrew Greig)

Pedro's mountain breakfasts

We're a couple of minutes late meeting our neighbour Pedro at the road junction for the 8 a.m. start to the mountain walk he'd suggested. We take the tarmac road for half a kilometre from our house, then an upward-trending unsurfaced track from there. We've been passing almond trees with a scattering of husks below. "Wild boar," says Pedro. I ask him how the boars manage to get into almonds. "Crunch them with their teeth," he says. "They're like machines but they break them so skilfully that the shell falls into two halves. Compare that with the way we smash the shells when we open them."

Pointing down into a steep valley with a few olive and almond trees on terraces in the bottom, he tells us that one morning, about 6 a.m., as he was walking quietly up this track, he looked down and saw an adult boar with half a dozen little ones. When I ask him where they lay up during the day he indicates gullies with thicker vegetation. "If goats pass, even very close, the boars don't move," he says, "but if the goats smell the boars they (the goats) veer off and make snuffling noises."

We've only been walking for forty minutes when Pedro calls a halt. From his small camouflaged rucksack he produces a large Milky Bar and a cylindrical cool-pack from which he pulls a bottle of chilled red wine. Not our usual breakfast. Troy contributes rather excellent small spinach tarts that Pedro eyes with suspicion until he has one and nods enjoyment.

On again, we pass over the col and he shows us three stones piled atop each other, marking the boundary of one of his patches of land. East from here you can see Mesa Roldán and the chimney of the power station at Carboneras with the Mediterranean beyond. South, even on an overcast day like this, the Campo de Níjar, the plain that stretches towards Almería, gleams with a pale expanse of *invernaderos*, the industrial greenhouses that provide northern Europe with vast quantities of cheap vegetables.

I ask Pedro whether a small building ahead, in a fenced enclosure, is some sort of weather station. "Yes, it sends data to Almería." Mounted on the small brick shed is a sizeable solar panel. Just beyond this, Pedro points to the stump of an almond tree and says he and his wife Isabel often used to come up here. The last time they were both here he drove them up in his 4WD a few years ago. Isabel always loved the mountains and they were both very keen walkers.

From the small three-stone cairn Pedro asks which way we want to go. Three options: left, right or back the way we came. We want to learn more about these hills and tell him we want to go left. There's a faint line across a scrubby hillside into a valley. "It used to be well looked after," he says, "but no-one uses it now and it's only a goat-track." We work our way down the valley, Troy and I in shorts, getting scratched to pieces. Pedro, himself a wily old goat, has long trousers of something like moleskin and forges ahead. Troy is crushing olives and smearing the oil on her legs to assuage the continual assault from the spiny vegetation. Pedro bursts into appreciative laughter.

We've seen a new house, still unfinished, down the valley, and now we reach it and see other ruins, it's clear this was obviously once a substantial community. "Los Loberos is the name of this place," Pedro says. He passes derogatory comments on the quality of the building work as we pass the stark red-brick house. We mention the name of the Romanian who we know is building it. "That's a gypsy name," says Pedro. "Nobody Spanish would have that name!"

"Around 40 people used to live here but the young people left and the old people gradually did too. José and Ana used to live there," he says, pointing to a ruin above where the Romanians are currently working. "They moved to a new house in our village". "When was that?" we ask, because José and Ana are our nearest neighbours and Pedro is talking as if this move was relatively recent. "Oh, 30 or 40 years ago," he says.

Troy says she's ready for a break. "Soon," says Pedro, "We're just about to reach the spring." We pass a huge ancient carob and there's the *fuente*, water trickling into an oblong concrete trough. He builds a fire from twigs and fallen wood from the surrounding oleanders and carobs. Out from his pack comes a stick of bread. We

78

toast it and he spears three hefty chunks of *morcilla* (black pudding) onto sharpened sticks. Add triangular wedges of soft cheese (remember *La Vache Qui Rit?*, that's the stuff) and wash it down with another plastic cup of cool red wine. We offer small bars of chocolate left in our fridge by recent visitors when they went back to the UK. It harks back, way back, to campfire discoveries we had when kids. Then more bread, and thick slices of pork that are 90% fat. It's delicious once crisped.

This place, again with a scattering of ruins, is called Granadino. Just before we leave Pedro indicates the remains of a house on the slope above and tells us that the man who used to live there shot himself. "He was the father of the guy who has the house below mine. You know, the couple who live in Barcelona now. He was living on his own and very ill. He obviously decided it was time. A single bullet," he says, pointing into his forehead.

"When I was young this *rambla* (riverbed) would have water in it for most of the year. Now it only runs once every eight or nine years." He's talking about a change that's happened within the last fifty years. The Sierra Cabrera is not a big mountain range and I don't think this is a tale of the water being taken for new urban developments or golf courses, as in other parts of southern Spain. It seems like a definite case of climate change, assuming that Pedro's memory is accurate. It also explains, he says, why a lot of the more remote terraces with their almond trees have been abandoned.

On another occasion, in fact the first time we'd been on the hills with him, we were up at the 601 m summit of Cerro de los Lobos. Immediately by the trig point are three stones, set vertically in the ground to form three sides of a square. We'd seen these before but only now realise that this is one of Pedro's 'mountain fireplaces'. However, he's sniffing the wind and he decides there's too much *aire* (breeze), so we drop 30 metres or so down the west side of the hill to another of his fireplaces.

We've brought apples, chewy bars and a bottle of water. Pedro has other ideas. He fishes three cool cans of beer from his rucksack, despite our (admittedly muted) protestations that it's too early. Sprightly for a man in his late sixties, he springs across the slope to gather kindling from under a nearby carob tree and within a couple of minutes has a fine blaze going. What appears to be a piece of slate is then set above the flames. We ask why it doesn't crack and he says it's some sort of special rock from Andorra and it's been treated with oil. Next, a slab of bacon from which three slices are taken with a Boy Scout knife, a stick of bread, cut, olive-oiled and heated, then *morcilla*. It's that old thing about how good food tastes in the open air, especially when it's as unexpected as this. To finish, or so we thought, oranges. Pedro's oranges are grown in heaven.

But he wasn't finished yet. A coffee pot appeared and small coffees followed. Then out came a bottle of *aguardiente* (fiery eau-de-vie). You toss a shot of the firewater down in one and pop a sugar cube in immediately afterwards: the culmination of a breakfast with a difference.

We go north-west from the 601 m trig point, down the ridge to point 579 m, then west. Looking north-west from here, down into the obvious valley, this is Rincón de los Buitres, Vulture's Corner. Within that, there's an obvious crag called Piedra de la Águila, Eagle's Stone. This is at spot height 456 m at grid reference 58721007 on the El Llano de Don Antonio map, sheet 1031-IV. These names are not on any map though. When the old folk who grew up here and roamed these hills finally pass on, these names will disappear too. Infinitesimally, the place will be further impoverished.

From there, we pursue a wandering course through the shrubby vegetation, nattering about plants, about who owns which land, the names of birds. *Camino de zorro*, says Pedro in answer to our question, it's a fox's path, as we follow a virtually invisible line amongst spiky bushes. Two minutes later, an involuntary cry from Troy. We look up and there, fifty metres away, a fox is crossing the adjacent slope.

Back down in the semi-agricultural zone, we work our way down terraces of almonds and olives. Some of these are overgrown and abandoned, their owners long gone to the cities. When we get to Pedro's immaculately kept terraces we ask him what the significance is of the upturned plastic bottles on canes, imagining them to be bird-scarers. "No," he says, "they're to tell the goat-man not to let his animals browse here."

Pedro remembers

Joe Moran, talking of modern environmental writing, suggests: '… that our lives gain purpose and meaning from the concrete particulars, the texture and detail of individual existences knotted together in unique localities over many years.' So, it seems to me, it is with our neighbours. Some time ago Pedro, he of the mountain walks, who now lives in a modern house on the site of the one he was born in, told me about his childhood in the valley. This would have been in the 1940s. My comments are in italics in brackets:

"The school was in Herradura, in a converted house, at the side of where Juan lives. I learnt to read and write a bit. Numbers, a little. Nothing else. The teacher was a trainee. There were only seven or eight pupils.

"We were in school between nine and one. In the afternoons I helped my mother in the house and my father and brother in the fields. My family and other families here had pigs, chickens, turkeys, ducks, rabbits, goats and sheep. Also dogs, but hunting dogs, not pets. We didn't have cows. There were cows in Mizala and at Cortijo los Arejos, four or five at each place, for milk. What wild animals and birds were there? Foxes, hares, martens, wildcats. The wildcats have gone; they're not here nowadays. There were more birds: eagles, for example.

"What did people grow? Well, it used to rain more. We grew wheat, maize, barley and rye for the animals, beans, peppers, tomatoes and chickpeas. There were threshing circles worked with mules, not with horses. There was a water mill at Granadino and five at Los Molinos de Río Aguas. The last mill was in Los Perales. Each mill used the water of the previous mill.

"There were 14 families here, usually with just two or three children but in the house below José and Ana there was a family of nine. In Los Garcías there were nine families *(Los Garcías is now a totally deserted hamlet at the head of the valley)* and five more families higher up in the *barranco* (ravine). In total, I reckon, more or less a hundred people.

"There were no roads or cars in La Rondeña then, just narrow paths. For transport there were just horses and mules. In the houses there was no electricity or water. Everyone got their water from the *fuente* (spring). There was always water but not a lot because there were so many people.

"I think every extended family had a *matanza* (pig-killing). The pigs weighed two or three hundred kilos. And *fiestas*? There were never *fiestas* in La Rondeña or La Herradura but there were in Gafarillos. Gacía Bajo didn't have a *fiesta* for 24 years until they re-started it this year.

"There were two shops in Gafarillos that sold everything. In Sorbas there was the market and some shops but not many. I went with my father *'con las bestias' (by mule, I think this means)* direct to Sorbas on the paths (*at least 12 km and very hilly*). When I was young we collected esparto (*a tough, wiry grass described in more detail elsewhere*) and walked to Carboneras to sell it (*again, a hilly 12 km*). The esparto was loaded onto boats. I was fifteen when I first went to Almería. There was a bus from Venta del Pobre to Níjar and then on to Almería. The first time I swam in the Mediterranean I was twenty. At that time there were only 11 farmhouses in the Campo de Níjar and four or five big farms at Fernán Pérez.

"When I was 18 I went to Andorra to work in a hydro-electric plant. Then, when I was 20, I went to Germany. There, I worked in a factory making metal products such as field kitchens for soldiers. (*Who were these soldiers in the 1950s? British and American forces stationed in what was then West Germany?*) There were a lot of Spaniards, Greeks, Italians and Turks."

We see Pedro quite often. We'll wave and shout a greeting across the valley from our garden, or he hoots as he drives past, as he has to in order to go anywhere from his house, or he'll come round as he did last Tuesday with, on that occasion, a bag of pomegranates, almonds and a tub of olives. To see Isabel we have to visit; she's been diabetic for almost forty years and is now housebound. We invited them round one Boxing Day and it was a major expedition for her. She has trouble seeing, though she watches the *telenovelas*, the Spanish TV soaps, so we time our visits to avoid them.

She has a keen sense of humour but she's harder to understand than Pedro. Because he was a Gastarbeiter ('guest-worker') in Germany for a while he is better at taking account of our linguistic limitations when he speaks. Despite her illness she's as sharp as a blade. They're characters both, a pair of dynamos. I'm less than five ten and they each only come up to my shoulders so they can't be much over five feet tall. They're feisty, opinionated, and we sometimes find we are looking on as they dispute some minor issue. As is the Spanish way, an exchange of opinions sounds to the untutored ear like an argument.

It feels a real privilege to have been taken under their wing. Isabel was suggesting a while ago that we try to learn ten new words per day. She's now reduced this target to two, a result, I suspect, of the way we regularly mangle *castellano*. We had some discussion about the fact that learning a language involves more than just vocabulary; there's the matter of verbs and tenses, of idioms. And of course we invoke the old chestnut about how much easier it is to learn a new language when you're young.

10. A historical perspective

'The writer Juan Goytisolo fell in love with the Almería desert on his first visit here in the early 1950s. Stopping for a drink in a bar in Sorbas, he could not contain his enthusiasm any longer. "It's the most beautiful landscape in the world," he blurted out. But the barman reacted in a way which Goytisolo had not expected. He stopped what he was doing, stared reproachfully at the writer, and replied in a voice which Goytisolo was never to forget: "For us, sir, it is an accursed country."'

(Michael Jacobs)

A historical perspective

Now for a little history. Gafarillos is our nearest village. It's at latitude 37° 3' 0" N and longitude 2° 1' 0" W. The old population sources for Gafarillos parish indicate that many more people used to live here. That's not surprising news; the ruined houses tell their own story. But one thing leads to another and I'm fascinated by the population statistics and the sheer extent of the change in the number of people, so I delve on into the past. Sorbas, the municipality that includes Gafarillos, proves to be one of the keys to the story. Goats prove to be another.

Sorbas town is a small place, with just a couple of thousand people. It's scarcely mentioned in guidebooks that cover the whole country. The *Rough Guide to Spain* refers grudgingly to Tabernas and Sorbas, saying: 'Both towns look extraordinary, especially Sorbas, whose houses overhang an ashen gorge, but neither is a place to linger, this is the middle of a desert.' Elisabeth de Stroumillo, in *Southern Spain,* accords it a fifth of a sentence, referring to 'the dramatically-perched pottery village of Sorbas'. In *The Shell Guide to Spain* Angus Mitchell ignores it. Even the *Rough Guide to Andalucía* finds space in its 650 pages for less than ten lines about Sorbas.

It's time for a historical perspective. In 1445 Sorbas formed a single administrative unit with Lubrín, a place of similar size. Sorbas is almost 30 km inland from the sea and Lubrín, although about 15 km north north-east of Sorbas, is almost the same distance inland because of the angle of the coast. The influence of Sorbas was substantial though. Down on the coast, just east of Agua Amarga, there's a Cala Sorbas, Sorbas Cove, about 30 kms from the town itself. Similarly distant, the main street in Carboneras also carries the name of Sorbas.

During the second half of the 15th century the Christians were wresting back large areas of Al-Andalus, southern Spain, from the Muslims, who had held sway for centuries. This was the Reconquest, which reached its peak under the Spanish monarchs Ferdinand and Isabella. Almería was taken by the Christians in 1489 and by 1492 they were at the gates of Granada. In that year the last Nasrid ruler, Abur Abd Allah, known as Boabdil in Spanish, surrendered to the Christians and abandoned Granada. He fled to the Alpujarras, then the coastal town of Adra, and finally North Africa.

Estimates suggest that a quarter of a million Muslims left the Kingdom of Granada or were killed during the hostilities. However, it is reckoned that a further quarter of a million remained in eastern Andalucía after 1492 and indeed had surrendered to the Christians on quite good terms. The Muslims who lived under Christian rule were called *mudéjares*. On condition that they stayed away from their fortified settlements such as Granada's Alhambra and the Alcazaba in Almería, they were allowed to follow their religion and retain their costumes and traditions.

In 1492 Sorbas and Lubrín were listed as belonging to the domain of Don Pedro Fernández de Velasco, *condestable* (more or less equivalent to commander-in-chief) of Castilla. Three years after this the towns passed to Don Diego López de Haro. At this time the area east of Almería, including the plains of Níjar and Tabernas and the Sierras of Alhamilla, Bédar and Cabrera, was known as La Axarquía Almeriense.

However, the situation soon deteriorated, with a revolt breaking out in 1499 after the hard-line Cardinal Cisneros, recently arrived in Granada, ordered the baptism of 60,000 Muslims. The rebellion began in the Alpujarras and spread through eastern Andalucía before being finally extinguished in 1501. All unconverted Muslims were thrown out of Andalucía, and those who had converted, known as *moriscos* (as opposed to *moros*, the general word for Muslims, and still today a rather pejorative term), were ordered to speak Spanish and wear western clothes. Nevertheless, according to the Venetian ambassador Andrea Navagero, who described Granada in 1526, the *moriscos* were continuing to follow their own faith, wear their own clothes and speak their own language. Navagero made a plea for tolerance of the *moriscos*' ways.

It was not to be though, and in 1568 Philip II made a renewed and stronger attempt to crush Muslim culture. A new rebellion began in Granada's Albaicín quarter and spread into the hills, becoming known as the Guerra de las Alpujarras (War of the Alpujarras). Not until 1571 was this revolt finally put down. The consequence this time was the final expulsion of all the *moriscos* from the Kingdom of Granada.

This was reflected even in the more remote parts of Almería province. A few days after the arrival in Sorbas of Don Juan of Austria on 6th April 1570, the population surrendered and the Moors were summarily kicked off their lands and dispersed, leaving the area almost deserted. According to Rosa María Piqueras: '...all the Moors from Sorbas, together with those of Lubrín, and some from Serena and Cabrera, were directed to the lands of the Marqués del Carpio in Córdoba.' From a total of 800 Moors expelled from Sorbas and Lubrín, fewer than half survived the journey to Córdoba. This left Sorbas and Lubrín virtually depopulated.

In June 1573 repopulation began, with 250 settlers brought from Murcia, Cartagena, Lorca, Aragon and elsewhere. A survey of Sorbas in 1576 recorded a series of rules for new settlers. They had to register their vineyards, trees, including mulberries, and both irrigated and dry land. They had to pay towards the clearing and maintenance of irrigation lines and the restoration of dams on the river. The use of flour and oil mills was free for the first six years, as long as they were kept in good repair. New settlers were obliged to farm and cultivate according to the customs of the area. Finally, they had to possess a sword, arquebus (an old-fashioned handgun), crossbow or halberd (a long pike) and a round shield.

But there were difficulties for those who were trying to settle. Many of the people who came to repopulate the area were from places with farming habits very different from those they found in the district around Sorbas. Some of them came from regions with far more water and they found adapting to dry-land agricultural practices very difficult.

In addition, because the area was so near the coast, it was at risk from raids. Many of the Moors who had been expelled had gone to North Africa and, knowing the Sorbas area well, acted as guides for incursions by pirates, who seized the people they found and sold them at slave markets in Algeria. J. A. Tapia Garrido tells us that in 1578 pirates pillaged Sorbas town and took the population captive. Shortly afterwards Sorbas was again resettled, this time with 30 people. By the end of the 16th century the population had stabilised but there were still large areas within the municipality with no inhabitants.

Things remained quiet and, a century and a half later, in 1749, work began on a large-scale census and statistical investigation called the Catastro de Ensenada. It was carried out under King Fernando VI and his minister the Marquis of Ensenada, hence its name, and it covered population, properties, buildings and other details. Its results, in 1752, showed that Sorbas, which was at this time part of the estate of the Duque de Alba, had '249 casas y 211 cortijos'. This would be 249 houses in the town itself and 211 farms in the outlying districts. So, 150 years after the expulsion of the Moors, there was again a significant settled population in the area.

Regular concrete evidence begins to appear over a century later, with the 1887 census, which tallied the number of dwellings in the municipality of Sorbas at 2,200, of which 1,383 were scattered in the areas outside the town. In the 130 years since the Catastro de Ensenada there had been a big increase in the total population to 7,462. It seems that many of the small population centres had their origins between the mid-18th and mid-19th centuries, no doubt growing around what were at first just single farmsteads. Gradually a pattern established itself that is still obvious today, one of simple nucleated centres, some with over 200 inhabitants, with a scattering of houses around and between them.

The historian Diego Molina Simón has investigated past population patterns in Gafarillos parish. One of his primary sources was Francisco Molina Méndez (1843-1939) of Granadino who, in a surviving photo, has a stocky head, short white hair and a steady determined gaze. He is recorded as saying: "The first inhabitant of La Rondeña was a wolf-hunter who came from Ronda in Málaga. Something similar happened with Los Loberos where some wolf-hunting families settled. In Granadino there was a wolf-hunting family who came from Granada. In the case of Los Gacía (Alto and Bajo) the first inhabitant was a Moor called Gacía".

As described in another chapter, the wolf connection is obvious from various place names on the map. Wolves are long gone from the Sierra Cabrera, though. In fact, Spain's total wolf population reached a low in 1970 of 400-500. Since then a slow recovery has brought the total up to 2,000 – 2,500. They are mostly in the north-east, with just a small population in the Jaén - Cuenca area of the Sierra Morena, estimated in 2005 at between 8 and 10 packs, numbering between 40 and 70 animals, and possibly slightly on the increase. So the nearest wolves to the Sierra Cabrera are now about 200 kilometres away, with no chance of a re-colonisation. (My editor, Helen, saw this and responded: "Never say never!" Well, personally I'd be delighted if wolves came back to the Cabrera but I can't see it happening any time soon.)

Depopulation

The 1887 census gave a population of 1,358 for the parish of Gafarillos and listed 13 centres of population, of which the largest were Mizala (229 inhabitants) and Gacía Alto (169). In 1910, the total was 1,344 and in 1930 the population level in the parish was still broadly similar and was split between 15 separate places: Alpañeces, Cerrada (Gafares), Arejos, Campico, Gafarillos, Gacía Alto, Gacía Bajo, Granadino, Herradura, Loberos, Mizala, Peñas Negras, Rellana, Rondeña and Varguicas.

By 1950, though, things were changing and the figures were showing a clear decline. Part of the variation in the figures for individual places is down to administrative changes but all the centres of population saw similar fluctuations, with the peak of population in the late 19th and early 20th centuries.

Times were harsh in the aftermath of the Civil War and many people left to find work elsewhere. Some of them did not go far, just to the Campo de Níjar (20 km) or El Ejido (80 km), for example, but many went to Cataluña or even Germany. Migrant workers are not a new phenomenon. By 1950 the number of people in Gafarillos parish had dropped to 1,028, a loss of over 300 people, mostly in the preceding 20 years, an average of 15 people per annum.

I have heard but not seen in any definitive source, that one reason for the depopulation of outlying villages in the 1940s and 1950s was this: the fascist government of Franco wanted to reduce the number of town halls. In order to do so it was focusing on small towns and it said that it would base its decisions on the total population, not in the town's whole municipality, but just in the town itself. At this stage Sorbas and Lubrín were pretty much neck and neck in this respect. The story goes that as a consequence the authorities in Sorbas (and presumably in Lubrín too) were reluctant to install services in the outlying villages and concentrated their efforts on trying to persuade people to move from the rural areas into the town where all manner of modern convenience could be had.

As for some of the component parts of Gafarillos parish, in the first half of the 20th century the population of Herradura fell from 225 to 102, of Los Loberos from 171 to 74, of Granadino from 68 to 8. In 1950, for the first time, a population count of zero was recorded, for Los Arejos (back in 1887 it had had 25 inhabitants). The same fate, total depopulation, had struck Los Alpañeces by 1970 and both Granadino and Los Loberos by 1991.

The biggest outflow of population was between 1975 and 1991. A key reason why people moved away from some of the more remote places was because of their 'grado de atraso', their 'state of backwardness', with no running water and no electricity. In most of the places in Gafarillos parish these services were not installed until the late 1970s or early 1980s.

Although places such as Granadino recorded no permanent population, some houses there were maintained and lived in for short periods, for example during the olive harvest, by family members whose fixed address was now elsewhere, such as in Carboneras or Almería. These are still used by those who previously moved away, as places for weekend visits or retirement, or to come back to at significant times such as the local saint's day. In the case of Gafarillos this is San Lorenzo, 10th August. As I write this on Viernes Santo, Good Friday, people are back in a couple of the houses in our valley that are normally empty. For these people, Semana Santa, Easter Week, is an important time to go back to their roots.

In 1857 the community where our house is was thriving; it had 115 people. In 1900 there were 109, and in 1950 still 69. But it was the same story as in other places; 62 in 1970, down to 40 in 1981 and down again to 17 in 1991. Now there are just a dozen people living here in six permanently inhabited houses. At weekends, in summer, and on varying family occasions, this increases with arrivals from Carboneras, Los Gallardos, Barcelona and even England because, of the dozen current residents, three are English. In some of the population centres, such as Peñas Negras, there are no Brits, but elsewhere in the parish most places have at least a couple and in some places, like Gacía Bajo, a cluster. Add the occasional Belgian, Dutchman, German and Romanian to the mix and you have the reason why the population figures have not fallen to even lower levels.

Of goats

If we go further back in the history (strictly speaking the pre-history) of the Sierra Cabrera, the pollen record indicates that 10,000 years ago the area was covered by woodland with an abundance of different species of oak, a consequence of both the climate and the limited presence of human beings in the area. However, by 5,000 years before the present, the Capsian culture was established in what is now Almería province. This was originally a Mesolithic culture of the Maghreb (North Africa), named after the town of Gafsa in present-day Tunisia. There is evidence from Neolithic times that this culture had domesticated animals of the subfamily Caprinae, which includes goats and the European mouflon, the latter thought to be the ancestor of modern sheep.

Historians consider the Capsian people to have introduced nomadic pastoralism to the Sierra Cabrera. As soon as this happened, the decline of woodland began and the range of flowers started to increase as a result of two factors, fire and grazing. Fire was the easiest tool with which the Capsians could increase the amount of scrubland that served as pasture for their animals. The number of animals, primarily goats, increased steadily until the Middle Ages. Since then, the landscape of the Sierra Cabrera, apparently semi-wild, has in fact been a direct result of human management and the increasing aridity of the climate.

The predominance of goats gave a name to both the mountain range and to a specific settlement, known since before 1500, and still today, as Cabrera. Bernard Vincent, director of the Centre de Recherches Historiques in Paris and an eminent researcher of Spanish social history, highlights the importance of livestock in the Kingdom of Granada during medieval times. As other historians confirm, a typical Muslim home in those times would have had an average of 18 head of livestock. Bernard Vincent also confirms the importance of transhumance, the seasonal movement of livestock to find better grazing. In major mountain areas such as the Alps this tends to be an altitudinal migration, but in southern Spain there was also a movement of livestock seasonally over substantial distances.

As summer comes on the grasses of southern Spain wither, so farmers and their flocks moved north in search of new pastures. But winter is cold in the north and fresh grass is growing in the south, so back came the farmers and their animals. As a consequence of this annual pattern of *trashumancia* a network of transhumance paths evolved, 125,000 kms in total, covering 1% of the land surface of Spain. These drovers' roads were overseen by the Mesta, an organisation of mainly sheep farmers which, at its peak in the early 16th century, was moving three million sheep each year. The *cañadas* along which the livestock could legally travel and graze under the protection of the crown were typically up to 40 metres wide. (For more on the old routes, see the chapter 'Lines on the landscape'.)

In the 16th century herds of livestock were brought into the area from elsewhere to forage on rented pastures. This increased after the *sierra* was cleared of its residents, who all fled to Africa in 1505. A clue to the rich flora of the Sierra Cabrera at that time comes from the fact that the fleeing inhabitants abandoned 88 beehives.

At this time Mojácar and Vera seem to have been the nearby settlements that had most influence on the Sierra Cabrera. In 1497, very soon after the Spanish reconquest, Mojácar council wrote to Vera council because of a dispute about grazing licences. The control and renting out of pastures continued to be an issue throughout the 16th century, with the municipal archive in Vera an endless source of detail on the matter. There it is recorded that over 2,100 sheep and goats passed the winter of 1530 in Vera, whereas the following winter only Juan Xarqui was there, with his 1,000 head of livestock.

Throughout the 16th century efforts were made to repopulate the settlements of Teresa and Cabrera, high in the *sierra*, but after the eviction of the *moriscos* in 1570 both remained deserted. The depopulation of the area became still more accentuated after the assault by the Moors on Cuevas del Almanzora in 1573, when 225 captives were taken to Africa. Over the next two centuries the recovery of the fixed population of the Sierra Cabrera proceeded only very slowly, but the goatherds remained, with their goat-pens alongside their remote hamlets.

Early in the 19th century, with the coast now fortified by the Castillo de San Andrés in Carboneras amongst other structures, the population slowly increased and began to exploit anew the resources of the mountains. Livestock farming became complementary to agriculture and to the exploitation of firewood from the mountains.

As well as supplying meat and milk, goats were useful for the clearing of weeds from the marginal areas around crops and for keeping shrubs trimmed to a modest size. This helped in two ways: it prevented the invasion of cultivated areas by unwanted seeds and it limited the risk of wildfires. However, it also restricted the re-establishment of trees in the area. So important did goats become that in the mid-19th century over 2,000 head were based in Turre, from where they grazed the surrounding area. At that time roughly 40% of the population of Turre municipality lived in the Sierra Cabrera, a state of affairs that continued virtually until the middle of the 20th century.

Back in the mid-19th century, Spain's network of *cañadas* or drovers' roads was still in full operation. None of the major routes, the *cañadas reales,* passed through the Sierra Cabrera, but the feeder routes linking into them did. On a smaller scale the pattern of animal grazing, with a rhythm linked to the seasons, and certain routes followed and nibbled down by the animals, created fire-breaks, a major factor in limiting wildfire damage. Although flocks of goats are still tended by the *pastores* (shepherds) on the Cabrera hills, there has been an overall reduction in grazing activity and this is thought to be one reason that wildfires (see the chapter 'Heat and wildfire') have been more frequent in recent years.

11. *Acebuches* and olives
'The truest gardening weaves the way of the wild within it.'
(Jay Griffiths)

Acebuches

Just outside our house, by the top of the steps that lead down to the terraces where we attempt to grow fruit and vegetables, is an *acebuche* tree. When we arrived here it was the only tree on the plot. The *acebuche* is the wild ancestor of the cultivated olive and produces smaller fruit. We were told that *acebuche* oil was one of the finest cosmetic oils available, so we collected some of the tiny *acebuches* and attempted a do-it-yourself pressing. It was a complete failure. We got no oil at all: the fruits seemed to be all stone and no flesh.

Normally we haven't bothered to harvest the *acebuche* with serious intent; the tree is on a steep slope which makes putting a net below it impossible and the minimal reward hasn't seemed worth the effort involved. Today though, needing a quiet and easy-paced activity to readjust my body and head after rather too much chocolate and wine over Christmas and the New Year, I took a green plastic bucket and began to pick the *acebuches*. Small purple missiles thudded into the bottom of the container. They were ripe, over-ripe I guess, because as I worked on, enough of the fruits burst for my hands to be stained in a way that suggested blackberry-picking.

After a good two hours I had almost a standard bucketful of *acebuches.* This amounted to five kilos, worth perhaps just over a litre of oil, not that we'd receive the oil from these hard-won fruits separately though. They would just go in with the other olives on our final trip to the mill for this season, delicate fruits with oil of reputedly high quality lost in the bigger picture.

Meanwhile, we'd already pruned our olive trees. The resulting branches lay in a mound on the middle terrace. Goats like olive prunings. As we drove home the other day, Paco the goat-man's flock was coming down the slope to the road a couple of hundred metres from our house, their activities guided by his dogs and a few well-aimed rocks from the man himself. I stopped the car, wound the window down and shouted up to him that we had olive branches. "The goats will have them when we come past another day," he called back.

Sure enough, a few days later I saw furious goat activity where I'd left the prunings, just across from our lower gate. I went down and had a chat with Paco. His hairy grey dogs were keeping the goats in check. "How many dogs have you got?" I asked. "Four here, and lots more back at home," he grinned. "Are they a special breed for working with the goats?" I wondered. "Yes," he said, *"perros pastores"*, shepherd's dogs. To the untrained eye they just look like a random assemblage of scraggy mutts. Within half an hour the flock had moved on, leaving a legacy of devastated twigs and thin branches with just the occasional leaf still attached. It was a thorough if somewhat untidy job with the remnant twigs scattered over a much wider area than the original pile, rather as if a small goatish rock festival had just ended, with a scattering of litter and the crowd staggering off happy and oblivious.

Diary: 31st Dec 2005

Helped Pedro finish picking his most venerable olive tree. He claims it was alive when the Moors ruled Spain. This would make it over 500 years old, perfectly possible. Small olives but lots of them. "No water, full of oil," he says. He reckons we'll get over 100 kilos of olives just from this tree. "When the sun goes down, we'll stop," he says. The sun goes down. Suddenly it's cold. We stop.

Picking Lindy's olives

Olive-picking is not a complex process. You lay out a *manta* (net) under an olive tree and pick, either by hand or with the use of neat little plastic rakes, thousands of those glistening bullets hanging among the slim silver leaves. Some of the olives are fat, glossy and black, some small and green, and many are on the continuum between these extremes; an endless range through purple and burgundy to reddish-pink and on into pale green.

A mid-January day: the sun is surprisingly strong, there's a breeze, and from up in the tree the view extends across many square miles of terraces, steeply eroded gullies, rocky outcrops and scrubby bushes. In a semi-desert way it is intensely beautiful. A kilometre away and some distance below is Cortijo Urrá, the house and field centre owned by Lindy Walsh, whose trees we are harvesting. Lindy offered us the chance to pick her olives, the deal being that she would have a proportion of the resulting oil.

Some of the olives are out of reach, so the pruning saw comes into play and a branch comes down, to be stripped of its fruit on the ground below. The fruits rain down onto the *manta*, a huge black oblong mesh of nylon, stretched as best we can organise it below the tree. Often, especially given that these trees have been relatively neglected, we spend fifteen or twenty minutes clearing the ground below the tree, removing feathery fronds of hogweed and sawing through the knotty stems of pungent shrubs so that we can lay the *manta* in such a way that when the olives spatter down onto it they won't run off the edge and be lost.

If you use the plastic rakes, the quicker method, you tend to bring down a fair few leaves and twigs, the biggest of which then have to be removed. It's a matter of pride to deliver olives to the *almazara* (an Arabic word meaning olive mill) without too much debris mixed in. It's also perfectly possible to pick by hand, pulling your fingers along the thin whippy branches, easing the fruits off and letting the leaves slip by intact. We tend to mix and match the two methods. Meanwhile, resonant cries somewhere across the *barranco* (ravine) indicate that 'Lindy's' jackdaws are about. I estimated 300 coming over the other day, like large flecks of soot, loudly celebrating their passage and aerial ability.

Initially we tip the olives from the *mantas* into those large black plastic buckets with two handles that are common here. If you are harvesting over a period of time though, the picked olives need to have an air-flow around them and so have to be stored in perforated plastic crates. We have a big stack of these in various sizes and colours, mostly scavenged from the municipal tip outside our local village, Gafarillos, in the old days, before it was closed in 2010. The ideal would be to take the olives immediately to be milled but this is not realistic. They're okay for a few days stored somewhere cool until there are sufficient to make a trip to the *almazara* worthwhile.

When we have enough olives we take our first batch down to the *almazara* in Gafarillos. It's run by Juan José, Juan-Jo for short. Juan-Jo is the local mover and shaker: as well as the olive mill, he owns the village shop, is a councillor in Sorbas and seems an entirely decent sort of guy. He's always quickly on the case when we go to tell him we have no water and there's a pot-hole in the road with water bubbling out of it and maybe these facts are connected.

At the mill the olives are tipped down through a grid into a hopper. They go up two steep conveyor belts and disappear. Juan-Jo then emerges and tells you how much they weigh and what he's going to give you for them. 116kg, he'll say, and here's the deal. 10c per kilo for processing them, and you get oil at the rate of one litre for every 5 kg of olives. So we pay €11.60 to have the olives processed, and this will give us 23.2 litres of oil. This is measured out by a dispensing machine with a digital readout on the front into 5-litre plastic containers. You can bring your own containers or pay 50c for each new one. So for a few days of not-too-hard work in the sun and fresh air, and a modicum of scratches from the less co-operative parts of the trees, we are set up with olive oil for the foreseeable future.

We've done some of the picking with our friends Marcus Field and Andrew Wilson. The olive harvest with these guys is a leisurely, sociable affair. We arrive at their house in the village of Los Molinos de Río Aguas, drink tea and have a natter, then gradually get our act together and drive off to begin the harvest. After a while we stop for a picnic of cheese, olive bread and satsumas then continue picking until the sun goes down and we're left clearing away as the almost full moon hauls its helpful light across the scene. As I write this, the four of us have harvested 140 kilos of olives, so that will be another 28 litres of oil, split three ways: a third to them, a third to us, a third to Lindy. Troy and I are finding that the longer we are here the more olive oil we use. We seem to be Mediterranean naturals, finding it hard to imagine how people can live without garlic and olive oil and red wine.

You can't leave trimmings and cut branches lying around. They have to be removed to avoid disease and diminish the fire risk, so we have to get these down to the fire-pit near the field centre. Lindy has a licence allowing her to have a fire, in a place she deems safe, during daylight hours between the beginning of November and the end of February. Fire permissions from the local council are season-sensitive. In the summer the whole landscape is like a tinder-box. I have photos taken from our house in October 2006 of vast plumes of smoke from wildfires to the east in the higher Sierra Cabrera. If you look closely at the pictures there are small black dots, insect-sized helicopters dropping water. On that occasion, after a few hours the insects won. The story was different in 2009 when extensive wildfires (see the chapter 'Heat and wildfire') ravaged the Sierra Cabrera over several days.

The new olive mill

We're just into 2011 and things have moved on with our local olive mill. It's moved from the old building in Gafarillos to a new site about a kilometre away, alongside the road to Peñas Negras. Custom-built, and with a reputed investment of over €1 million, the place is clean, spacious and efficient. It operated for the first time in the 2009-10 season. So this is the second season for the new *almazara* and a notably good one for olive production. The rain early last year was the key factor, so the locals say. And this year's harvest began a month earlier than normal, another result of the propitious weather.

Since November, particularly at weekends, the valley has rung to the sound of continuous chatter as families make their annual visit to gather their olives. On one occasion we heard the steady chug of an engine and picked out, through binoculars, a couple of guys using a tree vibrator, a machine that clamps onto the tree and shakes it viciously to free the fruit. Our traditional neighbours, those that still live here all year round, wouldn't be doing with such a new-fangled and surely harmful device.

The hefty investment at the *almazara* means that now, instead of using an off-the-top-of-the-head formula such as 1 litre of oil per 5 kilos of olives, a more sophisticated system prevails. As before, the olives are tipped through a grille into a hopper, weighed, and then taken up a conveyor to be processed. A quirky device on the conveyor with a scoop on the end of each of its four arms is turning and dipping into the olives as they pass, thus taking a representative sample of the crop. This goes into the lab, where that sample is tipped into a small mincer that crushes the fruits and exudes olive sludge from the bottom. Some of this is then smeared onto a glass slide over which a cover is clamped shut. This is then slotted into a spectrometer which takes several readings before averaging the results and providing a print-out of the oil content and acidity of the olives. A quick multiplication of 'weight of olives delivered x percentage of oil' determines how much oil you receive.

The whole process is simple and quick. On one of my three visits to the *almazara* this season I was in and out in less than half an hour. The last batch I took, which included our five kilos of *acebuches* in the mix, came in at 90 kilos and registered 24.5% oil, giving us 22 litres of oil. Overall this year, we had 389 kilos of olives which earned us 90.5 litres of oil. There's an undeniable satisfaction in seeing the plastic 5-litre containers lined up, their contents gleaming gold-green and promising endless future delight.

Soon after we came here we got our neighbour Pedro to tell us what type each of our olive trees is and then promptly forgot what he'd said. The only olives that are easily recognisable to the incomer (to me, at least) are the *picuales*, which have quite large fruits with a distinct asymmetrical point at the bottom. We have some *manzanillas* too, I think; these are the ones, picked green, that are found as eating olives, often stuffed with anchovies or almonds, in tins in supermarkets. When it comes to taking the olives for oil though, they are all just tossed in together.

The nine trees we have, all still young, produced 35kg of olives in 2008 when still very small, then only 6kg in 2009 and 136kg in 2010. This alternating yield pattern, whereby trees can be very productive one year and then bear almost no fruit the next, is known as a *vecería*, a mysterious phenomenon that, with luck, science will not be able to divine for some time yet.

Olives to eat

If you were pushed for time, you probably wouldn't get involved in processing green olives. First you have to bash them with a stone to split the skin. They tend to splatter so it's best to wear old clothes for this, or you can be less authentic and less messy by slitting them with a sharp knife. They then go into a solution of sodium bicarbonate for 24 hours. After this they go into soft water which is changed every day until they taste ready; this is when they have lost their bitterness. This will typically take a couple of weeks but you will only know by tasting them. At this stage they are put into jars with added ingredients for flavour: herbs, garlic, cumin, orange peel... Everyone you ask has a different favourite combination.

You can process olives when they've turned black too. This also involves splitting them open. Then you lightly salt them and spread them on trays to sun-dry. This is an easy way to preserve them but they do end up very salty.

And by the way, if you are eating olives with stones in them, save those pits, especially if you have a wood-burning stove: they make excellent fuel. Many commercial olive oil makers burn their pomace, the solid residue from olive processing, consisting mostly of the stones, in furnaces or even sell it as biofuel to power stations.

Drying can be trying

Though we spend much of our time working in our garden, I'm not covering gardening in any detail here. However, some of the incidental lessons learnt along the way, such as what follows, have somehow sneaked into this account.

In 2011, faced with a glut of fruit from our single apricot tree, Troy hurried to the internet where her research suggested drying the fruit on trays inside the car on the basis that this would be a hot place and would be fly-proof. So the apricots were halved, spread on a tray and put on the dashboard. The following morning the car was full of what we now know are vinegar flies. Also, the heat had been so intense that the fruit seemed to be cooking rather than drying. The next move was to try the trays on the broad front shelf of the campervan in a bigger, airier space. They were duly put in there. There was not a vinegar fly in sight. The following morning the campervan too was full of vinegar flies.

Off to the agricultural supplies emporium Ramblizo to buy fine-mesh netting. We had by now realised there was a use for some of the wooden frames we had rescued from a cowboy English joiner (name available on application) who had supposedly been making our window shutters but had stalled for two years and who clearly never intended to complete the job. In no time Troy had cut and stapled the mesh over a couple of frames and glued the edges to ensure a fly-proof join. Putting one frame over the other created a fly-proof space with plenty of air-flow.

By now the apricot season was past and we were on to tomatoes, which were coming fast and furious. Quartered and spaced apart, they were put into the frame, which was tilted towards the sun. Could this be the solution? Within 24 hours the tomato wedges were shrinking. They were also fly-free. Gradually the tomatoes dried and darkened. By the time they were deemed fully dried they were very dark and very chewy, much darker and chewier than commercially available dried tomatoes, in fact, but none the worse for that.

Once fully dried they can be stored in jars, either as they are or in olive oil. The drying intensifies the flavour so a couple, cut up into smaller pieces and added to stews or curries, really add an extra dimension. It's important to make sure they are fully dried before storing them though. One of my early attempts at tomato drying foundered because I packed them into oil in a jar, thinking them entirely dry, only to find in a week or two that they were fermenting and trying to fight their way out of the jar.

Sometime later our quince tree produced its annual glut of large, slightly furry-skinned yellow fruits. We were giving them away to all and sundry and discovered that our Spanish neighbours didn't really know how to use them. In previous years Troy had made *carne de membrillo* (quince jelly). This is traditionally eaten with cheese and it's a tasty juxtaposition but there's only so much quince jelly you can eat; ditto quince crumble. It begins to lose its novelty after three nights in a row. A couple of quinces will make a substantial crumble, so we are always on the lookout for new ways of using quinces. We were fairly sure that because quinces are a hard fruit they wouldn't dry successfully in the 'ambient air mesh drier', so we needed a different solution.

Then one evening on TV the garden presenter Alys Fowler was describing how to make fruit leather. Troy latched onto this and made, at the cost of much effort and time, a thick gloop of cooked and sieved quince, which was spread very thinly onto several metal trays. Two of these were put into the oven at a low heat for the best part of a day. Another was put into one of the drying frames described above and tilted towards the sun. This was in January, during a period of hot sunny days. In both cases the result was a thin, chewy, malleable and very tasty layer of fruit leather, which could be cut into strips, rolled up and stored easily. Whether the flavoursome outcome was worth all the hard work on that first occasion was a moot point, though with more experience, softer fruits and a liquidiser, fruit leather has subsequently proved much easier to make. A further initial snag involved the difficulty of separating the fruit leather from the greaseproof paper with which the metal trays had been lined. The solution was to use baking parchment or Teflon baking sheets instead, dispensing with both metal trays and greaseproof paper.

And now, two years on from the first attempts, and with 2013's glut of apricots, the drying frames have done their stuff successfully and the fruit leather has worked perfectly. The thin layers of apricot pulp facing the sun inside the mesh frames dried in just a day or two. Some surplus melon was also mixed in with the apricot pulp and this worked fine. In such ways the steady process of learning new skills to preserve our produce continues.

Olivo Milenario

Spain has about 2.5 million hectares dedicated to the cultivation of olives, with over 300 million olive trees. Olives, along with cereals and vines, formed the basis of Mediterranean civilisation as far back as records go and no doubt beyond. The Phoenicians, Romans and the Moors all processed olives for oil, so it is perhaps not surprising that some very old olive trees have survived, given the longevity of the species.

Almería province contributes five records to the Inventario de Olivos Monumentales de España , a database of the biggest, and generally therefore the oldest, olive trees in the country. One of the best known of these is in the Rambla de las Viruegas, about a kilometre inland from Agua Amarga. This particular *olivo* (olive tree) is reputed to be at least a thousand years old. In a recent book published under the auspices of the Diputación de Almería (the Regional Council) and the Instituto de Estudios Almerienses, a photo of this very tree is captioned '*Olivo milenario*' ('Thousand-year old olive tree'), adding veracity to the claim. Indeed some have dared suggest it may be twice that age.

It's easily found: take the road inland from Agua Amarga and after just a few hundred metres, and just before a sharp right-hand bend, turn onto an obvious track on the right. This is perfectly driveable in an ordinary car. After some distance it veers left and soon the ancient olive tree comes into view. It's about a kilometre from the road.

At the base the tree's circumference measures nine metres. The trunk is six and a half metres round and its height exceeds eight metres. Its four main branches support a canopy that creates a shady area of more than ten metres in diameter. So much for statistics, because the unobservant eye might not even notice such a tree. The trunk is pale brown and the foliage is a pale silvery green. The surrounding rocks are cream. Most of these colours tend to be washed out by the fierce sun. And to someone used to the trees of northern Europe it certainly isn't particularly big.

Yet, in the context of eastern Almería, of the semi desert, it is astonishing to think that a living thing has survived so long here. To stand under its dense, quiet shade and look closely at the gnarled bosses and scars of its massive trunk and to think of the North African pirates who may have done likewise can be a rich experience.

The Cariatiz-based artist Thomas Neukirch has made a vivid and compelling work based on the Viruegas olive tree. It's a big painting, 162 x 96 cms (64 x 38 inches) and he titles it, with a nod to its venerable age, *Römischer Ölbaum* (Roman Olive Tree). I haven't seen the original but when I saw a reproduction of the painting I knew immediately that it was the Viruegas tree, even though only the lower part of the trunk and a small portion of the canopy appear in the picture. The right-hand half of the picture is filled with the trunk, swirls of oils from across the palette giving vibrant life to the ancient beast. In the top right and top left corners of the painting, foliage stabs and curves into life; catching light on the right, silver and green and blue, and darker, green through to black, more subdued, on the left. The trunk hefts itself out of red earth and beyond it lies a landscape of lemon, dark green, grey, cream, and finally, a line of low brown hills. Framed between the trunk and the foliage is a patch of sky, diagonal irregular bands of blue and white with a hint of pink.

This is not a precise description. I am not an artist and my vocabulary for colours is limited to the predictable, but these are most definitely not the colours you normally see in the Almerían landscape; at least, not all at once. Yet this *is* most definitely immediately recognisable as the Viruegas *olivo*. It has the raw energy and swirling power of Van Gogh. Thomas Neukirch is not painting the tree in front of him; he's celebrating the joy of being here, of spending time in the presence of this tree, expressing the privilege of being able to live here, near this tree and in this landscape.

And yet, for all its colourful celebration, this huge painting is grounded by the presence of a car, centre frame. Just left of the massive tree trunk, and dwarfed by it, is the car in which the artist arrived. This is the real world. The artist did not arrive on foot as an ancient pilgrim might. He drove here. But the car is smaller than perspective might require. Maybe he's telling us that the natural world will be here long after we and our possessions have disappeared. It's a highly affecting work, *Römischer Ölbaum*. It makes us smile and it makes us think.

In an interview with the English writer and journalist Marcus Field in 2009, Thomas Neukirch admitted: "Moving to rural Spain was a crisis for me because I'd never painted landscapes before, only interiors. But gradually I learnt to accept the place where I live." Asked whether it was hard to find a way to paint the Almerían landscape, he goes on to talk about trees: "And the trees can make beautiful shapes because they are isolated, not like a wood with lots of green stuff. Olive trees are so personal; they are very close to human beings. Each tree has its own personality. So I discovered that the landscape could be very rich here."

After this I look again at *Römischer Ölbaum*. Isn't the ancient olive not just an old tree, imbued with vibrant colours by the artist, but a metaphor for the delight we can take at the decisions or twists of fate that have brought us to this superficially barren corner of Spain which, if only we take the time to look closely, reveals all manner of unexpected riches?

A week or two later I email this piece of writing to Thomas Neukirch and in reply he tells me of a recent article in the newspaper *El Pais* that dates the Viruegas olive tree to between 1,500 and 2,000 years. Another study Thomas has seen suggests that a circumference of 4.7 metres can mean an age of 1,000 years. However, this depends on the nature of the ground, whether it is *secano* or *regadío* – dry or irrigated. Maybe we'll never know the age of the Vireugas *olivo* and maybe it's fine that it should remain a mystery.

12. On the wing

'Why is it that people who are absorbed by something are seen as sad? For me, it reverses the true state of affairs. To be engaged is to be a part, to be absorbed and fulfilled. To be cool, to be detached from things and to have no passionate feeling is the real sadness.'
(Mark Cocker)

Was that a golden eagle?

Diary entry: 'Wednesday 9th November 2005. We've been here for not quite a month. After lunch, we set off for Cerro de los Lobos. It's sunny and breezy. Tracks lead most of the way, then there's easy climbing to the summit with the trig point at 601 metres. Huge views down and beyond our house, over Gafarillos; away to the higher tops of the Sierra Cabrera; over the sea of *plasticos*, following the double thread of the motorway towards Campohermoso; the flat top of Mesa Roldán; the upper part of the red and white chimney marking the coal-fired power station at Carboneras. Troy drops back to the col and is scanning from there when a raptor drifts low over her. She assumes I've seen it but I'm still back at the summit taking photos. We both lock binoculars on it for several minutes and have great views: our first golden eagle here. A superb addition to the local list.'

It's almost eight years since then and we've yet to see another golden eagle in the Sierra Cabrera. So is that really what it was? We've seen short-toed eagles, irregularly but on quite a number of occasions, and several Bonelli's eagles, particularly in the last couple of years, but never another golden. Over the course of many mountaineering trips to Scotland spread over 40-odd years I've seen golden eagles on maybe fifteen occasions, a few white-tailed eagles and plenty of buzzards in all sorts of places, so I have some familiarity with that range of species. And we had such close and lengthy views that day at the top of the hill. Yet, the more time that passes with no further golden, the more inclined I am to think that somehow it wasn't a golden eagle that delighted us that afternoon with its low passes above us.

Birding at Las Salinas

We had a day at Las Salinas de Cabo de Gata, the saltpans, on 2nd January 2006, our first visit since buying a house in the area. We deliberately avoided New Year's Day, when the roads are notoriously risky with some drivers having spent much or all of the previous night imbibing. The death toll is high on January 1st.

Since our previous visit some months earlier the Environment Ministry had been very active at Las Salinas, completing an 11 km fence enclosing the whole lagoon system to keep out dogs, foxes and unsuspecting humans. There had previously been just one hide; now there were five and information boards had sprouted to match.

The original hide has one of those heavy telescopes fixed to a mount, swivelling like something on an ancient warship. You put in a euro for a few minutes' dubious magnification and wrestle the thing around, just getting the hang of it when your money runs out. Fortunately we had our own telescope, not top of the range but fine for us, with its 27x magnification. It revealed a superb array of birdlife.

Hundreds of flamingos were scattered across the pools. In flight the vermilion and black on the wings seems even more improbable than does the standard gangly pink bird with the wonky bill. Additionally, and listed in no logical order, we saw: curlew, Kentish plover, avocet, grey heron, black-winged stilt, redshank, cormorant, shelduck, common sandpiper, yellow-legged gull, dunlin, common tern, black-headed gull, sandwich tern, black-tailed godwit, greenshank, stonechat, sanderling, little stint, great-crested grebe, wigeon, teal and little egret. Experts would have no doubt identified additional species and given the list in a more scientifically acceptable order.

Two days later we were there with a couple of friends and added spoonbill, shoveler, little gull, mallard and hoopoe to the list. Towards dusk in January the sun glows in at the saltpans from out to sea, a quirk of this particular stretch of coast being that it faces west, soaking the birds in rich late light, a scene close enough to perfection for the average human.

Bee-eaters

Involuntarily, I duck. I'm doing 70 kph through the sequence of curves between Gafarillos and Peñas Negras and a bird I haven't seen has risen up from the tarmac and is coming straight for the windscreen. Somehow it keeps rising and misses the glass. "Didn't you see it?" says Troy. "There were three of them on the road."

Only a couple of minutes previously, as we came over the crest of the hill at La Rellana, I had had to brake. Several bee-eaters were sitting in the road and seemed very casual about taking off. Their plumage, a less vivid version of the chestnut, yellow and green of the adults, marked them out as young birds, clearly still not fully aware of the danger vehicles pose. Later the same day, on a different road, we passed the mangled remains of a bee-eater glued to the tarmac, no doubt another recently-fledged juvenile, one emerald wing skewed upwards from the mashed corpse.

The sky above the valley has been alive with these birds through most of the summer, with just a temporary lull while nesting occurred. That moment when the bee-eaters first come back here is a sign of summer's arrival, like when the swifts are suddenly screaming through England's skies in early May. The bee-eaters get here much earlier than May though and usually it happens during an evening. Out of nowhere the air is full of a new sound. The birds are always heard before they're seen. A rolling, lilting, far-carrying burble has us scanning the sky and they're there, elegant, pointed shapes emitting a bubbling chorus that suggests nothing more than sheer delight in the ability to fly. Field guides to birds always attempt to transliterate birds' songs and calls but I've rarely been able to translate their efforts back to what the birds really sound like. Bee-eaters apparently, go 'quilp', 'prrup', 'pruuk-pruuk' or 'prrüt'. None of these is a bad shot at the noises bee-eaters make but somehow they all simply point up the fact that it's virtually impossible to represent bird calls in human language.

I don't keep a full record of the arrival of all summer visitors. Neither my birding skills nor my commitment are up to that but in the year I'm writing this, 2010, swifts arrived back here on March 13th, red-rumped swallows and barn swallows were here on March 20th, and bee-eaters arrived on March 23rd. By the evening of the 29th, around 7 p.m., we had a flock of at least 100 bee-eaters over the valley. In 2009 we were away throughout March so have no 'first date' for bee-eaters but when we got back on April 1st there were at least 20 performing over the house. In 2008 there's an entry in our 'Garden and Wildlife Diary', which is far more intermittent and random than that title might suggest, on March 26th, as follows: 'Last night I said I thought our first bee-eaters would appear today. So they did, here at 10 a.m., then also at Peñas Negras and Los Molinos.' I hope I'm not as much of a smartarse as that makes me sound.

Serin

A characteristic cat noise comes from the large porch beyond our back door then with a small commotion Minx, our black and white, year-and-a-half old female, comes in through the flap. I breathe relief as I had interpreted the sound as the one she uses to announce the delivery of a present. Only yesterday I rescued a mouse from her claws and released it, quivering and traumatised, amongst the prickly pears. A couple of hours later she killed a Sardinian warbler, so it was good to see her empty-clawed this time.

A few minutes later I went out and instantly saw the reason for her call: a scatter of fragile yellow and grey feathers and a small corpse on the doormat, wet and ragged, its bill almost too small to see. It looked familiar and my heart sank, but I checked anyway, in Peter Hayman and Rob Hume's book *Bird*. Serin, weight 12-15g ($^3/_8$ - ½ oz), 'the serin is a tiny, lively bundle of colour and song, especially common in Mediterranean areas'. It goes on to suggest what may have been this individual's undoing: 'Serins feed mainly on the ground and in low herbs,' prime cat hunting territory. Weeks have gone by without any kills on Minx's part, or at least none we're aware of, but the evidence is becoming incontrovertible that she needs a collar with a bell.

Butterflies

I'm no lepidopterist. I simply start from a layman's perspective that butterflies are intriguing and wonderful to watch. That's an easy enough stance to have as our garden here evolves and attracts more and more of these insects. Their innate mystery, their delicate and apparently random flight, their fabulous patternings, their sudden appearances, these things endow them with an ability to make me, at least, smile and gaze in wonder. Something of this was captured in an eloquent review by Richard Mabey in *The Guardian* of Patrick Barkham's lovely book *The Butterfly Isles*. Mabey says of the author: 'For him the universe of butterflies is like Alain-Fournier's Lost Domain, a place of elusive and endangered beauty, charged with the lost freedoms and the magic of childhood.'

Butterfly scientist Matthew Oates, who knows approximately a million times more about butterflies than I do, takes this notion further, prosaically and with angry strength. Quoted by the aforementioned Patrick Barkham, he says: 'We have to reforge our relationship with natural beauty. To us, nature is something we do through the BBC Natural History Unit and a television screen. It scares me rigid what's going on. Our whole relationship is remote and not experiential. We underestimate the importance of beauty and wonder in our lives at our peril.' Which suggests, among other things, that precise identification in every case, or even most cases, is not necessary for an appreciation of butterflies. That's a relief because precise identification is a skill I have yet to fully develop.

It's mid-May 2012. After a cooler than normal spring, the temperatures have risen and with the warmth butterflies have become much more evident. For a month or two there will be plenty of butterfly activity but then, as Patrick Barkham explains, things will quieten down: 'In southern Europe the biggest problem for butterflies is summer, when it is too hot and dry and food plants die off, threatening butterflies and their caterpillars with starvation. Most butterflies deal with extreme heat with a diapause, a form of summer hibernation during which insects stop growing and go into suspended animation.'

For now, wall browns are very active and for the first time I've seen several marbled whites in the garden. Previous encounters with them on the summits of Cerro de los Lobos have been fairly frequent but are they Spanish marbled whites or Iberian marbled whites? It doesn't much matter in the great scheme of things, I guess, but there are fairly clear differences between the two that I should be able to spot and it would be good to know, so I must try harder.

Almost all year the antics of butterflies provide intriguing entertainment on the Lobos summits. What is it exactly that attracts them? The plants seem no different from those further down the slopes. Is it something about the air currents? Could it be that butterflies, like me, revel in the airy feel of a summit and a 360° panorama? Then, by chance, I come across a reference to 'hill-topping' in the *Collins Butterfly Guide* and this sets me off in pursuit of more information.

Hill-topping, I discover, is a mate-location behaviour seen in many species of butterflies and other insects. Male butterflies may be found flying up to and staying on a hilltop, for days on end if need be. Females, looking for a mate, fly up the hill. Males dash around the top, displaying their aerial skills and competing for the 'best' part of the area, usually the summit itself. The male with the best territory at the top of the hill will have the highest chance of mating with any female which arrives. She will know the 'top male' must be strong and thus genetically fit. Female butterflies at hill-topping sites have been found to be predominantly unmated individuals. Presumably, that is, until they reach the top of the hill. Studies have shown that even slight elevation differences on flat terrain can trigger hill-topping behaviour and that the concentrating effect of hill-topping on butterfly populations makes such locations of special conservation significance.

So now I'm intrigued enough to go back to the brief records I've kept of my ascents of Cerro de los Lobos, with various references to the three tops at heights of 603 m, 601 m and 579 m. On 5th March 2007: 'Swallowtails seen on each of the three tops,' then nothing until 24th Sept 2008: 'Painted lady at summit of 601 m'. On 17th Jan 2009: 'Red admiral and frits flying in sun at 603 m summit'. Then three times between 8th and 15th May 2009, more references to butterflies; swallowtails on two occasions and a painted lady once. Then on 29th May 2009 I had a new hilltopping species: 'Scarce swallowtail on 603 m.'

During the hottest months, July and August, either we are away or I rarely go up the hills because of the heat, so my records are consequently patchy. I don't have the scientific records to support or disprove the notion of a diapause, a summer hibernation. From late September 2009 there are more mentions of red admirals and painted ladies, with the addition of swallowtails and orange tips. On 14th November: 'Painted Ladies still about.' Between 19th March and 19th April 2010, there are several more references to red admirals and painted ladies and, on 4th April: 'Visited all three tops. Loads of butterflies incl. Spanish (?) marbled white.' Even on Christmas Day 2010 there was a red admiral at the summit of 601 m.

I'm sure that on many days when I saw hill-topping butterflies I didn't record them. It was never a particular focus. I'm equally certain I've under-recorded various brownish butterflies I couldn't identify. Nevertheless, these very unscientific records give anecdotal evidence of hill-topping behaviour by at least seven butterfly species before I even knew of this biological phenomenon.

As I'm checking through these records I realise I've recorded, in passing, many birds at the summits of Cerro de los Lobos too. I've mentioned earlier the possible sighting of a golden eagle on the first occasion we went up los Lobos. At other times, on, over or close to the summits, I've seen swifts, barn swallows, house martins, crag martins, bee-eaters, red-legged partridges, Thekla larks, kestrels, black wheatears, ravens, corn bunting, spectacled warbler, rock bunting and on 19th October 2009 'Great views of a short-toed eagle'. Do birds indulge, I wonder, in hill-topping too?

2009 was a year when the population of painted ladies exploded and mass migration took place. This is a phenomenon that occurs from time to time, when certain conditions coincide. In mid-February of that year a Spanish researcher, Constanti Stefanescu, reported seeing hundreds of thousands of painted ladies emerging in Morocco after heavy winter rains in North Africa had triggered the germination of the plants on which its caterpillars feed. Favourable winds followed, bringing vast numbers of painted ladies to Spain by April. They continued north through France and on 21st May large numbers were first reported flying over Portland Bill, Dorset. Soon afterwards there were more and more reports. 18,000 painted ladies were seen in a few hours at Scolt Head Island on the north Norfolk coast, arriving at a rate of over 50 per minute. An invasion of Britain involving literally millions of painted ladies followed. This great swarming was evident in our Spanish garden too. Our tiny patch of green in the semi-desert of south-eastern Spain was attracting tens of painted ladies every day for week after week.

My 'Garden Butterfly List', however, could hardly be a less scientific affair. On a small square piece of paper taken from a phone-pad some years ago, once pink but now faded, are written the names of the species I have definitely seen in the garden. The list goes like this: meadow brown, wall brown, painted lady, clouded yellow, red admiral, small white, large white, swallowtail, scarce swallowtail and silver-studded blue. I have photos of most of these so I'm clear about exactly what they are. But my list couldn't be sketchier; there are no dates, no suggestions as to numbers, no references to food plants, though I know from the photos and from memory that the now widespread statice in our garden is a favourite. The list of species is certainly not complete because I have seen others, including fritillaries which I haven't precisely identified, and the marbled whites. It isn't even up to date; as I check it I see that I've not yet added my favourite among our butterfly visitors.

I have photos of it from the first time I ever came across it, on 18th September 2009. Then I saw it in the garden again just a few days ago, in June 2013. It's as big as a swallowtail. Its fore-wing uppersides (upf in the parlance) are a pale orangey-beige, whilst the hind-wing uppersides (uph) are a delicate olive green which shimmers like shot silk in the light. Prosaically, the guidebook says 'uph olive-green suffusion often extensive'. All the upperwings are delicately patterned with wavy lines and dots in black. The underwings are different again; the hind-wings are jade green with fine white markings and the fore-wings are a striking palette of yellow, orange, jade and black. It's a stunner. It's the cardinal fritillary and before I saw one I'd no idea such a thing even existed.

Being a butterfly beginner is fun. You can learn so much when you know so little to start with. The cardinal fritillary, for example, is univoltine in much of Europe, between mid-May and early July. I had to look that up too. It means the species has a single annual brood. But, says the guidebook, it is bivoltine in north-west Africa (May/June and August/September) and possibly so in parts of southern Europe. Given that our climate here in eastern Almería is basically identical to that of North Africa, I'm sure this explains why my first sighting was in September; it would have been the second brood of the Almerían cardinal fritillaries.

Piecing this together gives me an irrational buzz, a feeling of wellbeing that makes me check that I'm not walking around like a grinning idiot. After all, I just know a little more than I did before about a rather obscure topic but there's something about that which makes me feel great.

13. Gold and murder

'It's a contention of Heat-Moon's – believing as he does any traveller who misses the journey misses about all he's going to get – that a man becomes his attentions. His observations and curiosity, they make and remake him.'
(From the back cover of William Least Heat-Moon's book *Blue Highways*.)

Rodalquilar rocks

It's time to head south again to a small geographical area that holds the key to both the eastern Almerían gold industry and the connection of the playwright and poet Federico García Lorca with our area.

Arriving uninformed in Rodalquilar, you can't help but be puzzled by what you see. Half the village is derelict. There are rows of roofless graffiti-covered houses lining overgrown streets, all behind tall mesh fencing with notices that prohibit entry. The other half of the village is neat: white single storey houses, with a few small bars/cafes among them. Slightly uphill from the residential part of the village is a series of government buildings related to the Cabo de Gata-Níjar Natural Park.

A little higher still, beyond the upper edge of the village, a group of bleak structures stands, obviously abandoned, against the hilly backdrop. Closer inspection, which is easily achieved as nothing is fenced off here, shows a series of open circular concrete tanks of varying sizes and tall industrial buildings, their windows now sightless, their walls drab. A roughly-surfaced track winds up through the complex. Above these curious relics an information board gives some clues, and from this height there's a panorama out across the industrial remains, the village and the Valle de Rodalquilar beyond.

So what happened here? The answer is that gold was found and for a while turned the place upside down, but to make sense of it all means delving back into the rocks. If detailed geology is not for you, skip straight to the next section.

The rocks of the Sierra de Cabo de Gata were formed during two stages of volcanic activity, the first from roughly 14 to 10 million years ago and the more recent from 9 to 7.5 million years ago. If all geological time, some 4,600 million years, is condensed into a single year, the volcanic activity in the then tropical seas of Cabo de Gata occurred on 30th December. Geologists refer to the period when this happened as the Miocene, 23.5 to 5.3 million years ago.

Volcanic activity involves magma. Magma is formed as a result of the partial melting of rocks at enormously high temperatures in the Earth's crust and the upper part of the mantle, the layer immediately below the crust. Magma comes in many forms but typically consists of liquid rock, water vapour and carbon dioxide, both dissolved in the aforementioned liquid rock, and crystallised minerals. Magma tends to be less dense than the surrounding materials in which it is forming and so it rises through the mantle and the crust, incorporating chunks of solid rock en route.

Magma may either reach the surface quickly or, alternatively, it might cool and solidify within the Earth's crust. If the magma reaches the surface quickly, volcanic activity results. When this happens the magma comes into contact with the air and cools rapidly, with the resultant rocks having a very small crystal size.

If the magma fails to reach the surface and remains in the Earth's crust, the cooling happens much more slowly and creates rocks known as intrusive rocks, of which granites are examples, with large crystals. During its slow ascent, the magma may find its way into fissures in the surrounding rock to form features called dykes.

The most explosive volcanic eruptions can eject many cubic kilometres of magma onto the Earth's surface. In some cases so much magma is blown out by one of these episodes that a void is left, into which part of the volcano collapses to form a vast depression. Such depressions are known as calderas. At Rodalquilar there is such a caldera, roughly oval-shaped, some 8 km by 4 km, the product of a series of major volcanic explosions in which a mix of ash, semi-molten rock fragments and very hot gas was released from the volcanic vent. Falling back, these red-hot materials streamed down the sides of the volcano creating, when they solidified, rocks that are rich in pumice and ash.

Now we need to return to intrusive action; that is, where magma is cooling within the crust. This can occur at depths varying between a few hundred metres and a few kilometres. Such cooling magma has a major impact on the surrounding crustal rocks. In the case of the Rodalquilar caldera, the upper part of the underlying magma is estimated to have been about one kilometre down. Heat from this magma raised the temperature of the surrounding rocks to 400-500°C. At the same time the magma gave off gases and hydrothermal fluids such as sulphurous and hydrochloric acids at between 200°C and 350°C.

As these fluids rose through the crustal rocks they washed chemical components such as gold, that were originally widely dispersed, out of them. As these complex fluids arrived at or near the surface they cooled and mixed with subterranean or marine water. The metals then precipitated in fractures and fissures as hydrothermal deposits. At Rodalquilar, where the hydrothermal processes are dated to 10.4 million years ago, there were many fractures in the caldera that allowed the deposition of gold.

Before the gold rush

We now need to leap forward a long way from these major geological events to the point where the landscape looked broadly as it does today, with humans part of the scene. If we place ourselves in the early 16th century we arrive at the time when deposits of alunite or alum-stone, a hydrous sulphate of aluminium and potassium, were discovered at Rodalquilar. Alum was widely used in paper-making, printing, dying and tanning. Francisco de Vargas, a prominent member of the Court of King Ferdinand and Queen Isabella (1474-1516), heard about the Rodalquilar alum and in 1509 wheedled from the Crown a monopoly to exploit all the alum in the Bishopric of Almería. De Vargas built a fortified village in the valley for the Italian miners he had taken on, the most skilled of the era, and protected his enterprise with the Torre de los Alumbres (Tower of the Alums), aka the Torre Fuerte (Strong Tower) de Rodalquilar. Though ruined, the tower is still standing, as mentioned in Chapter 5, about one kilometre in from the coast, close to the Rambla del Playazo.

However, in 1520 a civil war broke out and took Francisco de Vargas away from Rodalquilar. Moorish pirates captured the village and subdued the locals. Mining stopped for over half a century and began again only in 1575, once the Moors had been expelled from the Kingdom of Granada. In 1587 Alumbres de Rodalquilar, as the village was then known, had 74 inhabited dwellings and a parish church, the site of which, just inland from the Torre de los Alumbres, is nowadays occupied by the Cortijada de la Ermita (House of the Hermitage). The beach now known as El Playazo was referred to as Puerto de los Alumbres in documents of the mid-16th century. The bay has a natural harbour at one end with bollards carved from the bedrock, though these haven't been accurately dated.

By the end of the 16th century a fall in the price of alum caused a further closure of the mining enterprise. With no work people drifted away. Field Marshall Antonio María Bucarelli y Ursúa made out the skeleton of the village when he was there in 1761 and indeed it appeared on a European map at the end of that century, shown as Alvi, a name derived from the initial syllables of Alumbres Viejos. Simón Rojas Clemente likewise made reference to the place when he passed by in 1805. Alumbres de Rodalquilar or Alumbres Viejos, its name evolving over time, was clearly clustered around the sites of the defensive tower and the old church. Close by, the crumbling remains of an old aqueduct and a waterwheel provide further clues to the relatively sophisticated set-up at that time. This original version of what is now called Rodalquilar was about two kilometres east north-east of the site of the current village.

All went quiet for much of the 19th century until records show that veins of lead were being worked, along with small amounts of silver, at Cerro del Cinto, a hill a couple of kilometres west of Rodalquilar. The workings at Cerro del Cinto revealed a Roman cemetery dating from the 2nd century AD. Amphorae recovered from sunken wrecks on the nearby coast date from the same period, evidence presumably that the Romans were aware of and possibly exploiting the area's mineral wealth.

However, before the end of the nineteenth century the lead/silver industry was in crisis. A solution was to present itself, though. Associated with the lead being worked at Cerro del Cinto were quartz dykes. Quartz was used as a flux in the smelting process. The only realistic way out of Rodalquilar in the late 19th century, for heavy materials at least, was by sea from Playazo, and via this route the lead and the quartz were taken north-east along the coast to the smelting works of Cartagena and Mazarrón. At the Mazarrón smelters traces of gold were discovered in the quartz. This wasn't a lot but it covered the costs of transporting the quartz from Rodalquilar to Mazarrón, a distance of 150 kilometres.

The rise and fall of the gold mines

In 1883 things stepped up a gear when more gold was found in the Las Niñas mine, just a kilometre from Rodalquilar village. But the amounts of gold were still relatively insignificant until 1914 when new finds created a miniature gold rush. Around 1915 a treatment plant was built at the Maria Josefa Mine on the slopes of Cerro de la Cruz at El Madronal, four kilometres west north-west of the present Rodalquilar. The process of registering concessions was fairly chaotic and numerous law suits ensued. At the same time, the whole Almería area was in a state of economic turmoil. Lead mining had declined and the other mainstay, grape production, saw its market slide into crisis. Many workers from the region emigrated to Algeria and later America.

In these fragile economic conditions, production of gold was sporadic until 1928, when a British company called Minas de Rodalquilar S.A. came onto the scene. Minas de Rodalquilar, under its chairman Fernando de Ybarra, imported machinery and methods from the USA and built a plant for extracting gold from the ore by cyanidation, which involves potassium cyanide. This is a process used when the ore is of low grade, so don't go rushing to Rodalquilar on the lookout for huge nuggets. Between 1928 and 1939 107,000 tonnes of rock were processed, yielding 1,125.5 kg of gold. After 1936 though, with civil war raging, production declined rapidly and fizzled away to almost nothing.

In 1940 the state, now under the dictator General Francisco Franco, commandeered the mines and handed the task of production to IGME, the Spanish Institute for Geology and Mining. Over the next two years only 37 kg of gold was recovered. At the end of 1942 responsibility passed to the Adaro National Enterprise for Mineral Investigation, whose mouthful of an acronym was ENADIMSA. This body focussed its efforts back on the Cerro del Cinto area, where a 4,000 tonne mass of mineralised rock was estimated to hold 4.5 grams of gold per tonne. The high point for gold-mining in Rodalquilar came during the 1950s. In 1952 work began on upgrading the mines and the whole associated infrastructure. 100 million pesetas was invested in this and about 700 manual labourers were employed in building an HQ for the mining operation, houses for the workers and other facilities.

A sepia photo from May 1956 shows a visiting General Franco posing for a propaganda shot with a gold ingot in the foreground. In the same year the writer Juan Goytisolo visited Rodalquilar and described the gold-washing facilities: 'Spread out on the slope of the mountain, various deposits sparkle in the sun, intensely red. There the gold ore which the trucks haul out of the mine is sifted and washed, before being passed on to the driers. At the foot of the pools the detritus has taken over the valley and formed a huge quagmire, cracked and yellow.' ENADIMSA could treat 600 tonnes of ore per day and at its height production reached 5,000 kg of gold annually. Rodalquilar's population, provided with astonishing amenities for a rural locality at such a time: a school, a social club, a pharmacy and a cinema, soared from 382 people in 1940 to 1,243 in 1960.

To win the gold the quarried rock went initially to a storage shed before being ground and sorted in vibrating sieves. Electromagnetic separation then removed metals other than gold. After this the concentrated minerals were mixed in two circular tanks with a solution of cyanide. In four even larger circular tanks, among the most prominent remains still at the site, the mineral and cyanide mixture was cleaned before undergoing further ventilation and filtering. The mixture was then added to zinc dust to create a precipitate. Drying, acid washing and filtration led to the final stage where, in an electric furnace, gold was obtained by fusion.

By 1961 Rodalquilar was responsible for over 90% of Spanish gold production. At this point the workers building the infrastructure had long gone and the mining and processing itself employed only between 200 and 300 men. The writing was on the wall though. Higher salaries and rising production costs due to the convoluted geology led to the closure of the final workings in 1966. By 1970 Rodalquilar's population had plummeted to 106 and soon afterwards it was down to 75. Speculative attempts to restart production in the 1980s came to nothing. Estimates suggest that some three tonnes of gold remain in the area but the complexity of the deposits means that exploitation is not economically viable.

The cessation of mining and the consequent departure of most of the population soon enough left Rodalquilar looking as if a battle had just ended there. Spoil heaps, machinery, miners' houses, industrial plant, all were simply left and began to rust, crumble and collapse, creating a scene of sprawling devastation.

Finally, in 1991, the Consejería de Medio Ambiente de la Junta de Andalucía (the Andalucían Government's Ministry of the Environment) acquired much of the site and began to take remedial action. Gradually Rodalquilar has picked itself up from the worst days of dereliction. A development of seven new apartments designed by architect José Luis Martín Clabo won a prize awarded by the College of Architects in Almeria in 1994. More recently an impressive geological museum has opened, as has an excellent interpretative centre linked to the El Albardinal Botanical Garden. When we were first looking to buy a house in the area in 2004, we were attracted to Rodalquilar. We went into the Medio Ambiente office to ask if it was true, as we'd heard, that much of the area was unsafe because of the presence of cyanide. No, absolutely not true, they said.

If you wish to explore the area further, you will find a rough vehicle track that winds up through the derelict gold-processing complex and heads inland. A kilometre or so along this track, look left for a tunnel, only twenty metres long, that has been punched through the rock wall. Inside the tunnel elegant, sinuous brown mineral deposits form a snaking pattern on the knobbly white surface of the walls.

From the far end of the tunnel there's a view of the ruins of the Cortijada de San Diego, one of the old mining settlements: a scatter of single-storey, roofless buildings, houses and storage facilities. This deserted hamlet has featured in many films including 1989's *Indiana Jones and the Last Crusade*. On the scarred hill behind San Diego, the levels and spoil heaps are slowly being re-colonised by encroaching vegetation but it will be a while yet before nature has fully disguised the evidence of human scratchings on the land.

Failing to see a quail

Once rejoined, beyond the richest of the old workings at Cerro del Cinto, the track forges north-west then veers due north. Here it is lined with agaves and is trying hard to be a stately avenue. It pretty much succeeds. This is, or once was, rich farmland. In the spring of 2010, after the very wet winter, you'd have imagined it as meadow, a swathe of strong colours fading to the hills beyond. It's a beautifully evocative landscape and is very unusual for this dry part of Spain. It's not 'unspoilt', but like almost everywhere in this area, indeed in Spain or the whole of Western Europe for that matter, it's a landscape shaped by human activities and decisions.

Down at ground level there are the pale mauve-green heads of bladder campion leading out to delicate white flowers, the purple-black flower heads of lavender topped with fragile mauve-blue tufts, the yellow-greens of euphorbia and great scatterings of blood-stained poppies.

From somewhere in amongst all this, as I'm down on my knees to get the poppies right into the camera, comes an unusual three-note call, liquid and endlessly repeated. I stand and walk towards where it seems to be coming from but the noise ceases. I retreat and it begins again. Once more I begin to approach, more slowly and carefully this time. The noise stops. I'm certain it's a quail. I heard one twenty-odd years ago near Tibshelf in Derbyshire, so it's not exactly a familiar call but it's one of those that is so distinctive that, when you put the call together with the habitat and the fact that whatever is making this noise is invisible, the complete package says 'quail'. And if my conclusion is correct, I realise I'm not going to see it. 'A mysterious voice in the cereal fields,' says Rob Hume in *Bird*. Exactly so. It's my first encounter with a wild quail in Iberia. My only sightings prior to this have been in the supermarket, where their tiny bodies are usually vacuum-packed in twos.

Blood Wedding

The track soon reaches a large low square building in a spacious setting. The sides of the square must measure about 40 metres so it clearly wasn't a simple farmhouse. With its sheer size it imposes itself on its immediate surroundings. Close-up it proves to be uninhabited and crumbling. Sheets of external plaster, pinkish-white and fading blue, are falling away in patches from the walls to reveal the stonework beneath. At one corner the chapel still has tall wooden doors in its huge arched entrance-way. Above, a square bell-tower rises from one side of the chapel's roof and is set off by a mature palm-tree a few metres away.

This is the Cortijo del Fraile, constructed by Dominican monks in the 18th century. Until late 2011 there was nothing to stop visitors entering the buildings. Just along from the front of the chapel, on the same side of the square, there are tall rooms with roofs of canted beams, musty but still intact. Their floors show deep, and fortunately dry, evidence that animals have sheltered here. On the far side of the complex from the chapel is a domed oven built of unworked stones, skilfully tapering to a rounded top. There is no access to it from outside the compound but step in through a hole in the wall to what is now a grassy courtyard and there is the oven access, literally a hole in the wall. Bread ovens in this part of the world are outside the living quarters. If you are in a semi-desert there's enough heat without having an oven *inside* your house.

Here, in 1928, a tragedy happened that later formed the basis of one of Federico García Lorca's best-known plays, *Bodas de Sangre*, known in English as *Blood Wedding*. The catalyst for the play was García Lorca's reading of a report about the events at the Cortijo del Fraile in the newspaper *Heraldo de Madrid*.

It concerned Francisca Canadas Morales, who lived at the cortijo with her father. The news report said she had a limp and a squint and prominent teeth. However, she also had a dowry, which is thought to have been a major motive behind what appears to have been virtually an arranged marriage. She was engaged, reluctantly, to be married to a labourer, Casimiro Pérez Pino, who in turn was reckoned rather dull. Casimiro, it seems, was being pressurised into the match in order to bring money from the dowry into his family.

The wedding date had been set but after an argument on the night before the nuptials, Francisca ran off with her good-looking cousin, Curro Montes Canadas, with whom she had had an earlier relationship. There had previously been tension between the families of the bridegroom and the cousin, to the extent that both the father and a brother of the intended bridegroom, Casimiro, had been killed at the hands of Curro Montes's family. This intense feud was taking place in a remote rural setting, almost a century ago, in a place where and at a time when the outside world barely intruded.

Lorca's play, *Bodas de Sangre*, was not published until 1932 and was first performed in Madrid in March 1933. For dramatic effect, Lorca had played around with several details of the actual events: he made the bride attractive and physically strong, he had the bridegroom shy and close to his mother rather than just dull, and he heightened the good-looking, virile characteristics of the cousin. Most significantly, he changed the time of the elopement, setting it after the wedding had taken place. During the wedding reception, in Act II, the bride runs off with her true love Leonardo (as Curro Montes Canadas is called in the play). She has been attracted to him since she was 15 but he is by now married and has a child. So the elopement of the bride and her cousin makes them guilty of adultery. This exacerbates the feud that already exists between the families and heightens the dishonour that both families feel.

In Act III Lorca has the lovers tracked down by the jilted bridegroom and his relatives. The pursuit ends with a knife fight during which both Leonardo and the bridegroom die. So in Lorca's version, the bride becomes a widow on her wedding day. Lorca also introduces The Mother of the Groom as a character. Her grief over her already dead husband and elder son, together with her fear for her remaining son's safety, creates an overwhelming sense of foreboding. And what she fears does come to pass: she loses her son on his wedding day.

In real life, as mentioned before, what occurred was that the lovers, Francisca and Curro, eloped on the evening before the wedding was to take place. Casimiro's brother realised what was happening and, either by chance or by a cunning interception, depending on which account you read, came upon the lovers and shot Curro dead. The assassin was convicted of murder but Casimiro, the intended bridegroom, reputedly never overcame his humiliation and never met Francisca or looked at a photograph of her again. Francisca never married and lived in seclusion until she died half a century later in 1978.

In her book *Andalusía*, published in 1968, Nina Epton, who travelled in Spain as a woman on her own when that was not at all common, mentions an encounter that adds a spooky resonance to the events at the Cortijo del Fraile. Visiting San José, on the coast not far away from the *cortijo*, during the 1960s, she was dining at the house of a wealthy landowner. A group of labourers was sitting outside on a long bench, waiting to be paid. Finally, Nina Epton accompanied her host Don José outside to speak to the men. She records what happened: 'Among them was a wizened old man called Casimiro whom I would not have looked at twice before I was told that a dramatic incident in his youth had inspired Federico García Lorca to take Casimiro for his model of the *novio* (bridegroom) in *Blood Wedding.*'

Neglect

In 1966 the Cortijo del Fraile was used by Sergio Leone as one of the locations for his spaghetti western *The Good, The Bad and the Ugly*. Since then it has deteriorated badly and intermittent attempts have been made to press the authorities over the state of the buildings. In 2008 protests intensified. A Facebook group called 'Salvemos el Cortijo del Fraile' (Save Cortijo del Fraile) mustered 1,600 followers and on one occasion mobilized over 300 people to attend a protest at the *cortijo*. For a time a petition was posted there, inviting visitors to sign in support of renovation work. The Mayor of Níjar, Antonio Jesús Rodriguez, confirmed that he wanted the building taken into public ownership and renovated but he only saw renovation as realistic if the place became economically viable. "It has to be compatible with some sort of economic activity that would develop the area," he said.

In February 2011 the *cortijo* was given status as a listed property but this was not linked to any practical action. In April of that year a wall was discovered to have collapsed and the Níjar branch of the political party Izqierda Unida (United Left) claimed that the owners of the *cortijo* were using it as a store, with heavy machinery going in and out of the building frequently. The owners were, and still are, La Mision, an agricultural enterprise based in Murcia. The implication seemed to be, given the precarious nature of the building after decades of neglect, that the movement of heavy machinery and the collapse of the wall might be connected.

In early September 2011, an architect and an archaeologist from Almería's Department of Cultural Assets inspected the property. Article 15 of the Andalucían regional government's Historic Heritage Law allows the Department to order the owners of listed properties to take whatever action is necessary to prevent deterioration of the building. Meanwhile, a spokesman for the Department, Antonio Lucas, said they were discussing the possibility of public ownership with La Mision.

Until recently, families who quite possibly know nothing of the *cortijo's* history, and nothing of *Bodas de Sangre*, would come on a Sunday to sprawl on their blankets and spread out their picnics. They'd turn up the music on the radios in their cars with wide-open doors and let their kids, chasing and squealing, have a great time exploring the crumbling ruins. Then, towards the end of 2011 the ruins were fenced off.

Just over a year later, in January 2013, an agreement was reached that ownership would be transferred to Níjar council but only once the present owners, La Mision, had paid the €30,000 they had previously been fined by the Junta de Andalucía for failing to keep the building in repair. At about the same time a judge in a hearing in Almería ordered Níjar council to take urgent action to halt the deterioration of the building. Catch 22, it seemed. The mayor of Níjar responded by saying that at that stage responsibility for the building lay either with the regional government or with the private owners. La Mision, with a €30,000 fine hanging over them, were said to be keen to get rid of the place as soon as possible. The continuing controversy over its future, they said, was proving more trouble than it is worth to them. By October 2013 the fine had increased to €41,000 after an appeal by La Mision had failed.

In November 2013 I was back at the Cortijo del Fraile. It was in a distinctly worse state than the last time I'd seen it, visibly crumbling. At the time of writing court proceedings are still under way to determine exactly who has the responsibility to restore the *cortijo*. According to the pressure group Asociación de Amigos del Parque Natural de Cabo de Gata-Níjar, the court order already in place includes a clause that Níjar council should act in place of the owners if the owners fail to comply with their obligations.

Unless something happens to redeem the situation the whole place will have collapsed long before the centenary of the events that gave rise to *Bodas de Sangre*. For the sake of this wonderful old building, let's hope there will be a positive outcome before that happens.

14. Leaves, pods, pads and spikes

'The botany of extreme climates has its special fascination. There is a thrill to be got from plants that surmount great natural difficulties, especially when they do so with excess and bravura.'

(Gerald Brenan)

Jardín Botánico el Albardinal

It is a speciality of plants in eastern Almería to do as Brenan says, that is, to 'surmount great natural difficulties'. I touched on this, with reference to jujube, sea daffodil, mastic, and purple phlomis in the chapter 'Coasting: Flatlands'. A good place to discover more on this topic is at El Albardinal Botanical Garden at Rodalquilar. Entry is free and you can learn a lot there in a couple of hours. Don't go on a Monday though; it's closed on Mondays.

The entrance area has a modern display showing the adaptations of many of the local plants. (In what follows, the Spanish names are italicised.) The very common yellow-flowered plant *albaida*, which is Anthyllis cytisoides in Latin but has no separate English name, grows in such dense groups that the infrequently falling rainwater is retained and only allowed to drip to the ground very slowly. The tall shrub *retama* (Retama sphaerocarpa, no separate English name), often seen with its feathery fronds waving in the wind, has long roots to search for water. It lacks leaves in order to minimise transpiration but it can photosynthesise through its green stems. The same strategy is used by wavyleaf sea-lavender (Limonium sinuatum in Latin, or *siempreviva azul*), which flourishes in saline and gypsum-rich soils. If you are still with me in this maze of names, statice is what gardeners call this plant, or its very similar close relatives. It's a favourite of butterflies and, as a bonus, its flowers retain their colour long after the plant dies. As I write, it is in the process of colonising large parts of our garden, whether we like it or not.

A whole series of plants have defence mechanisms to deter hungry animals. Wolfbane (Periploca angustifolia or *cornical*) exudes a very irritating milky latex if anything tries to eat it. *Rascamoños* (Launaea arborescens, no English name) protects itself with vicious terminal spines on its branches. *Retama*, mentioned above, contains the alkaloid sparteine, found also in some species of broom, a substance that herbivores find particularly unappetising and, for the same reason, the sage-leaved rock rose (Cistus salviifolius or *jaguarzo moriscos*) has a high concentration of tannins.

This information and more can be gleaned from the indoor exhibition and many of these plants can also be seen for real at El Albardinal. The gardens have notices showing which plants can be used for medical purposes, such as rosemary (Rosmarinus officinalis, *romero*) and for building, such as giant cane (Arundo donax, *caña*). Amongst all this there are some entertaining surprises; for example, the leaves and stems of purple phlomis (Phlomis purpurea, *matagallo*), it turns out, can be squeezed into a ball for use as a scourer. And with that it's time to move on and say a little more about a few of the most iconic plants of the semi-desert areas of eastern Almería.

Prickly pears

Certain plants play a big role in defining the character of eastern Almería, especially in the rural areas. Of the apparently wild plants that are common, one of the largest and most obvious is the prickly pear (*chumbera* in Spanish). This is the species Opuntia ficus-indica, originally from Mexico, and it's particularly widespread in our area. With clusters of thick pads covered in spines, it was widely planted on farms and *fincas* (country estates) in the 19th century. Its fruits were eaten and it also formed stock-proof hedging. Nowadays it rarely has the latter function but any fallen pads root easily and the plant can reach tree-like dimensions, its ear-like pads mildly comical in the landscape. Once established, prickly pear develops into a ferocious green tangle, creating impenetrable thickets which can form an effective firebreak due to its high water content.

The pad-edges produce abundant yellow flowers in late spring followed by fleshy fruit, initially green then gradually turning a deep golden-red. These apparently innocuous and attractive fruits carry very fine defensive hairs that are to be avoided at all costs. They are carried at the base of the larger spines and are called glochids. Once in your skin these are irritating and very difficult to remove. One method for getting rid of the hairs is to put sticky tape onto the affected area of skin. When pulled off it will hopefully pull out at least some of the hairs.

With care though, the fruit (*higo chumbo*) can be harvested, optimally in September when it is changing from green to yellow/red. By November, when the fruits are deep red, they are too far gone. Collected with the help of strong gloves as protection against the spines, the fruits are topped, tailed and peeled of their thick skin to reveal a soft, deep red, edible inner containing many seeds. Local knowledge (our neighbour Pedro, to be specific) has it that the fruit, picked first thing in the morning and eaten after being cooled in the fridge for half an hour, is particularly good for the stomach. Goats, of course, can eat both pads and fruit straight from the plant.

Prickly pear jam takes some making but has novelty value and actually tastes rather good. Having made a batch in 2008, I presented a jar to my Spanish teacher, Guadalupe, at Christmas. She seemed delighted at the time and then, when classes began again in the New Year, made further noises more positive than might be demanded by mere courtesy.

As for the recipe; collect a bucketful of prickly pear fruits as they turn from green to red and carefully remove the thick outer skins. Put the fruit into a thick-bottomed pan and, stirring it from time to time over a low heat, reduce it to a pulp. It then has to be sieved to remove the seeds and weighed before being returned to the pan. Now add about 750 g of sugar and 150 ml of orange juice for each kg of fruit liquid. Add a generous slug of lemon juice for pectin. You can also add such things as grated orange and/or lemon peel, cardamoms, a cinnamon stick, rosemary, etc., in whatever combination, to customise the recipe to your taste. Mix well and reduce over a low heat to an appropriate consistency, then bottle as with any jam.

In fact, I've just made some again (October 2013) and this time it was perhaps better described as prickly pear syrup rather than jam; I couldn't get it to set. Delicious on ice cream though.

Why, you might ask, would an awkward customer like the prickly pear have been imported from Mexico? The answer is that the *conquistadores* found that both Opuntia ficus-indica and Opuntia coccinellifera are host plants to the tiny parasitic Coccus insect (*cochinilla* in Spanish), which lives on moisture and nutrients from the plants, and whose dried body is the source of the vivid dye cochineal. Prickly pears were brought back to Spain, especially the Canary

127

Islands, to found plantations where the beetles could proliferate and be harvested to provide dye for bright red military jackets, carmine food colouring and lipstick. For about thirty years from the mid-19th century the production of cochineal was the main source of income for the Canary Islands.

In the 1880s synthetic aniline dyes were developed and the demand for cochineal tailed off, leaving a legacy of attractive but hazardous prickly pears across the landscape. Old plants can be enormous, their bulbous and twisted woody bases rearing among the skeletal fibrous ovals of long dead pads, providing a playground for rats living in their ferocious fastness and feasting through the winter on lingering, squishy fruits. The story doesn't quite end there though because cochineal is still used in certain items of food and drink as, unlike the chemical alternatives, it is not highly toxic.

Esparto

On our local hill slopes are wild grassy tufts up to a metre high. These are esparto grass (Stipa tenacissima or *esparto comun*), which also occurs widely on the coastal steppes of Cabo de Gata, where it can cope with saline influences, and on uncultivated or abandoned mountain slopes. Not an exciting plant visually, it nevertheless is literally woven into the local culture. A stem of esparto is easily broken when green but has immense strength once dried. For generations the country people have used it to make ropes, *alpargatas* (espadrilles), baskets, panniers, harnesses and straps. Now esparto is used almost entirely for decorative souvenirs, for baskets and other artefacts found alongside the *jarapas* (rag rugs) piled high in the tourist craft-shops of Níjar, rather than being put to use in the outhouses of rural farms.

From the mid-nineteenth century the best quality esparto was harvested and sent to the UK for use in the papermaking industry, particularly in the production of printing and lithographic grades of paper. It had to compete with esparto from Algeria and Libya but it provided a seasonal livelihood for many farmworkers. Níjar was one centre of production with, even in 1950, 11,518 hectares under esparto. At the same time Tabernas had over 5,000 hectares of esparto and Sorbas over 3,000. The middle altitudes of the Sierra

Alhamilla, the southern slopes of the Filabres and the Sierras of Almagro and María were all important areas for esparto too.

Once harvested, the esparto was tied into bales and taken by horse-drawn cart to ports such as Aguilas (just over the border in Murcia province) and Carboneras. It also came to coastal villages such as El Pozo del Esparto just south of San Juan de los Terreros. Here there were seawater pools (*pozos*) made by constructing low walls of stones in sheltered parts of the coast. The esparto was softened in these *pozos* then taken to local factories, of which there were about 20, to be plaited or woven into ropes, baskets, mats and so on. This work was mostly done by women. In time the factories all closed as more durable materials such as plastic and nylon displaced esparto as a raw material. The export trade also faded as the costs of collection and transport increased and particularly when wood pulp from Scandinavia began to dominate in the production of paper.

Once in a while, until very recently, our nearest Spanish neighbour José, well into his seventies, would sit on a chair at the front of what would be his garage if only he had a car, weaving esparto with measured skill, his hands working on automatic, the pattern for what he's weaving stored down the generations in his head. When I suggested that this was becoming a lost skill that the young had no interest in learning, he made a noise which I interpreted as suggesting that this is simply how the world is. It could equally have meant that he'd never thought about it. Or even that he hadn't a clue what I was saying.

José has an extensive repertoire of noises, sounds I merely guess at rather than understand. A small but telling insight into country ways or, more accurately, the lack of awareness of incomers, occurred soon after we came here when I asked José, who was still at that time mobile enough to use a mule as his routine transport, what the mule was called. He looked at me, his face like a brown nut with weather and age, slightly tilted with bafflement, and said: *"Mulo."*

Carobs

Carob trees (*algarrobo* in Spanish) are scattered around the hillsides near us and were deliberately planted to provide food for livestock. Tough and slow-growing, even carobs of moderate age appear gnarled. They have character. The leathery dark-green leaves and seamed, twisted trunks, often bent by the prevailing wind, make each carob tree an individual and a feature of the landscape. Carobs produce clusters of long pods, initially bright green, maturing to dark brown. Goats love them, though the small beans or seeds are indigestible, even by our neighbour's mule. When the piles of grassy turds that Mulo occasionally leaves on the road are run over by traffic, broken up and scattered by the wind, the last things left as evidence of Mulo's diet are always the tiny brown discus-shaped carob seeds.

Carob pods last for ages and are thought to have been the 'locusts' that John the Baptist lived on in the wilderness. One of its Spanish names, *Pan de San Juan*, St. John's Bread, refers to this. And because the seeds are so consistent they were used in former times by the Greeks, Arabs and Phoenicians as a measure of weight for diamonds and gold. Each seed weighs 0.18 grams or six thousandths of an ounce. This was later standardised as the official unit of weight, 1 carat, at 0.2 grams. The word carat comes from the Latin name of the carob tree, Ceratonia siliqua.

Carob pods are edible by humans too and widely used as a chocolate substitute. They're fairly chewy but fine to eat straight from the tree and the distinctive chocolate-like taste is immediately evident. In times past the pods were a popular treat for local children. No doubt today they'd expect a fancy chocolate bar or an ice-cream instead. Carob has a high sugar content, up to 45%, but hardly any fat, unlike the cocoa bean. It also contains calcium and iron and is considered an aid to digestion, as well as being helpful in cases of diarrhoea, vomiting in children, and intolerance of gluten. An infusion of the whole pods is recommended as a general anti-inflammatory in the case of, for example, conjunctivitis and can be used as a gargle to treat pharyngitis.

A book we bought soon after we moved here had a recipe for carob cake so I thought I'd give it a try. The locals look on carob pods as nothing more than goat food but we have plenty dropping into the garden from a tree on the edge of the cliff and as I'm a fan of 'food for free', this seemed too good a chance to miss. Processing the carob pods was a minor epic in itself. The book suggested pressure cooking the carob pods then cooling them and putting them in a blender until a powder was produced. Sadly a powder didn't result and I settled for cutting the pods, with difficulty, into small pieces. That's before even getting to the recipe.

Then you discover the ingredients include loads of honey and walnuts and butter, so certainly it's not food for free. The recipe was vague on quantities but very specific on baking the cake at 250°C. Troy said this was ridiculously hot but I asked her not to interfere and baked it at 250°C. It came out of the oven encased in carbon and the smell of burning pervaded the house for three days. Once we'd chiselled the black external casing off, which was no easy task, the inside tasted good though the carob was totally overwhelmed by the honey. I haven't made carob cake again.

Oleander

Surface drainage is uncommon here. When rain comes it is often heavy and, if prolonged, it sluices down the normally dry watercourses, the *ramblas*. With the occasional exception, notably the constantly flowing sections of the Río de Aguas, the riverbeds are, as a rule, wide expanses of sand, gravel and boulders, with the water table somewhere below the surface. This supports the growth of a specific community of plants including oleander and cane.

Oleanders (Nerium oleander or *adelfa*) are also found widely along the central reservation of the Autovía del Mediterráneo. In summer the motorway has an endless, dense line of oleanders covered in blooms ranging from white, through the spectrum of pink and apricot, to red. It has a tolerance of aridity, an evergreen habit, and grows into substantial bushes, providing a good barrier. Although oleanders are a mainstay in gardens, the central reservation of a motorway is probably the safest place to put them, as all parts of the plant are very poisonous; even goats won't touch it. Just a small amount of oleander can cause death to animals or humans due to its effect on the heart. Inhaling the smoke from burning oleander or even eating honey made from its nectar can produce poisonous effects.

A final thought on the motorway oleanders: in a spectacular example of poor management, the authorities always seem to choose to prune the oleanders just when they are in full flower. The maker of the decision is a highway engineer and not a gardener, I suppose.

Giant cane

Giant cane (Arundo donax or *caña*) is a widely-used material in the Spanish campo. Clumps of this plant that looks like bamboo but is actually a giant reed are common along the banks of *ramblas*. Cane helps to limit erosion but, because it grows fast, up to 10 centimetres per day and up to two metres in its first year, and spreads via rhizomes, it can be regularly harvested without destroying the clump. In local houses it was traditionally tied across wooden beams and covered with a layer of mud to make a ceiling, with tiles above that. Now, with the drying brown sheaths stripped off, it's more likely to be seen in gardens, making the frame for runner beans to climb up or the support for tomatoes and peppers to be tied to. *Caña* doesn't last a long time out in the weather, a few seasons at most, but it's free, abundant and local. On a wider scale cane is seen as a good biofuel and also as an ideal plant for below-ground carbon sequestration. On the down side, it provides virtually no food source or nesting habitats for wildlife. In fact, in New Zealand it is listed under the National Pest Plant Accord as an 'unwanted organism'.

Caña played a part in a wildlife first in our garden in July 2012. Troy was passing a raised bed occupied by climbing French beans that were supported by a frame made from parts of an old pergola and *caña*. The pergola had been destroyed by wind a few years earlier but that's another story. As she walked past the bed she heard a soft thud and there was a vivid green creature, 20 cm long, with a shield-like head, lying on the ground: our first ever chameleon. Maybe it had lost its hold in surprise as she appeared. Over the subsequent minutes it clambered slowly back up the *caña*, watching us as we tried to manoeuvre into position with our cameras. Its legs were surprisingly thin for its size but it moved with ease, deliberately placing its odd club-like feet and using its long prehensile tail for grasping. Its skin, although hide might be a better word, is armoured over its entire area with tough-looking green bobbles and ridges. Most strange though, is the face. A chameleon's large bulbous eyes, apart from the pupil, are also covered in the green armour but they swivel to keep a check on the situation. The large horizontal mouth extends far back into the head, two ridges extend from just above the mouth back over the eyes, and the back of the head has a hard ruff. The whole combination suggests something prehistoric and gives the creature a lugubrious, world-weary expression that can't help but bring a smile to the onlooker.

As we took our photos the chameleon moved with careful deliberation, its beady eyes keeping tabs on us all the while, onto some horizontal canes that linked the top of the bean-frame to a nearby vine, where it hid among the large leaves. It was perfectly camouflaged and if it hadn't initially fallen we would almost certainly not have seen it. A few days later I mentioned the encounter to our neighbour Pedro and he said that in his seventy-odd years he'd only ever seen one chameleon.

Capers

At irregular intervals by the sides of the track that winds up towards the summit of Cerro de Los Lobos, there are in winter, prostrate, dead, woody shrubs. Some of them poke improbably from cracks in cliffs where it would seem there could be no nutrient to sustain a plant. From the end of May onwards these woody skeletons transform themselves into vibrant green plants with short-lived pink and white flowers of exquisite beauty. Each flower opens early in the morning and dies in the roasting heat a few hours later. These are capers (Capparis spinosa in Latin). The prized parts of the plant are the flower buds, *alcaparras* in Spanish, which can only be picked by hand and then only with great care, as the stems have vicious backward-curving spines. The smaller the heart-shaped flower bud is when picked, the tastier it will be. The best are reckoned to be those that are no more than 7 mm across. If the buds are allowed to flower they then produce fruits that look like tiny striped green rugby balls. These, *alcaparrones* in Castilian, are also picked and processed but do not quite have the same striking flavour as the buds.

When picked the buds and/or fruits should be put into brine (2 teaspoons of salt to a pint of water) as soon as possible and left for two months. They are then taken from the brine and bottled in wine vinegar. This allows the distinctive tangy taste to develop. And as well as their unique flavour, capers are good for you. Around the Mediterranean they are known as a treatment for scurvy and rheumatism, and the Romans used them as an aphrodisiac.

If you wish to gather capers, as well as taking care to avoid the barbs, you have to beat the goats to the plants. We were 'capering'

133

on the hill across the valley one day when Paco the goatman came into view with his flock. When he realised what we were up to he said: "You carry on along there and I'll take my goats this way." All three of us knew that goats like nothing more than to browse a delicious caper bush, spines and all.

Agaves

There are approximately 300 species of agaves. The commonest agave in eastern Almería is the inaccurately-named century plant, aka American agave (Agave Americana/*planta del siglo* or *pita*). It's another striking incomer from Mexico. From a dramatic basal rosette of strap-like fleshy leaves, often well over a metre long and armed along their edges with short but vicious spines, the agave throws up a hefty flower spike in much less than the hundred years suggested by its common name. The time from seed to flowering is more typically between 10 and 30 years. Atop the wooden, trunk-like flower spike, evenly-spaced and elegantly curved side branches hold sprays of almost insignificant flowers which evolve into hard pods that fall to produce a new generation of tiny agaves. This is assuming the house sparrows, which are attracted to the seed pods like wasps to jam, don't consume all the seeds first. The spent parent agave is monocarpic; it flowers just the once, then dies. Locals know this agave as *pita*.

The *pita* trunks make handy poles and beams for construction in the campo. Fifty metres away from our front gate, on the lower slopes of the ridge opposite, there stands a very basic double carport, clearly 'do-it-yourself', constructed of *pitas* wired together, with plastic sheeting sandwiched between wire mesh for the walls and roof. The fronts of the two bays are open. Not attractive but functional. Outlay for the construction costs was almost certainly approaching zero. This was made by 'the gypsies', who had lived nearby, though when we arrived here several years ago they had already moved away. Two ancient cars mouldered quietly in the *pita* garage, together with bits of old bike and rusty tools scattered across the dusty floor. One day *los gitanos*, with the jet hair and dark complexions of stereotype, arrived out of the blue. They saw me and came over to ask how much we had paid for the house, a query to which I contrived a truthful but evasive answer. They then somehow got the cars started and vanished. More than half a decade on, the *pita* carport still stands proud against the frequent strong winds and the occasional torrential rains.

It seems that dead *pitas* last well above ground in the dry conditions which are usual here, in fact they seem to last for ages in situ, spearing the sky from their silently-drying basal rosettes, but their somewhat spongy centres rot in a few years if they're set into soil or anywhere damp might attack.

The steep slope at the bottom of our land and immediately above a road that peters out 200 metres further on is home to a thriving population of agaves. When their time is due they fling up their woody flower-spike at a rate of 15 centimetres per day. This agave can reach a height of 12 metres, making it perhaps the tallest flower on the planet. The angle at which they grow on our slopes means that from time to time a flower-spike will spear out horizontally, two metres or so above the road surface, impeding the very occasional traffic.

Soon after we came here I realised that one of the *pita* flower-spikes from our land, and therefore presumably our responsibility, was resting on the cables that linked the street lights along this road. Spotting Gabi Ramos, the local JCB man, working in the valley one day, I intercepted him as he came back up the road and asked if he could do something about the problem. He sized up the situation instantly and, delicately raising his bucket, eased the *pita* off the wires, nudged it sideways, pushed it down out of harm's way and then, with a wave and a grin, chugged off up the steepening road. And so a couple of years later, when we were having major building work done, Gabi was called in to dig our foundations.

In 2008 I hit on a new use (new to me at least) for *pitas*. With a surfeit of good, woody pita stems available in the abandoned parts of the nearby campo, it occurred to me to use them to make raised beds for growing vegetables. The method is simple. First, dig the bed, let's say two metres by one and a half, so you can reach into it from around the edges. Then cut *pitas* to length, so they can be two deep and will fit snugly at the corners. This means you need eight lengths of pita per bed. The four lower lengths are checked for fit, then can be drilled with a hole near each end. Through each hole will be hammered a piece of rebar 50 cm long, leaving it protruding high enough for the upper piece of *pita*, after careful drilling in what is measured to be the correct place, to be threaded onto it. Once this is done the rebar can be hammered down flush with the top of the frame of the raised bed. I finished the job by tacking lengths of heavy-duty black plastic as a moisture-retaining lining inside the *pita* walls, then filled the bed with compost and well-rotted manure.

A final use for the *pitas*, the agave stems, is one that I suspect northern Europeans brought to the area. We first had the idea from an Englishwoman who at that time was living nearby. The top metre and a half of a spent agave stem makes a fine Christmas tree. The tapering shape of the side branches mirrors, with a small leap of the imagination, the traditional festive conifer, the drying woody structure and uptilted seed pods are ideal for taking a silver or white spray and the whole is perfect for hanging baubles and tinsel. The unavailability of real Christmas trees here is another good reason to recycle a *pita*.

A relative of the agave americana is sisal (Agave sisalana), a superficially similar plant but smaller in all respects and reproducing in an additional manner: the candelabra spreading from the spike holds pods and miniatures of the parent plant, which easily root to produce a field of young at the feet of the mature agave. The fibres from the leaves of agave sisalana were formerly used in the manufacture of sacking and ropes. No longer grown commercially, rows and rows of the plant continue to grace the steppes of Las Amoladeras between Retamar and San Miguel de Cabo de Gata.

In Mexico the agave is called the *maguey*. There the sap is extracted from the heart of the *maguey* to give a fresh, nutritious drink called *aguamiel*, a brown nectar containing 70% fructose. *Aguamiel's* fermented relative is *pulque*, similarly fizzy, milky and slimy. Known as agave beer, it's been brewed in Mexico for over 2,000 years. These drinks are connoiseurs' beverages, I thought, when I tried them a few years ago at a basic Mexican roadside bar called a *pulqueria*. When distilled, the equivalent liquid from a related species, Agave tequilana or blue agave, produces the celebrated *tequila*.

I thought I'd learnt quite a lot about agaves and then my friend Carol Jepson, in the process of proofreading my text, provided another snippet. She sent me this: 'You can get agave nectar in

Waitrose. It's used as a sort of honey for people who don't like honey.' For more on agaves in the local area see the latter part of the chapter 'Río de Aguas: *acequias* and mills'.

15. Heat and wildfire

'The Andalucía sun starts singing a fire song, and all creation trembles
at the sound.'
(Federico García Lorca)

Heat

Figures from the Spanish met office, AEMET, based on equipment at Almería airport, show that the summer of 2010 was one of the hottest on record. Average temperatures in the province for the summer months, including daytime maxima and night-time minima, were: June 22.7°C, July 25.7°C and August 26.4°C.

July and August vie for the 'Hottest Month' title. During those months, what isn't done by 10 a.m. is unlikely to be done that day. On a hot day in the UK you can expect the hottest time to be somewhere around 1 p.m. or 2 p.m., after which the temperature begins to dip. Not so in Almería's semi-desert; after 2 p.m. it seems as if the temperature keeps inching up. At 6 p.m. it feels as hot as it did at midday. In fact the air temperature is dropping during the afternoon but heat radiating back up from the ground makes it appear otherwise. The constant grating buzz of cicadas forms a background; external sonic wallpaper. The birds fall silent. The cats disappear to the cool of the window ledges round the back of the house or to some shady place they've found in the valley. If they stay in the house they find the coolest tiles they can to lie on.

As the heat builds, however, it usually brings with it a breeze. This is still warm air but at least it's moving, bringing a small measure of relief. With doors and windows open, fly screens rattle and, depending on the wind direction, sooner or later a door will slam. Gauze curtains flow like clouds across the bedroom; our decision to have two sets of French windows there has the unanticipated advantage that the breeze is usually enough to keep us cool. We rarely have to resort to the air-conditioning; more unexpected brownie points on the green balance-sheet.

Wildfire

In the 1980s wildfires began to occur more frequently in the Sierra Cabrera. Fires didn't happen so often while goats were intensively grazing the hillsides, says the historian Clemente Flores, or at least such fires are not recorded in any of the documents he has consulted.

At the height of the summer of 2009 the midday breeze was a wind of searing heat day after day. The vegetation was frazzled to a pale shadow of its former self; all moisture had long been sucked from it by the relentless sun. Relative humidity was just 5%, the wind was reaching 30 kph and the temperature was close to 40°C. On July 15th a wildfire broke out in the Sierra Cabrera. Before it was extinguished it had devastated about 4,000 hectares of the mountain range. During the afternoon of Thursday July 23rd a second fire started and, fanned by ferocious winds, scorched towards Turre and the coast. That same evening, 3,000 people were evacuated as the flames came to within a few metres of the ancient hill-top village of Mojácar. At dusk, residents of Mojácar Playa peered through the hot smoky wind to see a line of flame on the mountain horizon inland from the town. Street thermometer displays were showing 44°C.

A Level 2 Emergency was declared, which allowed outside help to be requested. An army of 300 *guardia civil, policía local* and others such as troops from the Unidad Militar de Emergencias, aided by a dozen aircraft, including fire-fighting helicopters and planes which arrived on the morning of Friday 24th, managed to control the fire and it was eventually declared totally extinguished at 7.30 a.m. on Saturday July 25th. Most residents had been allowed back to their homes late on the 24th and were relieved to find that very few properties had been damaged. The winds had fanned the fire at such a speed that it burnt the mountain scrub in seconds and quickly passed on, so that it actually went round obstacles such as garden walls and didn't stay in any one place long enough to do serious damage. But even after the fire had been extinguished odd trees suddenly flared up and hot spots persisted for days.

Rumours spread as quickly as had the fire itself: conspiracy theorists had it that drug dealers had set the fire to divert the police; extreme environmentalists said it had been done to damage the Sierra Cabrera so it would be easier for developers to gain a toehold. There was speculation that arson was the cause but no official sources said this. There was no lightning at the time of the fires, but it needs only one discarded bottle to concentrate the sun's rays on these tinder-dry slopes. It was confirmed though that a further 2,600 hectares of scrub had been destroyed by the second fire and, given the speed at which it advanced, all ground-dwelling wildlife such as lizards and snakes and even many birds, will have been incinerated. As for tortoises, some that were above ground and didn't have the time to bury down may have perished, but since wild fires normally occur in the hot summer months when tortoises are aestivating underground, the majority of them will have survived. Tortoises bury themselves head down, so the top rear end of their carapace, the part that may be sticking out above ground, is sometimes scarred as a result of wildfire damage. Such damaged shell normally regenerates and the animals remain quite healthy.

In an article published soon after the 2009 fires, Domingo Ortíz pointed out that geological and archaeological evidence shows that wildfires have always occurred in the area. Yet in recent years the increasing frequency and size of the fires, together with more irregular rainfall, is heightening the risk of desertification and is worrying state organisations.

Historical records, says Ortíz, show a long history of conflict between crop-growing farmers and owners of livestock. He refers also to the destruction of mountain vegetation for fuel for local foundries and for firewood in the 19th century. Judicial documents from the period show 183 separate conflicts involving the destruction of firewood and grazing resources by either ploughing or burning for clearance. It was a tradition in the Sierra Cabrera, he says, to burn wooded areas and scrub. In the Archivo Histórico Municipal de Vera the growing incidence of mountain fires is shown by the number of disputes lodged: 12 during the 17th century and 130 during the 18th century. Of this latter total, 107 were in the Sierra Cabrera. With very few exceptions these were deliberate fires designed to bring formerly wild areas under cultivation. These fires were an ecological disaster, with the loss of many trees, particularly *acebuches*, carobs, cork oaks and pines and other resources such as the 100 beehives belonging to the vicar of Lubrín which fell prey to the flames in August 1691.

Ortíz finishes by pointing out the urgent need for more active policies to prevent the increasing number of modern fires from becoming even more of a socio-economic and environmental problem than they already are. A hefty hardback manual, dating from the time not too long ago when there was plenty of EU money sloshing around, details the restoration techniques used by the forestry services of Andalucía's environment ministry after wildfires. These are partly aimed at limiting the loss of soil by building dikes with stones or logs across the courses of streams to reduce the erosional impact of flash-floods. However, the large extent of many wildfires means that it is unrealistic to try to replant entire burnt areas.

Spur-thighed tortoises

After the devastating wildfires of 2009, in the summer of 2010 the Junta de Andalucía's Environmental Delegate Clemente García announced that about 100 tortoises had been released into the wild in the burnt areas of the Sierra Cabrera and that 80-100,000 trees of native species would be planted in October. Whether this actually happened and whether the trees survived I have not found out. The town hall in Turre organised small initiatives to replant a few hundred trees here and there, using the voluntary labour of its citizens under the supervision of specialists but, to use an inappropriate metaphor, it's a drop in the ocean. By and large the vegetation has to return on its own and is remarkably good at doing so. Clemente García pointed out that the burnt areas were recovering more quickly than expected, in part due to the weather conditions during the autumn and winter, cooler and wetter than normal.

The tortoises that were released are spur-thighed tortoises, one of two species found in Spain. They are distributed principally in North Africa from the Atlantic coast of Morocco to north-eastern Libya, but are also found in three areas of Spain. There are small populations in the Doñana National Park and the Balearic Islands, and a population of greater extent in the provinces of Murcia and Almería, especially the former.

The south-eastern Iberian population occurs in mountain ranges bordering the sea between Mazarrón and Carboneras. This area includes the Sierra de Bédar and the Sierra Cabrera, where the scarce rainfall produces scrub vegetation such as rosemary, thyme, *retama*, *cornicabra* and esparto, that provides ideal conditions for the animals.

Spur-thighed tortoises are herbivores and particularly go for the parts of the annual plants that give the most energy, namely the flowers, leaf-buds and new shoots. They weigh up to one kilo. Females are bigger than males. As with all reptiles, the species is cold-blooded and so needs an external energy source to heat it up. In south-eastern Spain the tortoises are inactive during winter (too cold) and summer (too hot). Spring and autumn are the periods of activity, with spring being the more important.

The breeding season begins in late February, when the males actively seek out the females. When they meet, the male courts the female by encircling her, biting her limbs, ramming her and mounting her. Then, during copulation, the male opens his mouth, showing his red tongue and making squeaking sounds. And they say romance is dead. The knocking together of their carapaces produces a characteristic noise, audible at some distance.

After copulation, the male leaves without ceremony to go and search for other females. The sexes do not form bonds and the species is not territorial. The female produces eggs between late spring and early summer, using her back legs to excavate a hole in which she deposits from three to five virtually spherical eggs the size of table-tennis balls. When the eggs hatch in the autumn, the young initially have a soft shell. During their early years they are at high risk of mortality from heat and cold, and predation by foxes, wild boar and magpies.

Spur-thighed tortoises are also seriously threatened by human activities. They are losing habitat due to the expansion of intensive irrigated agriculture in their natural range, for example on the plains around Vera and Antas and the foothills of Almagro, Almagrera and Los Pinos. They are now practically confined to the mountains, with populations that are in effect isolated from one another. Urban and tourist developments along the coasts of Murcia and Almería provinces have further reduced their former range.

A second factor threatening spur-thighed tortoises is their capture and use as pets. From the later years of the nineteenth century the various species of tortoise in the Mediterranean area were subjected to an onslaught of collection amounting to hundreds of thousands of animals annually. In Spain the trade did not reach such major dimensions but until the 1960s tortoises could be found for sale in markets and pet shops.

The species began to receive protection in that decade and since then the pressure from collection and trade has declined. Rural depopulation and an increasing environmental awareness amongst the human population have also been positive factors. Since 1984 all species of Mediterranean tortoises have been protected under CITES (the Convention for International Trade in Endangered Species). They *can* still be owned by private individuals but may not be sold or exchanged without a licence.

At present the spur-thighed tortoise is given 'vulnerable' status on the Red List of Threatened Species compiled and maintained by the IUNC (International Union for the Conservation of Nature and Natural Resources). Areas totalling 243,000 hectares in south-east Spain have been proposed as protected habitats for tortoises under the Natura 2000 Network. Almería province has three such areas: Almagro, Almagrera-Los Pinos and Cabrera-Bédar.

Despite their protected status, spur-thighed tortoises continue to be captured and kept in gardens as *'animales de compañia'*. This is on a local scale and not for commercial gain. Nevertheless, it is thought this is continuing to seriously affect the species and hastening local extinction in areas near villages. This is doubtless in many cases a matter of innocence, a simple lack of awareness. Incomers to rural areas in south-east Spain in recent years have been almost all non-Spaniards and almost certainly they are people who do not realise that tortoises are legally protected and under serious threat, as the story below illustrates. They have in some cases come to renovate ruins in remote places where, since the former residents left a few decades ago, the tortoises have been relatively undisturbed. It is also no doubt the case that many rural Spaniards are oblivious to the precarious situation for their local tortoises.

A few years ago we came to know a couple who lived in the Cariatiz area. They liked dogs to the extent that they eventually had seven. The dogs were well looked after and exercised daily in the *campo*. One result of this was that a dog would return home from its countryside romp, from time to time, with a tortoise in its jaws, fortunately unharmed. The response of the couple who owned the dogs was to build a small pen for the tortoises and keep them as pets on the basis that if they let them go, the dogs would only find them and bring them back. There is a well-meaning, albeit misguided, logic here. The couple's relationship did not last and neither of them now lives at the house in question. As to what became of their dogs and the tortoises, I can't say.

Meanwhile, back in the Sierra Cabrera, the recovery of the fire-burnt areas has been visually astonishing. Within a year of the major fires, what had been great expanses of scorched, blackened land had a flush of vivid new green. Trees that had been flash-burnt sprouted tentative new leaves. In these circumstances, olives are particularly good at recovering, coming back even when seemingly totally destroyed by fire. Birds came back quite quickly, of course, though no doubt other creatures will recolonise at slower rates. It's an object lesson in the obvious; nature is hard-wired to survive and will do so long after we are no longer here to create environmental mayhem.

The American thinker and writer Gary Snyder, in a recent essay about southern California, points out: 'California has a predictable summer drought and a high-risk fire season absolutely every year. That's what is called a summer-dry Mediterranean-type climate.' I mention this because this is exactly the climate we have here in eastern Almería and Snyder goes on to say a few pages later: 'Flood and fire are perfectly natural,' and: 'The experts have been telling us that the best way to prevent forest fires is to start lots of little fires each year to reduce the underbrush.'

The 'old fellas' in the *campo* and the authorities here know this. Each spring the ground around the olive and almond trees is ploughed to turn in the plants that have sprung up during the cooler, damper winter and that will otherwise shrivel to become wildfire-fuel as the year heats up. Between March and November it's illegal to have an outdoor fire. During the late winter it's common to see fires where people are burning undergrowth and scrub but even at that time of year you have to get a permit from the local town hall. This will give a fixed period within which the fire must take place, specifying the times of day and insisting on common-sense measures such as having water available by the fire and ensuring it is fully extinguished when it dies down.

144

How fires start

The final day of August 2012, about eleven in the morning. I'm in the house, tapping away at the keyboard, when I hear a series of strange noises, a kind of fizzy thumping, outside but close. I run out to see the overhead electricity lines sparking and crackling. On a derelict plot adjacent to ours, several agaves have sent up their woody flower spikes amongst the power lines. Last night we did have rain and strong winds. Something in this combination, the moisture, the weight of the agaves, the wind, has finally created a problem. Our electricity cuts out.

I walk up the road to our neighbours and meet one of them, Alan, coming the other way. His power has gone. We are just by Ana's house at this point, and so go to check the situation with her. Someone will need to call Endesa, the electricity company, to alert them to the problem. As we reach Ana's back door there is a cry of: "¡Fuego!" Flames are licking around the base of the agaves, just a few metres from our boundary. Shrubs and dried plants, shrivelled into tinder after a scorching summer, are everywhere on this abandoned plot.

I sprint back, heart pounding. The only thing I can do is use buckets, filled from the tap at the base of our rainwater tank. At least last night's 7 mm of rain, collected across our various flat roofs, will have put something into this tank. I race round the house side, slopping water, but the fire is beyond a steep bank topped with a tall wire fence. The fence is one I'd put up earlier in the year to stop the incursions of the neighbours' new dog, Combate, a huge Alsatian; friendly, but a nuisance.

Already my mouth is dry, drier than I ever remember it being. The flow from the rainwater tap is slow. Meanwhile, I'm unclipping the fence to get access to the fire. Along one side of our house is a huge woodpile. Then there are the thick wooden poles of the terraces. I have visions of the whole lot going up. The first bucketful of water launched onto the flames brings forth a great spew of steam and smoke. I slither down the bank, run round the house, collect another bucketful, pound back, scramble up the bank, try to assess where I can most effectively throw the water, get scarred by agave blades, eyes stung by smoke. Repeat many times.

The fire, partly contained by an old ruin, has by some miracle not spread. Attempts to run a hose across the scrubby slope from Ana's house have failed; it's too short. A guy in maybe his 30s, who I've not seen before, but who is presumably related to Ana, is using it to fill a second bucket though. And then serious help arrives. A chunky guy who I think I recognise from the next hamlet has spannered open a junction in one of the big pipes leading out from the village *deposito*, the water tank, which is close by. Three of us manhandle this big hose and soon enough the fire is extinguished. My heart is still hammering.

At various intervals after this the *guardia civil* arrive, then two 4WDs from the fire department in Carboneras with a high-pressure hose, civil protection vehicles, several Junta de Andalucía vans, and finally a helicopter buzzes in, describing close circles above us to check the state of affairs. It's an impressive response, albeit after the event. When it's clear that there is no longer any danger they gradually all leave. An hour later two guys from Endesa show up, borrow a saw from me and, with the aid of a long, extendable hook and a fair bit of cursing, between the three of us we fell and disentangle the five offending agaves. The power lines are surprisingly strong, seeming to cope easily with having the curved, woody upper branches of the agaves wrenched from them. That done, the power is restored and it is almost as if nothing had happened. The terror I felt was all too real though.

I'm still hyped up for a couple of days. The emergency services were clearly edgy too. Just a week earlier there had been a fierce wildfire in the Bédar/Serena area, just a few kilometres away. More than a thousand people were evacuated as over 2,000 personnel plus the usual planes and helicopters fought the fire. About 30 properties were damaged and a couple of fire-fighters suffered from smoke inhalation but as always the response was impressive and effective. Much of the 374 hectares that were burnt, mostly scrub and pines, was in the environmentally sensitive LIC (Special Conservation Area) of the Sierra de Bédar. In the days following the fire the hills looked like a war-zone, with stark tree skeletons, incinerated slopes, remnants of old terrace walls revealed from below the scrub for the first time in years and a pervading stink of smoke and ash.

The press reported that two men, a 30-year old and a 43-year old, who had been using an electric saw to cut a steel drum, had been arrested. Escaping sparks had started the disaster. They had tried and failed to put out the flames themselves but had also failed to call the emergency services.

Closer to home, back in the spring I'd seen the potential for problems as the agaves threw up their flower spikes like tree-trunks, so quickly you could virtually watch them grow. I planned to saw them down before they reached the wires but suddenly they were there, touching the lines, and it was too late. How could I have been so stupid as to let that happen? Next spring, any agaves that throw up flower-spikes near the power lines, beautiful and evocative of the semi-desert though they may be, will be coming down in good time.

16. Rain and flood

'But nature ain't an easy ride. You have to be prepared for loss and suffering too.'
(Richard Mabey)

Trapped by the rain

October 2007 was seriously wet. The 18th is a date etched in our diaries. We had been invited to Urrá for a meal by Lindy Walsh, who had suggested we go in the campervan to give ourselves the option of staying over if we wanted to have a drink. Continuing rain gave us pause for thought but we decided to chance it. This proved very wise, for the following reason. In the early 90s she and her late husband Bill had laid down a reasonable cellar but as things turned out their stocks of wine exceeded demand. On the basis that you can't take it with you, Lindy had extracted three bottles for the evening between five of us, including one abstemious driver in the other couple. The wines were awarded high scores by the ad-hoc panel. A decision to round the evening off with something Hungarian, virulent and bright green is best glossed over. So we slept in the campervan. It rained all night during which time, had we but known it, our earlier wise decision was beginning to look less wise.

Two attempts to negotiate Lindy's drive at 9am next morning failed. The drive has since been improved but at that stage was still made of gypsum. This dries quickly after rain but during a prolonged wet spell becomes slippery and treacherous. After various desperate phone-calls we walked up the drive and our neighbour Mary drove over to rescue us.

Much mountain down

By now the rain was even more intense. Our rainwater harvesting system, newly installed at that stage, has a capacity of 2,100 litres but was overwhelmed within minutes. The lower tank, set into a steep bank in the garden, overflowed and the water gullied its way down into the earth by the recently-finished lower steps, undercutting them to the point of collapse. Somehow they held. Huge fans of slurry and grit overwhelmed several of the vegetable beds below. The foundations of the lower tank were undercut, so it developed a list and the adjacent upper steps were soon deprived of support and lurching towards their doom.

The roof terraces had become lakes, their drainage holes quite incapable of coping with the intensity of the downpour. Damp patches appeared on a couple of ceilings and water began to come into the living room steadily through the hole where the chimney was due to be built for the wood-burner. The front door allowed a steady trickle of water in and this contrived to get under the kitchen units. For 24 hours after the rain eventually stopped it oozed quietly out from under the kickboards.

The back of the house is just a metre or so from a cliff that varies from six to eight metres in height and is of such complex geology it's difficult to guess what it will do next. Except fall down. "Oh my God!" I heard Troy say as she looked out of the window at a vast pile of rock-fall. We'd heard nothing as several tonnes of rock and soil had come down and wedged themselves against the house. It was a salutary lesson.

Mary had told Magnet, one of our Romanian builders, about the rock-fall and he was round here the following day building the aforementioned chimney. I showed him the debris. Mary told us later that when he got back (he and his partner Lily were living at that time in an apartment that is part of Pete and Mary's house), he said, with his lopsided piratical grin: "Much mountain down, Mary!"

Firewood

The leaden overcast we awoke to on that Thursday morning in October 2007 was clamped low over the Sierra Cabrera. In mid-afternoon we were expecting our first delivery of a €300 lorry-load of firewood, a mix of olive trunks, olive roots, and orange tree trunks. The price didn't seem excessive when you consider the scarcity of trees round here and that a lorry-load should last about one and and a half Spanish winters. Barely had we paid Francisco Crespo, the wood-man, when the rain began.

He then set off back to his yard near Alfaix for another load for Pete and Mary who live in the next hamlet, a few hundred metres away. At just this time Mary was at the airport dropping Pete who was going back to the UK, so we were left in charge of their wood delivery. We showed Francisco their house and kept a watch through the rain for his lorry coming back across the valley. I finally saw it coming and stationed myself, inexplicably clad in only a tee-shirt and jeans, by their gateway. Francisco manoeuvred into their front garden and tilted the bed of the truck so the wood slid out skilfully close to their pool, as requested. By now sodden, I paid him and jumped in the car. I had to go to the end of the road to turn and when I came back his wagon was still there.

"*¡Problema!*" said the head poking out of the cab as the wheels created spinning mayhem with Pete and Mary's gravel on the awkward little slope up to their gateway. Finally the two mini-skirted teenage girls who were (also inexplicably) in the cab of the lorry joined me in pushing. To everyone's relief the lorry finally scooted forward in a flurry of flying gravel and disappeared. I was drenched.

The rain in Spain

A late January night in 2010 and I'm not sleeping well. I register wind and rain lashing against the French doors that face east from our bedroom. Drifting in and out of sleep, in each phase of conscious recall I'm aware of rain stinging the glass.

The alarm on my watch sounds at 8.30. I cancel its beeping and burrow back below the duvet, searching out some extra warmth from Troy. An hour later I get up. She stays in bed. Beyond the window is a louring, wet sky. At least, with the front half of the house entirely rebuilt, the old problems in the main room, with its roof like a colander and its leaky front door, have gone.

The rain is intense. Such heavy rain is a semi-desert speciality. Once again the volume of water is too great for the downpipes that lead from our roof-terraces into our rainwater storage tanks. So when it siles down, water backs up on those terraces and inevitably finds any weakness, hence damp patches on the ceiling. I wrote that word, siles, then the computer's brain underlined it. It's a word I distinctly remember from my Lincolnshire childhood, so although I normally ignore red underlining, I checked, and Chambers English Dictionary has this: 'sile, seil. (*dial.*) – *v.i.* to rain heavily', and suggests a Scandinavian origin. Is it too fanciful to imagine that, having grown up on the Lincolnshire coast, having had classmates with Scandinavian and Baltic names like Eskesen (Danish) and Riekstins (Latvian), this is why this dialect word enriched, back in the 1960s, my tentatively growing grasp on our endlessly rich language?

Sheets of cardboard and strategic buckets are put into position, water is mopped from the wooden floor, and I reassess my plan to drive the twenty twisty mountain kilometres into Sorbas for various errands that can easily wait for tomorrow. From the window at the south end of our main room I can see that the terraces in the valley that falls away below the house are filling, the olive and almond trees marooned in silt-thick floodwater. The rain piles down. I dodge out to empty the rain gauge before it overflows: 106 millimetres so far. When it seems that it can't get worse, it does. Behind my shoulder I sense a flicker of lightning beyond the window. Thunder trails a wide rumble through the whole sky. I check the house again and find two more places where water is coming in. Another shard of white brilliance, another moment of charged airs crashing against each other, and the electricity goes off.

We light a couple of candles, more for cheer than utility, feed a couple more logs into the wood burner and sit back with our books. Reading seems the only option, albeit by the barely adequate grey light which is all that's available. We clearly can't do anything in the garden today. With no electricity the phone doesn't work, the laptops likewise once the batteries have run down. There's no water being pumped into the house, so we capture what's arcing off the porch roof. We do have gas to cook on, though of course no electric ignition, and we have the constant kettle on the woodstove. This is not hardship.

But Troy has an appointment with the physiotherapist in Carboneras at 6 p.m. and it suddenly occurs to me, mid-afternoon, that we may not be able to get there. At 3 p.m. I decide to drive down and take a look at the two *ramblas* we will have to cross to get out. In two places, high earth banks have slumped across the road but it's passable. At the first *rambla* the drainage pipes are overwhelmed and dense beige floodwater is streaming 15 centimetres deep across the road. Further on, where a small field of trees is entirely flooded to the left, the gale is flailing against the branches and a rain of unpicked olives is spattering down, small explosions dashing the brown water surface. Rocks have been sluiced onto the road. Shallow drifts of water speed past them.

At Gafarillos the *rambla* is a sandy torrent. I stop. At the house on the right a man I take to be the husband of Mercedes (I know her vaguely, but not him) is leaning on his wrought-iron fence, watching events. I ask if he thinks a car can get through. He is friendly but non-committal. I suggest this is more rain than normal. He agrees. I tell him where we live. He shows mild interest. Then a van appears from the direction of Peñas Negras and, cleaving a course through the flood, emerges unscathed. Mercedes' husband and I nod to each other.

The goat man and his wife come by, each hefting on their shoulder a massive bale of straw. Fifty metres away the animals are hunched, sodden, in their pen, an awkward wire enclosure on a steep rock-studded slope. Today there is no chance to take them out grazing. As an afterthought I ask Mercedes' husband if their electricity is on. "No", he says, with a hint of 'What do you expect in this weather? This is Spain.'

Back at home, I empty another 110mm from the rain gauge. We set off in plenty of time and, arriving early at Carboneras, drive through the town and on to the Playa del Algarrobico where, under a sky greyer than ever, grey water is thrashing down the wide braided *rambla* of the Rio Alías and fighting its way into a dark and wild sea whose waves rear and smash at the colourless beach.

After Troy's appointment the rain has stopped. We have a coffee and a *tapa* in a friendly bar where the owner explains his low prices as a response to *'la crisis'* (economic, not meteorological), then we drive home. The water is lower in the *ramblas* but the street lighting in our hamlet is still out. The rain gauge has another 12mm, a total of 238mm for the virtually continuous period of rain stretching from 25th January overnight into the 26th. We let ourselves in to the dark house, avoid standing on two squeaking cats and, by torchlight, try the trip-switch. The lights come on.

More than two years later I discover that back in December 1990 Gafarillos had recorded 177mm of rain in 24 hours. We appear to have beaten that total but to put it in perspective, the most extreme 24-hour period of rain recorded in the province involved 600 mm, a two foot depth of water, in Zurgena in October 1973.

152

Wet, wet, wet

Three months on. It's almost the end of April 2010, after the wettest winter in, and beyond, living memory. We recorded 164mm in December, 334mm in January, 104mm in February and a further 129mm in March. Four times more rain than normal, the media tell us. It hasn't been like this in a hundred years, say the local statisticians. In the last few days the temperatures have finally risen. People are at last commenting on the sun's heat, something that you'd expect fairly frequently a month earlier in a normal year. Each evening we at last make a conscious decision about whether or not to light the wood-burner after months of firing it up automatically.

The landscape is still intensely green, a patchwork of greens shot through with dots and patterns and swathes of colour: scarlet poppies, white cistus, purple-blue viper's bugloss, yellow broom, a bonus for the goats that come our way every few days and for the bees on foray from the many hives on the hillslopes. As I write this, Paco the goat-man has his flock chomping and farting contentedly in the unseasonably lush fields below our house. The word 'meadow' springs immediately to mind but would never normally do so here.

Floods

Heavy rain and drought might seem to be opposites but they can interact in darkly dangerous ways. On Friday 28th September 2012 significant rain was predicted for the first time in months. On cue, the skies darkened and the rain began. We were mightily relieved, as all attempts to keep things alive in the garden during one of the driest and hottest summers for decades had become a battle against the odds. As the rain intensified the power went off and the rain gauge steadily filled. It's instructive, how many things you can't do when there's no electricity. I resorted to filling in my tax return.

Five or six hours later the rain petered out and we had power again. We'd had 83 mm in total, and apart from the power cut and a bit of mopping up, we had no problems. It was only a day or so later, when we began to get emails and phone calls from friends in the UK who had seen the news, that we realised we must have been on the fringe of the storm. We were lucky. Phone calls to people we know living up remote tracks and *ramblas* revealed that most of them were stranded, their lines of access having been washed out, potholed or scoured down to impassable bedrock. We went over to Cariatiz to visit friends and found the tarmac road leading to their access track undermined and broken into great tilted slabs, utterly destroyed. We passed the Rambla del Chive, the only way to many houses, en route. That too was totally scoured out by the floods and impassable even in a 4x4.

Only later still did we realise the full extent of the disaster. Up to 254 mm of rain fell during the Friday morning alone. Eleven people died in the resulting floods across Andalucía and Murcia provinces, four of these in Almería. Vera, Antas, Huércal-Overa and Pulpí were officially declared disaster areas. 4,500 properties and 900 vehicles were badly damaged in Almería province alone. TV and online footage showed cars being swept away, smashed into each other, upended against trees and reduced to mud-filled hulks of crumpled metal. A sewage treatment plant in Antas was damaged, causing raw sewage to flow into the Río Antas for nearly a week. The Junta de Andalucía's José Manuel Ortiz reported that 20,000 animals had been drowned on ten farms in the Huércal-Overa area. A motorway bridge near Lorca was destroyed and many other lesser bridges and roads were taken out, for example the Los Carasoles bridge, a key link in the Zurgena area.

Houses in the Pueblo Laguna area of Vera, the worst affected place, were inundated with huge unstoppable waves of silt-laden water two and a half metres high. A 52-year old British woman resident in Pueblo Laguna was swept out to sea. Her body was found five days later by fishermen in Cabo de Gata, 70 kilometres away. Many residents were subsequently told by insurers that their apartments had been condemned as uninhabitable. Weeks after the floods, possessions utterly ruined and made almost unrecognisable by thick coatings of silt were still being dragged from the houses and piled in the streets.

The worst part of this storm was very intense and localised but the long summer, both drier and hotter than usual, was considered to have played a part in the severity of the flooding because the ground was so baked that the rain was not able to penetrate and simply became instant run-off. Damage in the Bédar and Serena areas was also thought to have been made worse by the wildfires that had stripped the vegetation from the hills just a few weeks earlier. With no plants to slow down and soak up the water, the run-off was made faster and more destructive.

José Cara of the Partido Popular accused the Junta de Andalucía of "inefficiency" in preventing the worst of the floods, saying it had spent only €133 million of the €431 million approved in 2002 for the prevention of flooding. He added that if the Junta had stuck to its plan, the Río Antas would not have caused such devastation in areas like Pueblo Laguna, Cuevas del Almanzora and Pulpí. The environmental group GEM accused local authorities and property developers of knowingly allowing and building holiday accommodation and other dwellings on flood-plains and in other high-risk flood-prone locations, a point it would seem difficult to counter. It was also suggested that the failure to clear vegetation and accumulated debris from dry river beds created obstructions which meant that the floodwaters could not flow away quickly.

Miguel Jurado, president of the Playa del Sur urbanisation, said: "We look to the authorities to take responsibility. The owners of these houses bought them with no idea they were on a flood plain. All the permissions were in place," and he added, "The banks of the river need to be reinforced and the vegetation cut down." On Monday 8th October at an emergency meeting in Vera, Juan Ignacio Zoido, regional president of the Partido Popular, revealed that the cost of repairing all the damage was expected to exceed €100 million.

17. Diverse dangers

"Geologists communicated in English; and they could name things in a manner that sent shivers through the bones."
(John McPhee)

Earth moves

The whole south-eastern corner of Spain is affected by the convergent boundary between the Eurasian and African tectonic plates. The movement of these plates against each other results in the presence of faults or, more precisely, fault zones. The difference is that a fault is a single clear boundary between the rocks either side, whereas a fault zone comprises at least two more or less parallel faults. A series of such fault zones, stretching between Almería and Alicante, has dominated seismic activity in the region. This sequence of faults extends for 450 kilometres and includes, from south to north, the faults of Carboneras, Palomares, Alhama de Murcia, Bajo Segura and Carrascoy, of which the first two are the most significant. In fact, the Carboneras Fault Zone is one of the most active in the Iberian Peninsula, with a length of almost 50 kilometres on land and a further 100 kilometres under the sea.

On land the Carboneras Fault Zone emerges near the mouth of Rambla Morales, close to the village of San Miguel de Cabo de Gata, and runs WNW-ENE, reaching the coast again near Carboneras and passing en route along the Serrata de Níjar and near to Sopalmo. The stresses are such that the land south-east of the fault zone is being pulled in a north-easterly direction. At its north-eastern end the Carboneras Fault Zone becomes the Palomares Fault Zone, which runs almost due north, paralleling the coast north of Mojácar. These two fault zones have created what geologists call a 'restraining bend' which has been largely responsible for the uplifting of the Sierra Cabrera.

Estimates are that, since some 16 million years ago, displacement along the Carboneras and Palomares Fault Zones has been about 35 to 40 kilometres laterally. This explains the fact that the Sierra Almagrera, which was originally part of the Sierra Cabrera, is now many kilometres north north-east of the latter range. Evidence of this can be seen from the main *plaza* (square) in Mojácar *pueblo*.

156

Looking north from there, the line of the Palomares Fault Zone is shown by the straight coastline and, in normal visibility, the detached mountain range of the Sierra Almagrera is clearly visible.

Research workers have estimated that lateral slip rates, i.e. the rate of movement along the faults, average one millimetre per year for the Carboneras Fault Zone and two millimetres per year for the Palomares Fault Zone. These rates of movement are similar to those along parts of the much better known San Andreas Fault in California. Of course, this is not smooth movement, as the rocks are snagged against each other. Tension builds over a period of time and then, when it reaches a critical point and the snag is released, there is an earthquake. In simple terms, the longer the delay, the more the stress builds and the bigger the eventual earthquake.

As for the seismic activity associated with these faults, historical records show a number of major earthquakes, such as those of 1518 and 1865 in Vera and several in Almería (1487, 1522, 1659 and 1804), registering up to 9 (out of 12) on the Mercalli Scale, equivalent to roughly 7.2 (out of 9) on the more modern Richter Scale. In November 1518 Vera was totally destroyed, whilst as a result of the earthquakes in Almería the Alcazaba was seriously affected, as were the Almadena neighbourhood and various coastal defences. Some research suggests that the coastline between Carboneras and Cabo de Gata has been uplifted by about two metres since the fifteenth century, perhaps as a result of some of the larger earthquakes.

Then, in a reminder that plate tectonics are not just remote bits of geology, on 11th May 2011, a magnitude 5.1 earthquake struck on the Alhama de Murcia fault system. The epicentre was 2.5 kilometres north-east of Lorca, a town of 92,000 inhabitants. "All the tiles on the floor were jumping," said Eliseo Lopez, co-proprietor of the Nissan and Renault concession in Lorca, "cracking as if they were alive."

The epicentre had a very shallow focal depth of one kilometre. Because of the combination of shallow depth and the magnitude of the earthquake, significant shaking occurred throughout much of Murcia province. Ten deaths resulted and dozens of people were injured. Widespread panic ensued, with many Lorca residents displaced from their homes and sleeping out in the streets on subsequent nights. Substantial damage occurred to older structures such as the Espolón Tower of Lorca Castle. In total the earthquake released a surface energy equivalent to 200 tonnes of TNT.

The Lorca earthquake was the result of strike-slip faulting. This means that there was very little vertical movement, just lateral movement of the rock masses relative to each other on the opposite sides of the fault. Estimates of movement at the location of the Lorca earthquake suggest that the African plate is currently moving north-east with respect to the Eurasian plate at an average of six millimetres per annum.

The 'Palomares Incident'

Back south-west again, it's not the fault of Palomares (pun intended) that it has been in the news for almost half a century for another disaster, although this one was man-made. The 'Palomares Incident' happened on 17th January 1966, at the height of the Cold War between the USA and the Soviet Union. It was while refuelling high over south-eastern Spain that a B-52G bomber of USAF Strategic Air Command collided in mid-air with a KC-135 refuelling tanker at an altitude of 9,450 metres over what was then the unknown fishing village of Palomares.

The B-52G had set off from North Carolina as part of a mission named Operation Chrome Dome. Chrome Dome involved continuous flights of B-52s armed with nuclear missiles within range of the USSR. Between 1961 and 1968 these planes were up there above us all the time and in fact the Palomares incident was just one of five similar accidents during this period.

On this occasion the B-52 required refuelling twice in mid-air over Spain and it was during the second of these operations that the accident occurred. The KC-135 tanker was totally destroyed when its fuel load ignited, killing all four members of the crew. The B-52G broke apart, killing three of its seven crew members. The other four parachuted to safety and were helped by local residents and fishermen.

Of the four B28RI hydrogen bombs carried by the B-52G, three landed just outside Palomares village and were quickly located. The bombs were not 'armed' but the non-nuclear explosives in two of the three bombs detonated when they hit the ground, contaminating a two square kilometre area with radioactive plutonium dust.

On 25th January 1966 the US announced that it would in future not fly over Spain with nuclear weapons and four days later the Spanish government formally banned US flights that carried such weapons over its territory. To defuse concern about the risks posed by radioactive contamination a photo-call was organised for 8th March. The Spanish Minister for Information and Tourism, Manuel Fraga Iribarne, and the US ambassador, Angier Biddle Duke, swam off the beaches of Palomares and Mojácar, smiling and waving confidently to the assembled press.

The fourth bomb fell into the Mediterranean and was found in 869 metres of water after a search lasting two months. It was recovered intact and lifted aboard the USS Petrel. Meanwhile, on land a clean-up was being attempted. From an area of 2.2 hectares, which was deemed to be the most contaminated, 6,000 250-litre drums of soil were removed and taken to the Savannah River Plant in South Carolina in the USA for burial. A further 17 hectares of land with lower levels of contamination were treated simply by harrowing and ploughing to a depth of 30 centimetres.

These remedial measures involved many personnel and enormous costs. The USA began paying €314,000 per year for plutonium contamination checks and blood tests for residents in the area. A free coach trip to Madrid each year isn't quite the same though, when it's overshadowed by the knowledge that you're going for a health check to see if you've been irradiated by a nuclear bomb. In 2004, a study revealed that significant traces of contamination remained present. There has, however, been no evidence of health issues caused to the local population by the Palomares Incident.

In October 2006 the US and Spanish governments agreed to share the workload and costs, estimated at €25 million, of decontaminating the remaining suspect areas. Spain does not have the infrastructure to store the contaminated soil, so it would have to be shipped to the USA. It seems though that nothing happened as a result of this accord.

In March 2009 *Time* magazine listed the Palomares Incident as one of the world's worst nuclear disasters. By this time the respected newspaper *El Pais* calculated that the incident had cost the US $1,983 million. In August 2010, the Spanish government announced that the US had stopped the annual payments it had been making to Spain because an agreement to do so had expired in 2009. This was 45 years after the disaster, which sounds a long time until you realise that plutonium-239 has a half-life of 24,100 years. One newspaper article at the time suggested that the remaining contaminated area would be fenced off with 'crime scene'-type tape and used for hunting rabbits.

Then in January 2011, the Spanish Foreign Minister, Trinidad Jimenez, meeting US Secretary of State Hillary Clinton in Washington, received a 'firm commitment' that the US would continue to work with the Spanish government to find a solution to the plutonium-contaminated soil at Palomares. Over three years later, perhaps predictably, the situation has still not been resolved and it would be an optimist who believed that any further remedial action will be taken in the near future, so the site remains fenced off for the public's safety.

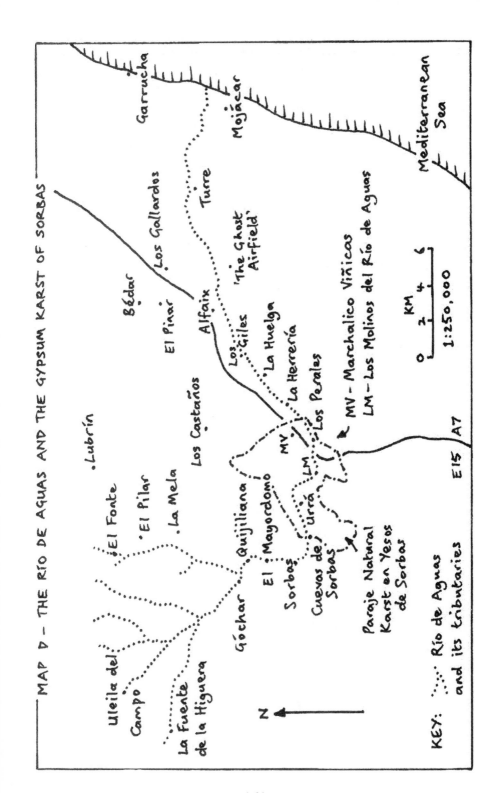

MAP D – THE RÍO DE AGUAS AND THE GYPSUM KARST OF SORBAS

Garrucha

Mojácar

Mediterranean Sea

Turre

Los Gallardos

'The Ghost Airfield'

Bédar

El Pinar

Alfaix

Los Giles

La Huelga

La Herrería

Los Perales

MV – Marchalico Viñicas
LM – Los Molinos del Río de Aguas

KM

0   2   4   6

1:250,000

Lubrín

El Fonte

El Pilar

La Mela

Los Castaños

MV

LM

Quijiliana

El Mayordomo

Urrá

Sorbas

Cuevas de Sorbas

Paraje Natural
Karst en Yesos
de Sorbas

E15   A7

Góchar

Uleila del Campo

La Fuente de la Higuera

N

KEY: ∵∵ Río de Aguas
and its tributaries

161

18. Río de Aguas: from the source...

'When I have a choice, I would rather travel down rivers on foot,
walking along trails that run the length of the river or, best of all,
wading through the river itself.'
(Kathleen Dean Moore)

Riverwalking

Another walk now, this time along a river. Following the
course of a river on foot has a pedigree. Invaders and settlers all over
the world, arriving on a strange coast, learnt early that rivers would
lead inland, usually by a relatively easy route, and that rivers and
fertile land and, by extension riches, go together. Only relatively
recently did people begin to undertake lengthy walks alongside rivers
for pleasure. In the UK there is now an official National Trail from the
source of the Thames in the Cotswolds to its mouth, a walk of 184
miles (294 kilometres). Lots of other, shorter rivers, such as the Test
in Hampshire, have similar bank-side walks.

More interesting than the organised leisure routes though are
individual explorations. We tend to only know about them if they
have been recorded. I have just been up to my bookshelves to check
on Robert Gibbing's book *Coming Down The Wye*. I remember it as a
luminously wonderful book, but it's not there. I'm not exactly
distraught but I'm puzzled as to where it went. Gibbings, an Irish
writer who was also renowned as a wood engraver and sculptor,
produced a series of acclaimed river books: *Sweet Thames Run Softly*
(1940); *Coming Down The Wye* (1942); *Lovely Is The Lee* (1944), the
Lee in Ireland, that is; and *Coming Down The Seine* (1953). Jim Perrin's
book *River Map*, a very personal revelation about a journey both
inside his head and along the River Dee (or Afon Dyfrdwy) in North
Wales, is a more recent example of the sub-genre.

All of which is leading up to the notion of following the course
of a local river. The Atlas de Almería shows the drainage basins of its
rivers very clearly. In eastern Almería the main ones are the Río
Antas, Río de Aguas and Río Alías. Further north, and a much bigger
proposition, is the Río Almanzora. The Río de Aguas, the nearest of
these rivers to where we live and the one with least development on
its banks, was my obvious first choice. I thought too that source to

mouth is the logical direction, if only so that you have a marginal amount of gravity on your side.

The puzzle of the *ramblas*

Following the course of a river in Almería province should be easy. After all, almost all the rivers are dry for most of the time so you can simply walk along the streambed, the *rambla*. There's no swimming or even paddling involved. But, assuming you plan to walk the line of the river downstream, you must first identify the source. This is where it becomes tricky.

According to the Atlas Almería, the Río de Aguas drains an area of 543 square kilometres and has a length of 35 kilometres but there is much more to the drainage system of the Río Aguas than that. It is the one river in eastern Almería that flows permanently, albeit only for part of its course. To find its true source, the logical plan would be to work upstream, following the map. El Nacimiento (The Birth), the group of permanent springs from where water flows, is named on the 1:25,000 scale map, sheet 1031-I Sorbas, a kilometre or so north of the village of Los Molinos del Río de Aguas. Upstream from there, the *rambla* is obvious enough as far as Sorbas, quite broad in places, and clearly a riverbed in times of heavy rain.

At Sorbas things become more complicated. This is where the *rambla* described above splits into two or, more accurately, given the direction of water flow, where two tributary *ramblas* converge to form the Río Aguas *rambla*. One of these comes in from the west where, just over a kilometre upstream, it is itself formed by the joining of the Rambla de Cinta Blanca and the Rambla de los Chopos.

The other tributary *rambla*, coming down from the north and looking much more substantial on the map, is the Rambla de Sorbas. About four kilometres upstream, near Góchar, this in turn changes its name. The major branch continues as the Rambla de Góchar in a north-westerly direction. The minor tributary that comes in here from the north is the Rambla de Mora, which is fed in turn by the Rambla de Zaga.

Continuing the quest for the source of the Río Aguas, the Rambla de Góchar is the biggest at this point and so seems to be the obvious line. It can be followed upstream from the eponymous village for about five kilometres before another fork, a three-way affair this time, presents a further choice. This is close to the hamlet of Albarracín. Here the Rambla del Salar comes in from the west (more or less), the Rambla del Aguador comes from the north-west and the Rambla de Garrido funnels in from the north. These *ramblas* are draining the southern slopes of the Sierra de los Filabres.

Looking on the adjacent maps, and tracing the *ramblas* as they twist, ever narrower and higher, into the Filabres hills, it becomes apparent that there is no obvious single point which can be determined unequivocally as the source of the Río Aguas. You pay your money and you take your choice. The Rambla del Salar looks as good a candidate as any. Following it west, upstream, onto the adjacent map, sheet 1030-II Los Yesos, its name appears as Rambla del Solar (rather than Salar: a cartographer's error or a local variation?) and then, still further upstream, the Rambla del Aguador. About three kilometres south-west of Uleila del Campo, the legend Fuente de la Higuera (Spring of the Fig Tree) is printed at the point where the *rambla* seems to have faded almost to nothing. The map symbol for a spring is not used, so it is not obvious from the map precisely where the spring is but nevertheless this seems like an appropriate spot to begin a 'source-to-mouth' journey.

Comprehensively lost

And so, on a fine May morning, I set off with Charlie Brown, a local friend who's also keen to explore the area. We have left a car at Sorbas, having estimated that a steady day's walk from the Fuente de la Higuera will get us that far. We've driven the other car to the start of our route, parking by a road bridge comprising two square arches (can arches be square?) in grid square 568113, just east of Fuente de la Higuera. The sun is already warm as we start east along the Rambla del Salar. Within two minutes, a haunting call from above produces a cry from Charlie: "What's that?" A glimpse of a sizeable green and yellow bird in loping flight, a green woodpecker.

A vehicle track uses the *rambla* and makes for easy going. This early, before the heat has built up, the walking is a pleasure. After a kilometre, as we approach another road bridge, the arch frames a building with a small tower perched on a bluff on the left bank of the *rambla*. This is Cortijo del Pocico. A line of fan palms and well-tended vines marks the left edge of the stony *rambla*. Terraces lead up to the *cortijo* which has the look, from its prominent position, of a small castle.

It's a good year for poppies. Drifts of them line the *rambla*, fragile vermillion flags in the sun. Huge piles of pads from prickly pear cacti have been thrown into the *rambla* at one point. At another, the carcass of a car with a fridge inside it quietly rusts into oblivion. Such features take on a strange kind of significance because it's not easy to see what lies beyond the confines of the *rambla* itself, even though it is working its way here only through a low, undulating landscape.

The going is easy and pleasurable: there's almost no gradient, there's no-one around and swifts and bee-eaters swoop in curves across a sky of sun and cloud. A plastic *invernadero* (greenhouse) rears up on the right, followed by large corrals for horses and donkeys. A figure some distance away sees us peering at the map and shouts: "Do you want anything?" "No thanks," we say, "we're just walking."

Just walking, just following the *rambla* downstream, a simple task. We pass under a hefty road bridge, then almost immediately a smaller one. Much later I realise, after poring over the maps, that this was the moment when we went wrong. Sheer carelessness: we had looked briefly at the map and decided we were at a point about a kilometre south-east of where we actually were. The bridge, the direction of the *rambla*, yes, it all fitted.

The going remains easy, apart from an unnerving encounter with an enormous, aggressive mule which seems to think it owns the *rambla* and repeatedly charges us. There are buildings above the *rambla* and also over to the left. This will be Góchar, I'm thinking, we're making good progress. Much later, with the luxury of hindsight, I realise it was not Góchar, it was Garrido. In fact we're going north but don't realise it. The route we had intended to follow trends south but is full of looping twists and we persuade ourselves that our *rambla* will curve back south soon enough.

We press on. I say to Charlie I have the impression that we are walking slightly uphill. He doesn't disagree. The *rambla* is narrower and the steep slopes of the Filabres are now much closer. There's no longer any doubt. Only for so long can you keep consulting the map and persuading yourself that you are where you should be, even when all logic and navigational skills tell you otherwise. We finally admit we are lost.

The problem is that by now we have walked off the map we have with us. We need the adjacent sheet to the north. We don't have it because we never expected to need it. And, in fact, neither of us actually owns it. So, trying to discern where we are and navigate our way out of the dilemma is well-nigh impossible. We press on, having decided to find someone we can ask. After a short while a *cortijo* rears up above the *rambla*. There are vehicles parked there, so we walk up a steep track, past a 'no entry' sign, past enthusiastic but fortunately chained-up dogs. I stick my head into the open door of a barn that is emitting noises of activity. A guy is some yards away, in oily overalls, doing something to a vehicle. Much nearer, a woman is standing, looking quizzically at me.

I explain that we're lost and ask where we are, exactly. She asks me where we're trying to get to. The answer 'Sorbas' produces bafflement. How could we be going to Sorbas but be so far from it, and on foot? Despite my asking a couple of times, the woman seems reluctant to reveal the name of her remote house. Much later, my best guess is that we were somewhere near Rincón de Marqués. She explains that we can take the obvious track that is visible curving across undulating olive groves below us, then disappearing round a low hill. That will get us to the main road and if we turn left there we will reach the agricultural co-operative at El Puntal, with La Mela beyond that. "How far is it to the main road?" I ask. "Two or three kilometres," she says.

I thank her and we set off at a good pace, buoyed by the knowledge that at least we now know roughly where we are, even though it's embarrassingly far from our intended route. As we stride briskly south, we realise it's too late to walk either back to my car or on to Charlie's car at Sorbas. We could try hitching, of course. But then a thought hits me. Our friend Helen lives near La Mela and is just the sort of kind soul to effect a rescue.

We make it to El Puntal and I call Helen. She asks me to hang on a second as she's literally in the middle of booking air tickets to Australia online. Confirmation comes through and she's instantly happy to help, although somewhat amused that a geographer has managed to get so spectacularly lost. Meanwhile, Charlie and I hover

166

in the shade of a strange tree with spiky bark out at the front of the agricultural depot. Soon enough Helen appears. As she drives us to Sorbas we sheepishly explain what has happened. She casts a wry smile in our direction. Next day, I receive a scan of a portion of the adjacent map (1014-III Lubrín) from her by email, covering the area where we got lost, and it's from this that I manage to piece together the last pieces in the narrative jigsaw of our cock-up.

A chaos of blocks

Life intervened, so it was almost two years before the walk was resumed. Charlie was too busy with his work to join me again or maybe he was just waiting until I had learnt to navigate.

Starting again from where we went wrong, I check with the compass to be sure I have it right this time. The *rambla* here is wide and ill-defined but with a clear vehicle track along it. This services a large, well-tended olive grove on the left and makes for very easy going. After a kilometre the *rambla* veers left in a big meander to reach a road bridge with a hefty central pier. Here the dry riverbed shows major signs of scouring from the torrential rains of late September 2012. This continues, with steep banks of gravel and rearing boulders as the *rambla* twists in its now narrow confines for almost another kilometre.

Suddenly everything changes. The riverbed falls away in a chaos of huge blocks, fluted rock walls and dangerous water-eroded slots, with the remnants of a few trees jammed here and there for good measure. In the rare times of heavy rain this would be quite a waterfall. There is no hint of this dramatic feature on the map, though the name Manantial (Spring) de los Charcones occurs nearby. The continuation of the *rambla* is visible some way below but how will I reach it? I make two attempts to work my way down this maze of rock but fail and have to reverse my moves. It's only climbing of 'moderate' standard, but I'm on my own and breaking a leg here would not be a good idea. I scramble out and up the left side of the valley to a goat-path, then stay above a nearby ruin to allow the crossing of a deeply-etched tributary valley coming in from the left which looks totally insignificant on the map.

Continuing along the hillside, I have to angle further up the slope to work my way round another tributary, even bigger and steeper than the previous one. There are signs of former cultivation, such as drystone terracing and the skeletons of almond trees, but all appears abandoned here now. I soon reach an overgrown vehicle track tilting towards the *rambla* and can see from the map that it leads to another *cortijo*. So it does but this is yet another ruin, albeit a large and spectacularly-sited one. The *rambla* is not far below now but is choked with trees and *caña* so I contour along for a couple of hundred metres more before regaining the *rambla* where the gravel and rock of the riverbed can be seen again.

Soon a clump of palms and a cluster of buildings up on the left tell me I've reached Góchar. The *rambla* sweeps round below the village in a big meander with huge pockmarked cliffs to the right and tamarisk and *caña* thickets on the left. After the cliffs diminish a narrow road dips across the *rambla*. This is the access to Góchar from the south.

Should you walk this route, take care here not to go up the tempting tributary *rambla* on the left that goes north to Moras. The main *rambla* twists south-east again, passing more *caña* and the small settlements of Quijiliana and El Mayordomo on its right bank. I walked this stretch early in 2013 with Troy and with Gabrielle and Gary Lincoln, who live nearby. Gabrielle was eloquently sad about the devastation caused by the storm of the previous September that had changed the riverbed entirely, ripping out familiar trees and washing away much of the vegetation.

The names Góchar and Quijiliana are both of Arabic origin. The Moors found good land on the inside of the river's meanders along this stretch and made fertile terraces. At the next hamlet, El Tieso, a narrow path leads up the riverbank to the shell of the one-room village school, its blackboard still intact. That building and the adjacent schoolmaster's house are both now crumbling. The next place, even smaller, is La Tejica, its name recalling the time when tiles (*teja* means 'tile') were made here.

A kilometre on, just beyond Zoca, a more contorted series of meanders begins. Sorbas is now visible, its church tower prominent. Soon enough Los Caños is reached. Here, with the houses of Sorbas perched high above on a cliff, is a double washing trough. As you face it, the older washing place, with stone channels, is on the left with a more modern concrete affair to the right. A small arch stands between them, decorated with the words DOS EPOCAS SEPARADOS POR UN ARCO (TWO PERIODS SEPARATED BY AN ARCH) facing one way and, facing the other way, the legend, partly chipped away: ...ARCO QUE UNE DOS EPOCAS XIII-XXI (...ARCH THAT UNITES TWO PERIODS XIII-XXI). Just beyond here a road angles up into the lower part of Sorbas, the potters' quarter.

Beyond the washing place, the *rambla* describes another tight meander, curving below the town. Heading south-west now, it approaches two high bridges just a few metres apart. A track on the left climbs up to the road and comes out directly opposite the Bar El Suave, a good option for refreshments. The older bridge, which carries the road up into the lower part of the town, has impressive arches. The newer, carrying the A-340 as it by-passes Sorbas, is in the brutal concrete style. Shortly after this, the *rambla* swings to the right with cliffs on the outside of the bend. Classic geography this, where the meander cuts away at the outside, with deposition creating flatter ground on the inside of the curve.

As the cliffs decrease in height, there's a strong and unpleasant smell. To the right is the sewage plant that processes the waste of Sorbas. This is locally notorious. Years of complaints and petitions from many people have led nowhere. It still stinks. Outflow from the works comes back into the *rambla*, creating less than salubrious pools in the riverbed. The only compensation is a green sandpiper, a striking wader, taking flight with loud calls as I pass. Another leftward curve with a tall cliff of complex geology exposed on the right, and the *rambla* is now heading north-east. To the right, tall eucalyptus trees line the bank. These sometimes hold golden orioles but none makes its presence known today. The old road from Sorbas to Venta del Pobre, the A 1102 (see the chapter 'The road of 100 bends') crosses the *rambla* on a seven-arched bridge just beyond which, on the right, are the buildings marking the Cuevas de Sorbas, the Sorbas Caves.

The next stretch of the *rambla* is wide. It makes several sweeping curves and passes the field centre at Urrá, (see the chapter 'Sorbas and the Gypsum Karst') which is marked by a couple of tall cypresses. Beyond Urrá the Río de Aguas *rambla* widens even further, to 100 metres or more. There is a waymark with white and yellow arrows on a nearby rock indicating that the route goes to the right.

Don't be tempted by the narrow, gravelly riverbed running north. The main *rambla* turns south-east then east in the vicinity of the abandoned Cortijo del Hoyo. Here there is a rarity: in a large ploughed field stands a particularly enormous tree, with a circular corral below it, allowing animals to make use of the tree's shade. A damaged wooden sign announces this as the *EUCALIPTO MAS GRANDE DE ALMERÍA* (THE BIGGEST EUCALYPTUS IN ALMERIA). Before long the *rambla* narrows and bears rightwards under a cliff. It is now trending south and soon a signpost is reached announcing El Nacimiento. Here are the first surface waters of the Río de Aguas.

19. Río de Aguas: *acequias* and mills

'La ruta nos aportó otro paso natural.' 'The path provides the natural next step'.
(A Spanish palindrome.)

Using the river

As explained elsewhere (see the chapter 'Sorbas and the Gypsum Karst'), the dramatic gorge immediately south of El Nacimiento is a direct result of water eroding the softer marl which underlies the deep layers of gypsum. The steep-sided valley leads up to fringing cliffs of crystalline gypsum. As the softer rocks below have been eroded, huge blocks have crashed down, hence the chaotic jumble of massive gypsum boulders just south of El Nacimiento. This appears to bar passage along the valley but it is perfectly passable on foot. There are tall stands of *caña* and oleander, many bent almost horizontal by floodwaters.

The Moors who settled here made use of the reliability of the river's flow by constructing a water channel to supply their settlement, now called Los Molinos del Río de Aguas, a few hundred metres downstream.

The village developed at the first point below the permanent springs of the Río de Aguas where there was space to build houses and mills and to cultivate the land. The bulk of the village was built on the south-west side of the valley. Various dates as far back as the twelfth century have been suggested for the founding of Los Molinos but no-one has definite evidence for this.

Water was brought from just below El Nacimiento in channels partly dug into the earth and partly tunnelled through the bedrock. These, called *acequias* by the Moors though I have heard that they have characteristics that might even suggest a Roman origin, serviced cultivation terraces on both sides of the valley, two tiers on the north-east side and possibly up to five on the south-west (village) side. These irrigation lines began at a pool adjacent to a rock face with twelve arched manifolds, still visible and functioning today, cut into the rock. The entrances, big enough to allow human access, allowed control of the water flow into a channel excavated inside the rock. The *acequia* was made at a slight downhill tilt so that the water would move by simple gravity flow.

Constant maintenance was, and still is, required to clear blockages and keep the water flowing along these lines. To make this easier in recent decades, deeper pools called 'tanks' have been dug in the channel, from which rods can be prodded along to keep the underground lengths of the *acequia* open.

The path from El Nacimiento passes between two enormous tilted gypsum boulders called El Fraile (The Monk). Yellow and white flashes on the rocks show the way onward under more (much smaller) tilted blocks. On the right are the remains of a small circular gypsum kiln and just beyond this, on the left, the tumbledown ruin, choked by vegetation, of a mill, the Molino de la Pena. The miller here was Gabriel Idañez. The mill's name denotes pain or woe, referring to the fact that it was a 'run of river' mill. It had no *balsa* (tank) to store a head of water and the water pressure therefore simply depended on the amount of river flow at the time. You might have to wait a while. People said you would throw a *fanega* of wheat into the hopper and then come back another day to collect your flour. Close by, just downstream, was the mill run by el Tío Nicolás Serafín.

The path climbs, twists and falls, often through stands of *caña*, crossing and re-crossing the *acequia*. At one of the high points an interpretation board explains, in Spanish and English, the 'Springs of Los Molinos'. At a small agave plantation, where the path forks, go right, uphill, then continue ahead, passing above the ram pump with its insistent watery thump and so into the lower part of the village.

Water mills have operated along the Río de Aguas and its less reliable tributary the Río de Moras, since the Middle Ages. Between El Nacimiento and La Huelga on the Río de Aguas there have been at least fourteen mills over the centuries. Records in the Libro de Apeo y Repartimiento de la Villa de Sorbas (1572) and the Catastro de Ensenada give many clues but few precise facts about the exact locations of these mills.

Two mills have already been mentioned above. The third was near the village but on the left (far) bank. The miller here was Tío Frasquito, whose real name was Francisco Fernández Molina. This mill was also referred to as the Molino de las Tejas. The building no longer exists, its materials presumably having been carried off for use elsewhere. Back on the right bank, and in the village itself, was the Molino del Tío Juan Barranco.

These were 'horizontal mills', which means that the water wheel was set horizontally rather than vertically. A spindle called a *rodezno* was fixed into the rotating water-wheel and was also fixed to the upper millstone in a room above, thus providing the motive power for the milling process. The lower stone was stationary. The millstones were typically 1.2 metres in diameter and 30 or 40 centimetres thick. They weighed about two tonnes (2,000 kg) when new. Grooves were carved into both upper and lower stones and the particular pattern of these determined the type and quality of the resulting flour. These grooves had to be re-dressed every few days to maintain the quality of the milling.

The number of mills along this stretch of the valley reflected the reliability of the water supply and provided far greater capacity than was needed to process just the grain from the village. In turn this meant that milling would have been an important source of income in the village.

From the water channel some way above the river, which was known as *la madre* (the mother), irrigation water was led to the terraces below. A branch, traces of which are still visible as a brick-lined channel, formerly ran above the village houses to a *deposito* (water tank). Each person maintained their own stretch of the irrigation lines, with the responsibility for overall co-ordination passed on every two or three years; it was very much a co-operative effort.

Near the centre of the village, another branch channel led off from *la madre* to a tall stone tower projecting some four metres above the slope around it. This created a head of water to power a water-driven turbine that generated electricity for the village and for Sorbas also, in the 1920s. Locals who were very young at the time still remember it operating. The Hidroeléctrica de Sorbas supplied energy to Sorbas between 1921 and 1925.

María Tomasa Fernández, who moved away to live in Sorbas in 1925, recalls her last years in the village: "At that time the whole village had electric light. But we didn't have it for very long. I don't know why it ended and we had to use an oil lamp...". The parents of María Sánchez Mañas remembered that, when the Civil War began, the machinery was taken away in lorries and carts. So the turbine is long gone but the tower, still referred to as *la central*, the power station, by the old Spanish people who used to live in the village, was refurbished a few years ago and is in good repair.

Different villagers were allowed to draw off irrigation water at specified times, according to a rota. This arrangement still applies. Each plot is surrounded by a bund, a small earth wall designed to retain water. Generally, during the hotter months of the year, each plot will be irrigated by flooding once a week. The water in *la madre* is fairly saline, so as far as possible the vegetable beds are flooded in the evening to minimise evaporation and avoid salt deposits collecting in the upper horizon of the soil. This water coming along the *acequias* is too salty (from the gypsum) for drinking and risky because of pollution from terrapins, so the villagers traditionally used a *fuente* across the river for their supplies of potable water. Nowadays the inhabitants of Los Molinos usually collect their drinking water, with cars full of plastic flagons, at whichever of the various public *fuentes* in the area they happen to be passing, at Cariatiz or on the approach to Sorbas, opposite the El Suave bar, for example.

Los Molinos

At its peak there were about 50 families living in the village. The greatest population, of maybe 200 people, was in the 1920s. The most sophisticated form of transport then was the donkey. The main street, below the A 1102, contours north-west along the valley side from the Barranco de los Barrancones. Always too narrow for vehicles and with the donkeys now long gone, it is these days used just by pedestrians with the occasional wheelbarrow.

The houses, mostly of two storeys, have clay tile roofs supported by eucalyptus beams from local trees. *Caña* laths are lashed to the beams with esparto to create the traditional ceilings. Beside some of the houses are conical kilns. These were used for burning gypsum to make plaster which was used on both walls and ceilings. There were at least four *eras*, threshing circles, in or near to the village, testifying to the times when cereal-growing was the norm. Just below where the current A 1102 passes through the village, there was also an *almazara* (olive press).

In times past, the men of the village kept the riverbed 'clean', clearing vegetation so that the flow of water was not impeded and the risk of flood was reduced. Twice a year lorries came and took

174

away all of the cane that had been cleared from the riverbed. Francisco Fernández Molina, aka Tío Frasquito, ensured there were just fifteen mature eucalyptus trees there at any one time. These were used to provide building materials such as roof beams. The wood was cut down and soaked for a year before being used. Fifteen trees were deemed just sufficient for this purpose. There are far more today, now the old Spaniards have gone from the village, and this creates a problem as the eucalpti soak up too much of the precious water.

After the Civil War, in the 1940s and 1950s, hunger and misery were widespread in Almería, as in much of Spain and particularly in those areas which had opposed Franco. Los Molinos probably suffered less than many other villages because of its reliable water supply. This allowed the vegetable gardens to be cultivated and the flour mills to run almost non-stop. However, most of the land was owned by just a few people and the others all worked for them. The dryland (non-irrigated) areas relied on rainfall but repeated droughts brought poor harvests and reduced some of the workers to the status of day-labourers. Life was becoming more difficult for the elderly Spanish residents and their children were not interested in living in a place without mains services. From the mid-1950s emigration began to drain the village of its people. Los Molinos was facing a similar fate to El Tesoro, Hueli and El Marchalico: total depopulation.

Things were to change though, with fresh blood from elsewhere. The very first incomer, in the early 1970s, was a Dutch geologist, Henk Pagnier. He was conducting long-term research on the Río de Aguas and realised it would be cheaper to buy an unoccupied village house than to pay hotel bills for several months. Amongst other early arrivals, also from Holland and as a result of the pioneering move of Henk and his wife Annerie, was Hanna Geertsema who came in the late '70s.

Hanna recalls that: "In summer, there were still Spanish people cultivating their plots, like Consolación and Emilio. I'll never forget his way of taking us on tiptoe up to El Nacimiento to show us the house where he was born. It was all really exotic for us.

"José Confite's allotment was the most beautiful of the lot. It seemed like a work of art. I recall Paco 'Espain' (the nickname of Francisco Idáñez) always working in his house and María and the builder Francisco who made the beautiful fireplace in my house in the upper part of the village.

"Tía Cándida came on Sundays to water the plants and clean the path in front of her house. I also remember old Elisa, the herb woman, walking with her stick, and Juan from Urrá with his goats but my strongest memory is of Cristóbal, el Pirri. From him I learnt to plant trees with the result that we made a small paradise around the house. He also showed me the difference between cooking with butane and on a small fire with straw. He was so nice.

"One morning in the 70s I remember waking to find there was no-one around in the village. I was astonished to discover that the old *vecinos* (neighbours) had gone to La Herrería to vote, walking all the way up over the *cuesta* (slope) and back. Amazing strong people."

By the 1980s a steady trickle of new people was coming to live in Los Molinos, especially those in tune with ecological ideals. Susan and Bob Harrington moved from Mojácar, which was becoming too touristy for them, in 1980. A friend had told them about a village with a river where they would be able to grow organic food and find themselves once again in real Spain. When they arrived they found that no-one was living full-time in Los Molinos. There was too little rain to grow grain on the dryland areas.

The village school had closed some time earlier. As far as I can discover, this was in the early 1960s, since when the children had to go to school in Sorbas. Hanna Geertsema says Emilio told her that he opened the school building up after many years and it was like stepping into a time-capsule.

Various people from Sorbas who had land in the village still came out to tend their plots though. Susan and Bob would sit round the fire eating *migas* (fried breadcrumbs) with Emilio, Consolación, Juan and María, hearing the old stories about the place; everyone's front door would be open on *fiesta* days with people coming from nearby villages to celebrate a wedding, the bride on a donkey with her dress trailing, petals used as rouge on the women's cheeks...

A key moment in the modern chronology of Los Molinos came when the charity Sunseed, originally called Green Deserts, established a presence there. The ideas that led to Sunseed, with its stated aim of researching and disseminating ways of living sustainably in dryland environments, were first mooted in the UK in 1982. The organisation bought its first house in Los Molinos in 1986. Sunseed has gradually grown and now owns several houses in the village, providing many beds for volunteers. Up to 200 come each year, mostly young, all idealistic, many of them students who want to experience and learn more about sustainable living. Sunseed runs open days and courses on such topics as organic gardening and the design and installation of photovoltaic systems. One measure of the impact Sunseed has had is that many people currently in positions of influence in environmental organisations and NGOs list a formative spell at Los Molinos on their CVs.

During these years other incomers - Dutch, English and Spanish - arrived, having heard of the possibilities for living a 'green' life among like-minded people. It's fair to say that Sunseed has played a large part in defining Los Molinos as an 'alternative village' or *ecoaldea*. Sunseeders, for example, maintain the ram pump, a fine piece of appropriate technology that uses the power of falling water coming along the *acequia* to lift and distribute, via some of its own captured energy, five litres of water per minute, 24 hours a day, to the village above.

But there are other initiatives in Los Molinos too. Tim Bernhardt, known to everyone as Timbe, is the driving force behind the Pita-Escuela (Agave School) in the village, a project that specialises in demonstrating and disseminating the many uses of agaves. The Pita-Escuela (www.pitaescuela.org) runs frequent workshops and activities in which an astonishing range of items, including musical instruments and 'magic villages' can all be made from agaves.

The Pita-Escuela sees the agave as having a significant place in future sustainable economies. It can produce high yields and grow on arid and semi-arid land, where it does not compete with conventional crops. Due to its many uses and low demand on water and soil fertility, the agave has enormous potential as a promising 21st century crop, a life-insurance plant for farmers in arid areas. The plant's uses range from various wood products, organic plastics and fertilizers, to the production of bio-fuels for renewable energy, as well as pharmaceutical and healthfood products. The aim is to spread the word about the agave as a resource in marginal dry-land environments as widely as possible. A 7-minute video which you can see on YouTube gives a fascinating insight into Timbe's work at the Pita-Escuela.

Higher up in the eco-village is the Casa de la Realidad, a project realised by David Dene, who has transformed ruins, with the help of volunteers from many countries, into a 21st century energy-efficient house. The Casa de la Realidad was applauded by *National Geographic* for combining low environmental impact with high living standards.

Barbara Hart Appel and Harvey 'Hogan' Appel are just two local residents who, attracted by Sunseed, decided to stay in the area. Barbara, a committed organic gardener, found that the trees on the plot that came with their house meant: "...we can pick fruit for breakfast right through the year." Many other people who initially came to Sunseed also found themselves hooked and now live nearby in places like Góchar, Lucainena, Los Perales, Urrá, La Mela and Lubrín.

The miller's tale

To focus on the mills along the river for a moment, the continuous flow of water for several kilometres downstream from El Nacimiento used to support many *cortijos* and water-mills, as well as the villages of Los Molinos, El Tesoro, Los Perales, La Herrería, La Huelga and Los Giles. Each mill took water from the river and then, after use, fed it back again lower downstream. A high level of co-operation between the different communities was needed to manage the use of the water.

An occupational hazard for the millers was the occasional but ferocious flood that would come tearing down the Río de Aguas. This seems to have been what happened at the enigmatically named Molino de Siete Suertes (Mill of Seven Fates) where all that remains is a bit of wall. In the mid 1950s a flood destroyed the mills of Tío Nicolás Serafín and Juan Barranco. By this time the Molino de la Pena had already closed.

In fact all the mills along the Río de Aguas had closed by the late 1960s and time and neglect have destroyed almost all of the buildings and machinery. Not a single mill still exists with its machinery intact. However, several people who remember the world of the mills were still living in the area in 2009 when interviews were conducted for the Sorbas journal *El Afa*. One such was Rafael Llorente Galera, who was born in a mill, grew up in a mill and worked in a mill for 30 years. To complete the set he also married a miller's daughter.

Rafael was born in June 1927 in the mill at Los Perales owned by his father José Llorente Lázaro and grew up in the family house close by, along with his five brothers. He was steeped in the work of the mill from an early age. There were two rooms in the mill; one contained the milling machinery and the other, the stables and *la limpia*. *La limpia* was where the grain was cleaned by a system involving pulleys and ropes driven by water power. Nowadays the mill is obscured by undergrowth on the riverbank and almost ruined and the modern access road to the village has destroyed part of the mill's *balsa* (water tank).

Because the river flowed all year the mill at Los Perales was in an advantageous situation. "In the mill there was always work. The winters were worse because more mills were running. All that area around Carboneras...in summer they came here because they had no water there and they couldn't mill...". Although the basic principle of a mill's workings was simple, the machinery was quite complicated and to keep it operating at optimum performance involved skills and tricks of the trade that only came with long experience.

Rafael explained also that the miller was always paid, not in money but by '*una maquila*', a quota of the grain milled. A *celemín*, a dry measure equal to about 4.6 litres, was a key part of this process. A *fanega* of wheat was 44 kilograms and for each *fanega* the miller would keep half a *celemín* of grain. For different grains, a *fanega* weighed differently; a *fanega* of barley was 33 kg and of millet, 40 kg. Although wheat and barley were the commonest grains, Rafael also milled chickpeas, carob pods, *sipia* (the refuse left after olives have been milled for oil) and even broad beans.

Before the Civil War the mills were allowed to work in a free and flexible manner. There were no restrictions on how much grain a mill could process but in November 1940 a law was promulgated, under the name of the Servicio Nacional de Trigo (National Wheat Service), imposing a quota on mills and a requirement to keep records of all their dealings: how many *fanegas* of grain entered the mill, how many kilos of flour left it, who they did the milling for and when.

Unsympathetic officials policed the new regulations strictly and closed mills that ran on an unregulated basis.

Then in the 1950s came a time of droughts. Plots were abandoned, yields diminished and as a result there was less business at the mills. Milling was no longer profitable. For Rafael Llorente Galera, who was still only thirty, the future in the Los Perales mill did not look promising. He gave up the struggle and emigrated to Venezuela to look for better opportunities.

20. Rio de Aguas : ...to the mouth

'No hay camino, se hace camino al andar.' 'There is no path; the path
is made by walking.'
(Antonio Machado)

Juxtaposition

After that diversion into the world of watermills, it's time to
continue the journey downstream towards El Tesoro. So, take the
narrow track through Los Molinos village and, just before a small
parking area at the Barranco Los Barrancones, take a path on the left,
steeply down below a half-built and abandoned tall brick house in a
dramatic position. The path is signposted PR A-97 with the neatly
incised but wrongly spelled legend EL TESERO 30', meaning it is half
an hour's walk to El Tesoro. This leads to a large pool in the river. Go
back upstream, 30 metres or so, to avoid the pool and cross on
stepping stones through the flattened *caña*, regaining the path on the
far bank. Yellow and white flashes on stones and low posts show the
way up to the ruins of Fuente Los Molinos. The path climbs steeply,
giving fine and sometimes sheer views down into the valley.

There's an aerial view down over the remains of the Molino de
Carrasco de Arriba (Upper), evocatively set off by a small clump of tall
palms. The path is high here and levels off, with the motorway lying
ahead, astride the valley on huge concrete pillars. Almost below it are
further ruins, those of the Molino de Carrasco de Abajo (Lower).

The path is easier now and, initially above the level of the
motorway, it soon drops to the abandoned village of El Tesoro. The
ruins are scattered but repay investigation. Up on the left is the old
school, built to the usual local formula and with a blackboard still on
the end wall of its single classroom, as at El Tieso many kilometres
back upstream. A slightly creased but intriguing old photo in *El Afa* N°
20 shows the school in the early 1930s, during the Second Republic,
not long before the Franco era. The schoolmaster, Don Joaquín
Fernández, is flanked by a squad of 21 pupils, variously scowling,
squinting or snotty-nosed, as kids were back then, with the republican
flag hanging behind them; it was clearly a thriving community at that
time. That flag provides a link to a darker facet of the village's past.
I've heard from at least three sources that, because of the socialist

181

leanings of the villagers, gruesome retribution occurred here during and after the civil war, atrocities that to this day make the old locals reluctant to say anything about the place. The first house, nearest to the mill, was the Guardia Civil *cuartel* (barracks) and I'm told that this is where the tortures occurred.

In some of the houses are features such as a second storey and neat arched mouldings over the doorways which show that, at one time, some of the villagers must have been relatively well off. There are many terraces, and with permanent river water, life here would have been good, if inevitably hard. It was once an idyllic setting. Now, with the motorway viaduct towering right over the ruins, the insistent roar of traffic and the painful secrets of the past, it is quite different. The simple juxtaposition of the old village and modern motorway, even without the darker dimensions of the village's history, is overwhelmingly poignant.

Cross under the motorway (there are yellow and white flashes on some of the pillars but they are heading off in another direction, so ignore them) and find the stepping stones among the *caña* to get over the river (if it's wet). This will allow you to have a look at the spectacularly situated remains of the Molino de la Cerrá del Tesoro. This is still easily visible to northbound drivers from the motorway as it dips across the ravine. In 1899 records show that this was owned by Don Aureliano Piqueras. Although now long disused, there are enough remains to show it was a substantial enterprise; a leat, a channel leading water to the millwheel, that is, and a sizeable *balsa* (watertank) are still obvious by the upper building, with a huge drop down an adjacent circular stone-built fall to the mill itself. If you explore here, do so with care and a healthy dollop of common sense.

Heading downstream is frankly, difficult and recommended only to the very adventurous. Here's why: storms in the autumn of 2012 destroyed part of the path and at the time of writing the valley bottom is an apparently impassable combination of pools, thick stands of *caña* and enormous fallen blocks, with no way through that I can find. Maybe the wild boars of the area will create a new way through in time, as they have in the past. I teeter back over the stepping stones and work my way up by the right-hand side of the motorway, then follow the high ground between the *autovía* and the steep fall into the valley, climbing abandoned terraces, crossing loose crumbly slopes, and staying to the left to avoid an area with unpredictable chasms among the shrubs on the *yeso* (gypsum) heights.

This route does provide almost aerial views down on to the carefully tended organic *huerta* (market garden) at Los Canales, with an isolated pinnacle spearing upwards by the farm buildings, and another lovely view down over the vegetable fields of Los Perales, held inside the curve of an elegant meander. Steep and unpredictable gullies lead down from the high ground to both places but look far too risky to chance, so I retreat, via El Tesoro, to Los Molinos. The English mountaineer Don Whillans once said something to the effect of: 'The mountain will be there another day. The trick is to make sure you are.' This isn't a mountain but discretion is, similarly, the better part of valour.

A few days later I try another tack, driving down the Cuesta de Honor to the Río Aguas *rambla* by Los Perales and then walking back upstream towards El Tesoro. The first section is easy, two or three hundred metres along the access track to Las Canales, then on to the pebbly bed of the *rambla*, hopping across braids of shallow water. So far, so good. The ruin of Molino de la Cerrá del Tesoro is visible ahead but huge boulders and vast stands of *caña* begin to block the narrowing valley. I manage some further progress by clambering, shimmying and ducking among these hazards, at the cost of a couple of cuts from surprisingly painful vegetation, but finally I have to admit defeat just a few metres short of another towering ruin, this time of the Molino de las Canales. All of this confusion is taking place in squares 583105 and 584105 on the 1031-I Sorbas map but the map itself doesn't give enough detail to help and there seems to be no way through. Or so I assumed until tantalising rumours reached my ears that there *is* a way between El Tesoro and Los Perales and that there are people who know it; further investigation is obviously needed.

Regaining the *rambla*

With those investigations still pending, my walk begins again at Los Perales. We are still on map 1031-I Sorbas, incidentally, in square 584105. From there it's possible to force a route downstream through the *caña* in the *rambla* or to follow the road as it loops up through the small village. I have tried both options. The latter one, once you have passed the final buildings, involves sticking to the left side of the terraced fields alongside a small deep gully to regain the main riverbed. Continue on animal tracks under the cliffs. I was last there in April 2013 but it's not possible to give precise instructions as the state of the riverbed can change at any time. There is evidence in the rock faces of where the old *acequias* ran in tunnels. After a bend, it's best to go up onto the next set of terraces, mostly disused, it seems. The farmhouse here, the Cortijo de Lentiscar (although stencilled above the door it says Cortijo Lentiscal), has, it seems, been partly abandoned and partly maintained.

Where a clear vehicle track comes down across the terraces and swings into the *rambla*, follow it. This gives easy walking for a while. Just at the point where La Herrería comes into view some distance ahead, the track hairpins back and it's time to take to the *rambla* again. Tracks come and go, leading off to patches of farmland, but it's a matter of following ahead, looking now and then for stepping stones or clumps of rush or *caña* to negotiate runs of shallow water. In spring the vegetation is alive with the strident calls of Cetti's warblers and the occasional blackbird's alarm call.

Just beyond where a pipe spans the rambla in a single leap, seven or eight metres up, the *rambla* reaches La Herrería by a tall drystone wall on the right. Here the road into the village, hugely widened for access to the high-speed rail works (see the chapter 'Lines on the landscape') comes down from the left.

The village itself lies slightly uphill on the right. The name 'Molino' on the lowest house leaves no doubt as to its former function. The road continues ahead, under the railway bridge but then when it swings up to the left, it's time to take to the *rambla* again. Heavy vehicles have been here and the *rambla* has been partly trashed, though in time it will no doubt heal. The riverbed holds pools; a green sandpiper flies off, scolding. A big ruin stands on a bluff on the right, behind an orange grove and a line of mature eucalyptuses. About here, we have passed on to the next map, sheet 1031-II Turre. The village of La Huelga, further back from the *rambla*, nestles under the slopes of the Sierra Cabrera then, beyond the prominent buildings at La Quemadilla, Los Giles hoves into view ahead. Soon enough I pass under a road bridge and beyond here, the valley is wilder and quieter.

The going follows an easy track until, within view of the Cortijo Suesa, dead ahead, the surface has been broken by erosion. It's quickly better again though, with citrus groves on either side in the now wider valley but then the view is ruined by big *plasticos* on a bluff on the north bank. South, there's a pitted cliff defining a meander and favoured by jackdaws.

There are tracks along here that cut the meanders and make life easier, whilst still giving the flavour of the river valley. I'm not a purist. I don't hesitate to use them. Yellow posts show the position of the gas line that was laid through here a few years ago; they announce GASODUCTO ALMERIA-CHINCHILLA and tell you the number to ring if there's a leak. Substantial and squat, the Cortijo la Panalera stands to the south. Soon there's a restored house high on the north bank in a commanding position. A large pool in the riverbed looks tricky until I discover stepping stones that take me across. The track continues past Cortijada les Flores, rising slightly to follow the northern edge of the *rambla*. There are sizeable terraced fields here but they seem disused. The track, now of tarmac, passes some smart buildings in Los Rodríguez and reaches Los López, both constituent parts of the scattered village of Alfaix.

At Los Lopez a 'proper road' is reached, with a white line down the middle. Almost immediately it swings sharply left though and it's time to continue ahead along the *rambla* again. Here the Río Jauto, the largest tributary of the Río de Aguas, comes in from the north. Looking up its wide empty bed, you can see three bridges less than a kilometre away, seemingly stacked above one another. These are the old road (the N-340a), the new AVE rail route and the A7 motorway.

The *rambla* is sandy and gritty here, patterned as I follow it at the end of March with the vivid colours of Bermuda buttercup, rocket, wild stock, broom and scarlet pimpernel. Beneath a cream house on a striated cliff, the riverbed begins to describe a big meander round a large citrus plantation edged with an elegant line of pines. Gradually the *rambla* narrows and deepens, with the river in a rocky slot choked with vegetation, a gorge, in effect. The point comes where it's no longer possible to follow the valley. You are looking from a high cliff down at the river's continuation: impressive scenery but tricky going for a foot-traveller.

My solution to the dilemma is to climb out onto the track that edges the citrus grove near some low breeze-block buildings and follow that. It goes south, away from the Río Aguas, because of another deeply-etched and uncrossable tributary, the Rambla de las Chozas. Across this deep cleft lie the Cortijo el Aire and the Cortijo Nuevo del Aire (see the following section) but there seems no way to negotiate the cliffs and precipitous slopes. Somehow I need to get down into the Rambla de las Chozas and follow it back north to regain the Río Aguas.

Whether there is any objection to pedestrians following the track along the citrus grove, I don't know. I saw no-one to ask, so I can't unequivocally recommend the route. I can't imagine a problem though; passage on foot does no harm, after all. Following the track beyond the fruit trees, the solution becomes apparent. A branch of the track begins to dip and can be seen ahead describing a long descent down into the Rambla de las Chozas (this is in square 594110).

So in the end it's easy enough. The low blue flowers of Barbary nut star the ground as I reach the bed of the *rambla* and start back north. Almost a kilometre of delightful exploration ensues, following a twisting line of gravel as it threads amongst boulders and oleanders to finally join the Aguas. I turn right, north-east, walking easily again now among bedrock, pools and boulders below striking cliffs.

Round another bend lies the Molino de la Higuera, now a house but from its name, form and position, betraying its origin as a mill. Ahead is the high arched structure of the Puente Vaquero with, higher still beyond it, the Cortijo de Buenavista perched on a bluff.

Ghost airfield

Now, another brief diversion from the river walk. About 300 metres due south of the Río Aguas, just before it reaches Puente Vaquero, lies a feature I first saw on the map several years ago. I've always meant to go and have a closer look at it and today we finally did that. This is the *Aeródromo* three kilometres south-west of Turre. The map shows a runway aligned north-east to south-west, about 800 metres long, with a building alongside, the Cortijo Nuevo del Aire. You can access it by coming out from Turre on the old road to Los Gallardos then, after two and a half kilometres, taking the left turn between pillars which is signed to Cortijo Grande. So far so good but ideally you need to have the 1:25,000 Turre map sheet 1031-II, as mentioned above, to follow the instructions from there.

On that map, take a right turn off the Cortijo Grande road, opposite a spot height at 143m. This turning is a little less than one kilometre from where you turned off the main road, so even without the map you can find your way. You are now on an unsurfaced track, perfectly passable if taken at a gentle pace. It descends, jinks across a small valley and then curves round to where, with a left turn, you can drive right on to the old airstrip. On the right is a line of tall rusting hangars. Just beyond these is the airstrip itself. You can drive along it and, although scrubby bushes are encroaching, especially at the north-eastern end, you could probably still land a light plane on it.

At the south-western end, on the runway itself, you can make out the remains of a tennis court with the tarmac painted a faded green and the white lines still clearly visible. Beyond the end of the runway, which is buttressed by a stone wall, the land falls away steeply to the Rambla de las Chozas. Looking south-west, you see a wild dissected landscape through which the Barranco del Aire threads a tortuous route. On the skyline are the pinewoods that stretch down to the hidden picnic site east of La Huelga. The Sierra Cabrera is an astonishingly complex mountain range, given that in the Spanish scheme of things it is so small. Then again, it rises from sea level to, in old money, well over 3,000 feet, so maybe we shouldn't be so surprised.

The Cortijo Nuevo del Aire is in remarkably good condition for a building that has been long abandoned. There has been fire damage, there are smashed tiles, the windows have gone and the graffiti merchants have been here but you get the distinct impression that, for a relatively modest spend, you could get this place up and running.

The buildings enclose a courtyard, now overgrown by huge oleander trees, two flowering red and one white. In one corner a twisting set of steps, still absolutely solid and safe at the time of writing, leads up to the octagonal control tower, its metal roof still entirely intact. This is a superb viewpoint: north-west past the citrus trees of La Noria and the conical hill, not surprisingly called Cerro Redondo, towards Los Gallardos; south-west, as described above, into the heart of the Sierra Cabrera; north-east, back towards Turre and the sea beyond. It always looked as though this place would merit a visit but both Troy and I were amazed at what a discovery it was: well worth searching out.

The airstrip was built, we were told, at a time when there seemed the possibility of the settlements of Cabrera and Cortijo Grande becoming a destination of choice for the rich and famous, and was used until a fatal accident in the early 1980s in which a pilot and his son lost their lives. Subsequently, the airstrip was used during the filming of *Indiana Jones and the Last Crusade*. A friend talks about rubbing shoulders in a local bar at the time of the filming with Harrison Ford, who clearly didn't wish to be pestered, and edging past Sean Connery as he drove a 4x4 along one of the narrow mountain roads. Not quite the moment to ask for an autograph.

The airstrip is perfectly accessible in an ordinary car driven carefully, but a word of warning. On the map there is a track which curves around under the south-western end of the runway and then passes a lake to regain the main Cortijo Grande road. This is passable but it is narrow, particularly where it passes over the dam that holds back the larger of the two lakes. The drop-off to the right as you drive along here is dramatic and scary. If you are of a nervous disposition, don't come this way; go back the way you came and regain the Cortijo Grande road via the track to the north-east of the runway.

Cowboy's Bridge

Puente Vaquero (Cowboy's Bridge, somewhat improbably, though '*vaqueros*' also means denim jeans) throws a high central arch across the river to carry the AL-150 linking Turre and the motorway. A sign by the road carries the name but, strangely, the map doesn't. Below, the *rambla* is flanked by high cliffs of mudstone.

Immediately below the bridge, concrete installations channel the flow with yellow and black depth scales going four metres up the vertical wall of the arch. I'm walking this stretch on a mid-January day of louring skies after the wettest December in half a century. The flow is steady but the painted notice low on one of the arches indicating *PROHIBIDO HACER HOGUERAS* (BONFIRES FORBIDDEN) seems, temporarily at least, redundant. The muddy path winds through dense thickets of tamarisk and oleander. Coming this way again in March 2013, I find all the vegetation scoured away and a big pool lying downstream of the bridge. There is a way through though, mainly sticking to the right-hand side of the *rambla*, sometimes using the narrow shelves of fluted mudstone on the cliffs themselves.

Three hundred metres on, a deeply-incised tributary *rambla* comes in from the right, spanned by a high bridge with an elegant single arch. At the roadside close by this bridge stands a building repainted in a combination of peach and deep blue, a striking if not entirely subtle colour scheme. Integral stone panels high on the building, and not highlighted by the makeover, inform the passer-by that this is a CASILLA DE PEONES CAMINEROS (ROADWORKERS' HUT) and the road is the CARRETERA DE GARRUCHA A LOS GALLARDOS Km 11. There are many such roadworkers' buildings in the region, identifiable by the mileages marked on their walls. There is one, for example, alongside the N340-a between the A7 motorway *salida* 529 and Vera, by the banks of the Río Antas.

Back in the *rambla*, beyond where the mudstone shelves have been undercut by the river, a line of tall eucalypts flanks the south bank. The Finca 'El Esparragal', shaded as *regadío* on the 1:25,000 map to indicate that it is irrigated land, displays a prominent notice 'GANADOS NO' (No Livestock), illustrated by a goat in a red circle, struck through with a diagonal.

On the north bank of the river near here, at Cadima, archaeologists Francisco Llidó López and Oscar Jiménez recently led a three-year long excavation of a site long known about but never previously investigated. The dig was financed by Adif, the company building the AVE high-speed rail line which cuts through the site. In February 2013 the archaeologists presented their findings, which included a 2,000-year old Roman villa with traces of mosaic, an underground heating system and sculptures. They also found a 9th century Arab settlement built on top of the villa. However, due to a lack of funds and to prevent further deterioration and the attentions of looters, the excavations were re-buried. Local historian Juan Grima bemoaned the regional government's (the Junta's) permanent lack of money, which means that there is no way to exhibit sites like this or the associated finds.

By now the *rambla* is 80 metres wide and much less vegetated. Concrete flood walls have appeared and the presence of nearby humans is more evident: a sodden, shredded mattress; fragments of a smashed bathroom suite; insulting and grammar-defying graffiti: *'Maricarmen son mongolos'*. In contrast, a solitary gorse bush blooms fiery yellow and to the south the high, crenellated profile of the Sierra Cabrera suggests greater height than the map shows. A modest cliff on the north bank of the *rambla*, its upper strata riddled with holes, is clearly a jackdaw stronghold. Their resonant calls ring round the rock-face.

The tower of Turre fire-station comes into view, then a bridge where a gap in the concrete wall leads to a ramp out of the *rambla* and, a few metres further, the pictograms on the Turre town sign promise golf, shooting and photography. There are also plenty of places for refreshment and sustenance.

Back in the *rambla*, there's another bridge 200 metres further on and the flood walls continue, shown as red-pecked lines on the 1:25,000 map. The riverbed here is a matrix of sand, gravel, pebbles and boulders. To the right are the works of Turre Aridos, producing sand and gravel. Making a racket, a great spotted cuckoo flies across the *rambla*, where a goat flock is attacking the scattered bushes that somehow retain a hold.

Over the next couple of kilometres, four concrete weirs each hold back extensive flats of finer material. Apart from the small drops at each weir, there's no discernible gradient. Ahead, as the riverbed begins a big rightwards curve, piercing calls alert me to a group of large waders. They fly off way before I reach them but it's clear that they are stone curlews. To them this raw *rambla* is the stony steppe habitat they like.

Where the concrete walls end, their continuation being merely loose material bulldozed into levees, a conical hill with a truncated top lies dead ahead. This is Cerro de Mojácar la Vieja. Remains have been found here dating from the 6th-7th centuries AD, indicating that there was first a Visigoth settlement and later a Muslim one, with the name Muxacra. It is from this that the present name Mojácar derives.

At this stage it's easier to go up on the left bank where there is a wide, level roadway. Mojácar *pueblo* lies ahead on its hill. Birds enliven the scene: a flight of little egrets, their yellow feet contrasting with black legs; a hoopoe, always an exotic flash of pink, white and black; and a twittering flock of serins.

Under the next road bridge it is best to cross to the south side of the *rambla* and take the obvious track, passing Servacon, another company processing sand and gravel. Where you can see over the loosely bulldozed levee on the left the *rambla* is full of *caña*. By now we are on map 1032-I Mojácar but you won't get lost without it.

Two hills constrict the river's course, Rincón del Mirador to the north and Cabezo de Guevara to the south. The next kilometre of the riverbank is frankly uninspiring with, on the south side, abandoned buildings, an electricity sub-station and a sad group of olive trees in a field of dust. To the north is the huge Hotel Marina Playa with, stepping up the hill behind it, an unfinished development called Atalaya de Mojácar, another victim of Spain's dire economic woes.

The Romans had a settlement called La Rumina at the mouth of the river. There were pottery kilns here, sited so that the products could be distributed by sea. This name persists, with Vista de los Angeles-Rumina on the present-day map.

The final reach of the *rambla* is more attractive: it's full of water, at least when I'm there at the end of February 2013. Coots, a few pochards and a cormorant dot the surface of the extensive pool and newly-arrived swallows and house martins hawk low and fast for insects. The road between Mojácar and Garrucha, the ALP-118, crosses above this long, *caña*-fringed lake, giving pedestrians a good view down onto it. The pool is separated from the sea by a sandy beach bar 100 metres wide.

And there it is, finally, the Mar Mediterráneo. There's an extra satisfaction to seeing those waves crashing onto the beach on this winter's day, at the end of a walk from the river's source, achieved intermittently over about three years, an absorbing journey through the surprisingly varied landscapes at the heart of eastern Almería.

21. Sorbas and the Gypsum Karst

'I am pleased enough with surfaces...the embrace of friend or lover...sunlight on rock and leaves...the face of the wind – what else is there?'

(Edward Abbey)

The Gypsum Karst

Visitors to the Sorbas area can hardly avoid seeing references to the Karst en Yesos de Sorbas, the Gypsum Karst of Sorbas. Before looking at that particular geological phenomenon though, the town deserves at least a mention. Incidentally, the 1:25,000 map showing both the town and the karst area is sheet 1031-I Sorbas.

The origin of the place-name Sorbas is disputed. It may come from the Arabic word 'chorba', meaning 'pot' and referring to the *alfarería*, the pottery quarter, at the lower end of the town. However, a very similar word, 'chórba', means a pimple, perhaps referring to the way in which the town sits on high ground surrounded partly by the dry *barranco* (ravine) called El Afa, a former meander of the Río de Aguas, and partly by the present course of the same river. Perched high above the gorge that almost entirely surrounds it, Sorbas occupies an impressive position, many of its buildings seeming to teeter on the very rim of the steep cliffs that plunge to the dry floor of the ravine below.

Now, the Karst en Yesos de Sorbas, the Gypsum Karst of Sorbas. It's quite a mouthful but it's not too difficult to deconstruct, as follows: gypsum is hydrated calcium sulphate, a kind of deposit laid down in very specific marine conditions that will be explained shortly. Karst is geologists' shorthand for landscapes shaped by the dissolution of soluble bedrock. The word karst originates in the Kras limestone area of south-west Slovenia and north-east Italy, where such landscapes were first intensively studied. The term 'karst landscape' is normally associated with areas of limestone, simply because limestone is much more common than gypsum. Limestone and gypsum karst landscapes have many features in common. The Sorbas karst is the most important gypsum karst area in Spain and one of the four top examples in Europe.

Sorry, more geology coming up! Only six million years ago, what would later be the Sorbas area was on the bed of the Mediterranean Sea. To the north lay the Sierra de los Filabres, along the coastal edge of which were coral reefs. The remnants of these reefs are evident today in many places, notably at Cariatiz, a few kilometres north-east of Sorbas. At this time, the Sierra Alhamilla and Sierra Cabrera, which now lie to the south of Sorbas, did not exist. The Sierra Alhamilla began to emerge about seven million years ago and the Sierra Cabrera about 5.5 million years ago. So at this stage what is now referred to as the Sorbas Basin was semi-confined by the mountains around it.

At roughly the time that the Sierra Cabrera was undergoing tectonic uplift and emerging from below sea-level about 5.5 million years ago, the convergence of the African and Eurasian tectonic plates closed off the connection between the Mediterranean Sea and the Atlantic Ocean. This led to the deposition of huge amounts of evaporites (gypsum and salt) in the central and deepest parts of the Mediterranean during what was technically called the Mediterranean Messinian Salinity Crisis. The thickness of the accumulated salt exceeded 1,500 metres in some places. However, it was some time later, during the period when the Mediterranean was refilling with new water, considered to have come from the Atlantic, that the Sorbas gypsum was deposited.

As mentioned above, the Sorbas Basin was 'semi-confined' or 'semi-restricted' by the surrounding mountains and was almost separated from the open Mediterranean by a shallow submarine barrier at its eastern end caused by the uplift of the Sierra Cabrera. Evaporation rates were high in the shallow waters of the Sorbas Basin and the result was the chemical precipitation of gypsum deposits that were up to 130 metres thick.

In fact, the 130 metre depth of deposits is not just gypsum but an 'evaporite sequence'. What this means is that it is in effect a many-layered rock sandwich in which banks of gypsum, up to 20 metres deep, are separated by layers of marly-limestones. The marly-limestones were laid down during what are called 'non-evaporitic intervals'. These 'non-evaporitic intervals' were the periods when the sea flooded into the Sorbas Basin. Especially in the higher, and therefore more recent, part of the rock sandwich, these marly-limestones incorporate remains of the calcareous skeletons of marine creatures.

Later still, as a result of continuing uplift, these varied sediments were pushed above sea level. Once this had happened, streams coming down from the Sierra de los Filabres, the mountain range to the north of the Sorbas Basin, began to develop a drainage network on top of the 'new' landscape. Very gradually, the sedimentary layers above the gypsum were eroded until, in places, those layers had gone and the drainage network came into direct contact with the gypsum. In the modern landscape the gypsum outcrops at the surface over an area of almost 25 square kilometres and it is this which is the unique and partially protected Karst en Yesos de Sorbas. The Centro de Visitantes (Visitors' Centre) Los Yesares in Sorbas, with its imaginative displays and re-creation of an underground cavern, is an excellent place to learn more about the Gypsum Karst area.

Dolines, tumuli and caverns

Where surface drainage first came into contact with the gypsum, it began to dissolve the gypsum to form hollows called dolines (*dolinas* in Spanish). Over time these were gradually enlarged and water began to penetrate deeper into the gypsum mass, finding both vertical and horizontal weaknesses that were slowly enlarged by solution. Over many thousands of years a complex network of underground passages, galleries and caverns developed, of a type that will be familiar to anyone who has visited any of the British limestone caves open to the public such as Peak Cavern in Derbyshire.

As well as the features of solution, more delicate structures are also part of the subterranean landscape. As water moves slowly through the gypsum, it not only dissolves it but also becomes saturated with it. The result is that, where water drips constantly, small crystals of gypsum are precipitated, gradually building to form stalactites, stalagmites, columns and curtains of great delicacy. One way to remember the difference between stalactites and stalagmites is to consider the middle letters; stala**c**tites grow down from the **c**eiling, stala**g**mites grow up from the **g**round; or 'tites (sic) come down and mites grow up'.

The surface of the karst also presents a distinctive landscape, if maybe less dramatic than the subterranean one. The rocky surface, often patterned with large, angular gypsum crystals, is pocked with the dolines, solution hollows. In the larger ones, more often than not, a fig tree, protected from nibbling animals, has thrived and provides a splash of summer green. Some of the dolines have fluted grooves and narrow, sharp fins leading into them. These are also the result of 'surficial dissolution', the action of rainwater to you and me, and are called lapiés.

The area around the abandoned village of Marchalico Viñicas (see the chapter 'The old way of life') is a good place to see both dolines and other characteristic surface features. Some years ago, a circular walk, the Sendero de Los Yesares, was devised and way-marked. It is well worth doing but not always easy to follow. At one time a descriptive pamphlet was available from the Centro de Visitantes in Sorbas but, at the time of writing, this is out-of-print. The route is shown on the Junta de Andalucía's 1:45,000 Cabo de Gata-Níjar Parque Natural map and on local information panels such as the one at Marchalico Viñicas.

A surface feature unique to the Karst en Yesos de Sorbas is the tumulus (túmulo in Spanish). These tumuli or mounds exist in their hundreds on the plateau surface. They are formed when the surface layer of crystalline gypsum absorbs a lot of water and expands. The result is a gently bulging dome up to several metres in diameter. As a consequence of the low dome forming, an air space is left immediately below it and in many cases, where the dome has cracked or subsided, this void is visible.

One of the most striking features of the Paraje Natural (Natural Place) Karst en Yesos de Sorbas is the deep valley carved into the landscape by the Río de Aguas in the Los Molinos area. This is a direct result of the interaction between water and geology. Rainfall filters into the gypsum, flowing and seeping downwards under the force of gravity. Like a sponge, the gypsum has the ability to hold a lot of water. However, below the gypsum there is marl, which forms an impermeable layer. Because the water that accumulates in the lower levels of the gypsum cannot pass through this, it is forced out sideways to emerge in springs. This is the source of the name El Nacimiento ('The Birth', i.e. the birthplace of the river), a kilometre or so upstream from the village of Los Molinos. Here water flows constantly from the base of the gypsum, creating in the Río de Aguas the only permanent stream in the area. This in turn explains the development of Los Molinos village and the several water-mills downstream from El Nacimiento (see the 'Río de Aguas' chapters).

The marl is a softer and more easily eroded rock than the gypsum. Consequently the Río de Aguas has steadily deepened its valley. High above the river, at the edge of the karst plateau, a distinct cliff formed as the valley sides became steeper. Through geological time huge blocks of gypsum have calved off this cliff and tumbled down the valley side. These can be seen in close-up along the footpath between Los Molinos village and El Nacimiento.

Urrá

The gypsum karst of Sorbas is but one of the geological riches of the area. With tectonic plate boundaries, faults, a history of vulcanicity and desert features, geologists are spoilt for choice in eastern Almería. The sparse vegetation and cuts for new roads also make geological details easy to observe. Students are fortunate too, because there is a field centre catering to their needs in the heart of the area. Gradually, after a chance meeting, we came to hear the story of the Urrá Field Centre.

In late 2004 we bumped into Lindy Walsh at a protest march against the Algarrobico hotel (see the chapter 'Coasting: Carboneras and Algarrobico'). We kept in touch with Lindy and bit by bit we heard the story of how she and her late husband Bill developed the field centre at Urrá. I've partly adapted this version of the tale from an article Lindy wrote for the local Spanish journal El Afa.

Lindy and Bill came to the Sorbas area in 1987. An inheritance had given them the good fortune to be able to work for just six months per year and spend the other six months, with some financial care, enjoying themselves. They decided to work through the summers and spend the winters somewhere in the south of Europe where they could live cheaply. They were looking to buy 'a small ruin' which they would then renovate, little by little, over several winters. They weren't builders but they had gained some experience from working on their 500-year old house in England.

They came to southern Spain initially to have a look at Sunseed, a project they'd heard about that had 'gardens in the desert' (see the chapter 'Río de Aguas: *Acequias* and mills'). Their Land Rover was over 20 years old and they were sleeping in a small tent. Once they reached Sunseed they thought their search might be at an end: friendly people, beautiful views, rare plants and of course the climate. They didn't want to be in the town but they didn't want to be too isolated either. They were getting on for fifty and what would happen if one of them broke a leg? And the other had flu?

Soon, searching the Sorbas area, they saw 'the *cortijo* with the cypress by the side of the river'. It was much, much too big but it was beautiful, what a situation it was in, and...it was abandoned. After a long process they bought the two *cortijos* at Urrá, with 90 hectares. Their two children already had their own adult lives and, after talking to them, Lindy and Bill decided to sell everything in England and make a new life at Urrá. But what were they going to do there? Their only advantage was being English and being able to speak with other foreigners in that language. In 1988 farmers in the area didn't have a very good life, so they realised they would have to use the buildings rather than try to make a living from the land. They didn't have the money for a luxury renovation; only enough for a basic job. What sort of people would like to spend time in a desert in simple accommodation? Young adults who are into the environment? University students studying dry-land geography? This was the logic that led to the founding of the Urrá Field Study Centre.

They knew Urrá was within the Paraje Natural de Karst en Yesos de Sorbas and wondered how this would affect their plans. They didn't want to change much; just to stop hunting and the grazing of goats over their land. They had a lot of problems explaining this in those days. Locals didn't understand at first what it was about but, Lindy believes, they have now come to realise they were simply making a zone of total protection for the plants and animals found within the Paraje Natural, something that was crucial for the studies their visitors came to carry out.

With these plans in mind they built dormitories and hot-water showers for 40 people, a big kitchen that self-catering groups could use (the Club El Tesoro, the local caving club, has managed to cook for more than 80 there), and enough space to study and relax. Andrés

Requena and his son Miguel led the rebuilding; Lindy and Bill were the labourers. After two years they welcomed their first group of visitors and within five years they had 500 clients every academic year. Over two decades on, and run for the past several years by Debbie Talbot, the Field Centre continues to thrive.

Bill succumbed to cancer in 1993 but said at the end that he wouldn't have changed anything of his last five years. Support came from many of the local people during the difficult time before and after Bill's death. Lindy continued the Urrá project, albeit at a slower pace. Getting connected to mains electricity proved an ongoing saga. In 2003, fifteen years after beginning the venture, Lindy opened the old *cortijo* where she was living as a *casa rural*, a bed-and-breakfast.

The main room of the *cortijo* is worth a mention. It's like the Spanish equivalent of a tithe barn crossed with a richly decorated baronial hall. There's a big fireplace at one end and behind long, heavy velvet drapes are enormous ancient wooden doors, battered and worn and patterned with metal studs. The roof is supported on cast-iron pillars reminiscent of a Victorian railway station, below which are floor tiles that look as if they were already old when the Moors held sway here. It's quite a place.

The cavers make an impact

In a 2009 article that lies in the enticing territory between elegy and hard-nosed reality, Juan García Sánchez looked back over a third of a lifetime at his involvement in the early exploration of the underground world of the Sorbas Karst and the subsequent attempts to protect the area. Much of what follows is based on his writing. He pointed out that the Karst en Yesos de Sorbas is signposted from the nearby motorway. By contrast, the same cannot be said of the quarries that are steadily consigning part of the area to oblivion.

Juan García recalled the early years of exploration, from 1978 onwards. The cavers were given permission to camp at weekends and to squat for occasional nights in the abandoned and substantial houses of Marchalico-Viñicas. They'd open an old chest and find heart-rending letters from family members who'd left and gone to Cataluña or South America in search of better opportunities. Protected by the walls and warmed by the hearths that had once been home to the writers of these poignant letters, the cavers would drift off to sleep thinking of the poverty and suffering that had been part of living there and the harsh conditions that had driven the young people away.

When the cavers first set foot on the karst plateau, the quarries were already there. The markets wanted gypsum and the attitude to the earth's resources in those days was simple. The plan for extraction was straightforward: strip off the top layer, then keep going deeper. At that time speleologists passed unnoticed; after all, they weren't a nuisance. They came to the plateau, explored and had fun discovering new caves and passages.

Soon enough the cavers realised the karst was something special. They found themselves exploring underground systems of huge extension and depth, all part of one great whole. Here it was possible to observe all the phases of karst development in a very specific material, gypsum. It was a rare treasure. It became apparent to them that they had to save the karst.

At that stage, from 1978 until 1984, the cavers formed 'la Sección de Espeleología del Club Almeriense de Montaña'. In other words, they were the Caving Section of the Almerían Mountain Club. They realised that they had to raise the profile of the situation, to let the public know that this priceless natural asset needed protecting. They also felt impelled to continue to make new discoveries and disseminate information nationally and internationally among cavers, researchers and universities. It meant beginning a campaign against the economic power of the quarry companies and the general point of view of the people of Sorbas who, because the quarries were the main local employer in an area with few other sources of work, were strongly in favour of them.

Francisco José Contreras, who has now made a successful business from the caves in the karst, confirms that the caves and cavers were looked down on 20 years ago. Working in the quarries was seen as the only way to make a living. When he started to go caving with other young people, his father used to say: "Are the caves going to put food on your plate?" His father, like lots of other Sorbas parents of those who went to discover the karst, were afraid of the unknown and, says Francisco, they weren't wrong. Besides, if your son at that time became a speleologist, it was like having a black sheep in the family, one of those who wanted to close the quarries. In retrospect, the cavers realised that they were used in those early years by the local powers-that-be to get from the quarry companies something they had always previously refused to give, namely support for new municipal projects.

Once the cavers began to campaign openly for the protection of the karst, the attitude of most Sorbeños to them became one of contempt. How was this made clear? Cavers were served reluctantly and with sour faces in some of the bars in the town; events designed to publicise new discoveries were boycotted and posters removed; lorry drivers from the quarries brought an intimidatory presence to talks and exhibitions. At the Encuentro Nacional Pro-Defensa del Karst en Yesos de Sorbas, a major meeting held in 1985, the electricity to the assembly hall of the school, the main venue, was cut and at the last minute the promised water supply for this major event with 300 delegates from all over Spain was denied.

The intimidation reached such worrying levels that the cavers feared for their own safety. They took to leaving one of their number on lookout duty on the surface while they explored underground. One day they heard a passing farmer on a tractor say: "Look at the layabouts from the canvas huts. They need persuading to mend their ways with a good solid almond-beating stick!" The cavers were seen as 'the delinquents from the depths', even though in those days they had quite respectable short haircuts. Working to achieve protection for the gypsum karst, they were a relatively small group. They found themselves virtually alone and without support from the older cavers in the province, especially after they split with the Club Almeriense de Montaña to form the Espeleo Club Almería.

At an institutional level Hermelindo Castro Nogueira, at that time provincial director of the Agencia de Medio Ambiente (Environmental Agency), together with Manuel Navarro Jiménez, the Agency's manager, were hugely important in requesting a technical report evaluating the karst, a necessary step in moving on to its protection. Sorbas town hall also played a significant role by requesting finance for the report to be carried out. Now for the first time the cavers could provide a rigorously detailed catalogue of the cave systems of the karst with the input of all those who had been active. These initiatives finally bore fruit and in 1989 part, but only part, a mere 2,375 hectares, of the gypsum karst area received a measure of protection as the Paraje Natural de Karst en Yesos de Sorbas.

Sustainability

Francisco José Contreras takes up the story again: after hundreds of enjoyable and exciting trips to the karst, many camping trips, hundreds of hours exploring caves and investigating topography, 1993 saw the birth of a project called Natur-Sport. It was supported by Andrés Pérez Pérez who, from his position at that time in the town hall, put in place the foundations for tourism in Sorbas. Natur-Sport's basic idea was simple: tourists, equipped with helmets and head-torches, would be led on underground visits to see for themselves some of the subterranean delights the cavers had discovered. The start of this business was questioned and supported in equal measure, not least because the young entrepreneurs and enthusiasts involved were from Sorbas itself. They were keen to work hard and had little to lose.

At that time the business created by Lindy Walsh and her husband Bill at Cortijo Urrá was already up and running. Lindy was always certain about the riches the karst had to offer, seeing the advantages that others seemed slow to recognise. She was a key early supporter of Natur-Sport, offering ideas and suggestions, providing links to other foreigners in the area, and sending customers in their direction. Her field-centre business brought a dimension to the area that others had not thought of. Year after year, universities from Britain and Scandinavia were bringing undergraduates of geology, biology and environmental studies, with staff members and post-graduates doing more detailed research.

At the time when Natur-Sport began to operate, Sorbas town hall set up a tourist office and together they took the first steps into the tourism business, promoting the *casas colgantes* (hanging houses), gastronomy and the *alfarería* (potters' quarter) and simultaneously highlighting the caves and the Río de Aguas in the nearby karst area. They wanted to attract tourists from the coast to come inland, to spend money at the caves and in the shops and bars, and in the process to begin to dispel the doubts of the local sceptics.

Within a couple of years new businesses provided more accommodation and catering, whilst existing enterprises found they too were receiving a boost. Sorbas was becoming more widely known and the flow of visitors was steadily rising. The caves were now both literally and metaphorically on the map. Natur-Sport had become a viable project and was putting food on the plates of the offspring of those Sorbas parents who had once been dubious about the whole thing. By 2009, with a visually striking circular restaurant opening at the Cuevas de Sorbas (Sorbas Caves), the business of cave-visits was directly employing a dozen people during the winter and over 20 during the summer.

Over 30 years things have changed substantially. Many of the inhabitants of Sorbas now have a different outlook. Most of the younger residents understand that they have something on their doorstep of which they can be proud: a unique natural area that can generate jobs and income over the long term with far less damage to the environment than the quarries. Since 1990 Sorbas has had its own caving club, the Espeleo Club 'El Tesoro', whose activities have helped involve local youngsters. Natur-Sport has proved to be a dynamic, sustainable business and, having shown the possibilities for long-term use of the karst, has even been the subject of some jealousy from the old guard.

Juan García Sánchez meanwhile hopes he won't have to wait another 20 years to see further positive developments in the management and protection of the Karst en Yesos de Sorbas. He thinks the karst has been massively underused as a resource. He would doubtless be pleased by Natur-Sport's optimistic plans.

In 2009 the companies with concessions to quarry the karst undertook an exercise in common sense. They renounced their wish to exploit the gypsum in the protected area. While this seems on the face of it to be a boost for the conservation of the landscape, it does not actually represent any advance in its protection. Activists would like to see such additional elements as 'cushioning', that is, perimeter areas which minimise the visual impact of the quarries and, going further, protection for karst zones that are currently outside the Paraje Natural. Meanwhile the slopes of Peñon Díaz (Diaz's Crag) and Sima de la Parra (Pothole of the Grapevine) between Los Molinos del Río de Aguas and Hueli, continue to be remorselessly eaten away as a result of gypsum quarrying.

As an aside, freight traffic from the port of Garrucha reached 3.7 million tonnes in 2012, being exported to 32 different countries. 98% of these exports consisted of gypsum with 120 lorries making up to 1,100 trips per day, back and forth to the Sorbas quarries.

22. The old way of life

'Most of the terraces were overgrown now, the dry-stone walls that held them up slowly crumbling away...'

(Jason Webster)

Marchalico-Viñicas

As you drive north on the Autovía del Mediterráneo past Km 510 and glance to your left, a scrubby slope sweeps up to the rocky rim of the gypsum plateau. Just below the top of the slope are two clusters of houses. To reach them you can take the exit at 510, from where a steep track climbs the slope. It's sometimes gullied and impassable to vehicles so you may have to park and walk the rest of the way. (It is also possible to drive to the same place from the N-340a; for this, see the section 'Bridleways' in the chapter 'Lines on the landscape'). When you get up to the village you find that many of the buildings are externally in pretty good shape but the whole place is deserted; the doors are hanging from rusty hinges or are gone. Inside the houses there are signs everywhere of disuse and decay: holes in ceilings, crumbling plaster, walls scarred with graffiti.

This is Marchalico-Viñicas, often known simply as El Marchalico. Marchalico or Marchal, a name of Arabic origin, means garden. A detailed picture of the time within living memory when El Marchalico had a thriving population was provided by Isa García Mañas in a lengthy piece in the journal *El Afa* in 2012. Life in El Marchalico, until it was finally abandoned at the end of the 1960s, would no doubt have been typical of many of the other remote villages of the area.

Much of Isa García's information came from interviews with former residents. Don Antonio Castro Padilla was born in El Marchalico on 12th June 1938. He lived there until he married at the age of 22 and moved to Los Collados near Los Gallardos. Another of Isa's chief sources, Doña María Padilla, known as María Bolea, was born in April 1922 in the village. Of nine children, only María and one of her sisters were still living when Isa conducted her interviews. María recalled that, although her mother had been left a widow with seven children, they always had sufficient to eat. She remembered too that, although they always wore trousers, they weren't well enough off to have underwear.

El Marchalico had no school or church or doctor. As a child, María went to school in La Herrería. Every day they went down the incredibly steep slope and of course had to climb back up it after school. Halfway up was a carob tree and, as kids do, they used to stop there to play with stones until their parents called them. María enjoyed studying. When the war came and families had sons away fighting, it was María who wrote to them because their parents didn't know how to. "I went to the cave where the spring is, there where the water comes out, in the open air, and I took an inkwell. The ink was powder mixed with water. The pen was made of wood. It was wet ink with a quill and there I would write three or four letters."

Strange treatments

If someone in the village was ill, Don Agustín Amérigo, who was the doctor in Sorbas, had to come by donkey or the patient had to go to Sorbas. In Los Perales there was a gipsy called *el tío* Penco (Uncle Penco) who now and then acted as a doctor. Everyone knew a lot about the plants of the area and almost all of the plants had a use, for both prevention and cures. They would use the castor-oil plant as a purgative and it was commonly given to children and pregnant women as an anti-viral. If a child had a cut, a spider's web would be wrapped around it to protect it from infection. For pain in the bones and muscles they used the smoke from a bonfire with essential oils, usually from rosemary, passing the affected part of the body into the fumes. Antonio Castro recalls how fires were made with fennel stems. "Stems of fennel are very spongy, like a reed, and they get very hot before they catch fire. You twist them into a sort of rope and make a fire with that."

For scorpion stings there was a strange treatment but the villagers were convinced that it worked. If a scorpion stung you, you put a handkerchief in your vagina (if you were a woman, obviously) then put it over the site of the sting. It worked for men as well but in that case they had to find a female donkey and go through the same process with the animal. Don Gabriel de Haro, Maria's husband, remembers one occasion when he saw how effective it was. "The guy at the Venta of Los Perales said that if you've been stung by a scorpion, catch a *burra* (a female donkey), put your finger that's been stung in its thingamabob and the pain will go. Once we were in La

Herrería collecting capers and a scorpion stung a little girl. What they did was take her to a donkey in the *barranco* (ravine), put her finger in the donkey, and the kid came back with no problem."

To treat a cold they collected figs, carobs and thyme and made a drink from them. They also made a sort of coffee by toasting and grinding barley or carob pods. For cold sores they would leave an iron frying pan out in the damp of the night then spread the rust from it with a finger onto the cold sore. However, Antonio said that when he tried this it didn't work. For stomach ache, the cure was to apply *boja*, a plant of the Artemisia family, externally, direct to the tummy.

María recounted a way in which she'd tried to cure her daughter's chronic asthma. She put the skin of a freshly-killed rabbit directly on her daughter's back and left it overnight, the idea being that the heat from the skin would help the child to breathe more easily. The problem was "not just the smell of it but it began to graft itself onto her own skin."

There were women called *parteras* who helped at childbirth. In those days women would give birth sitting or crouching. The husband would help the midwife and mother-to-be by standing behind her and squeezing her belly to help the baby come. Women nearly always had their babies at home. On average they would have six children but not all would survive. It was rare to find a woman who had not lost a child, either at birth or afterwards, and it was not uncommon for women to die in childbirth.

In villages like El Marchalico people made their own entertainment. A popular pastime was cards and one of the villagers, Andrés Morales, who emigrated to Argentina, reputedly made a big fortune by playing cards there. And of course there were always dances, usually in the biggest house, where they would dance *'las carreras'*. Unless it was harvest time, Sunday was a day of rest and that's when the dances took place. The women used to hold hands and dance from one side to the other while the rest made a corridor and sang songs such as *La Campanera* and *La Raspa*. Sometime in the 1930s María met Don Gabriel de Haro from Los Perales at such a dance. They courted for several years and married on 25th March 1940. After the wedding they went to live in Los Perales in the house of the paternal grandparents of Gabriel.

There were traditions, of course. At Christmas, folk would go round the nearby hamlets, knocking at doors and asking for *un agilando* (a gift). They'd get at least a *chatillo* of wine. This is like the old British custom of wassailing, going from house to house, singing and being rewarded with a glass of ale or something similar. Sadly, there was not always a happy ending to these celebrations. Antonio Castro has a tale that one Christmas a gypsy called Pizoco, who squatted in one of the empty houses in El Marchalico, got so drunk that he died. Life in those days was not all sweetness and light.

Each village house had an oven but there was also a communal one called the 'Polla' oven which was used for making fritters and *roscos* (bread rings or rolls). Sometimes, for the same purpose, they used the oven of *tía* (Aunt) Cojica, a woman who lived alone and gave carob pods to the children in exchange for *cantaricas* of water. Anyone out there know exactly what a *cantarica* is?

A surprising number of people lived in El Marchalico, given the fact that it lacked what nowadays would be considered the basics. There was never a drinking water supply to the houses. In contrast to that, Gabriel says: "I remember the day water was put into Sorbas. It was inaugurated by Don Manuel Urbina Carrera at the time of San Roque in 1948."

Gypsum for everything

In El Marchalico the use of gypsum in traditional architecture reached its highest expression. The whole village is built with it. Gypsum mortar held together stones of gypsum, and gypsum plaster adorned the interiors. It is a unique example of an architecture that lasted for many years and fitted perfectly into its surroundings. Antonio Castro's father was a builder, the imprints of whose hands are still visible on the walls of the village houses he made. As for the plasterers, they made wooden moulds, fixed them to the walls and filled them with gypsum to make the fireplaces and other internal features of the houses. Gypsum is easy to work, especially for decoration, as evidenced at the Alhambra in Granada, where all the frescoes, stuccos and murals are made from it. Impermeable clay called *launa* was brought up from the river to line the ovens and to cover the *solanas*, the sun-rooms, in their houses. Various types of wood found in the area, poplar and *pita* (agave stems), for example, were used for structural timber.

In the Los Molinos/Marchalico-Viñicas area two architectural styles overlapped. El Marchalico shares a flat-roofed, cubic architectural style with the typical buildings of the Campo de Níjar, a low-lying agricultural area not far away. But it also has, in common with the more mountainous and wetter terrain of the Sierra de los Filabres, a style of pitched, tiled roofs. A panoramic view over the village from above, from the plateau edge, shows that the first houses to be built had flat roofs and no tiles. These were the lowest down and are in the poorest state of repair. The houses built later, the higher ones, were more substantial, incorporating a second storey and a tiled roof. At first the flat roofs were covered in the local impermeable *launa* clay. Later, when people were better off, they could afford ceramic tiles.

The upper parts of the two-storey houses were used for drying grain, storing straw and food from the gardens and also meat from the *matanzas* (pig-killings). In some houses they also incorporated pigeon-lofts. The oven in each house was made entirely from gypsum with a clay lining. All of the houses had fireplaces beautifully decorated with plaster mouldings; no two were the same. There was obviously a very talented plasterer in El Marchalico. Everything, larders, attics and feedings troughs, was made from gypsum. At the side of many of the houses was a *zahúrda*, a small gypsum pen with a cupola-shaped roof at one end. These pens, which were very typical of El Marchalico, were for fattening pigs and some had the exact dimensions of a single pig.

Water and war

The basis of the village economy was agriculture, both dry-land and irrigated. Vegetables and fruits were grown in the irrigated gardens, with olives, cereals and legumes on the dry land. There was a system of skilfully designed *acequias* (irrigation channels) dating from the time of the Arabs. Each landowner was responsible for keeping clean his section of the water channel. The water went from the spring, which never failed, in sequence to the vegetable terraces every 10 or 12 days and to the cereal terraces (wheat, barley, millet), which needed only occasional irrigation, every 24 days. The water came from a spring deep in the Cueva del Agua, which is part of a huge system that has only partly been explored and mapped. This is the subject of a recent film, *La Cueva del Agua: un reto colectivo*, which shows some of the sinuous chambers and delicate underground features already discovered. Exploration of the Cueva del Agua system is continuing.

The ravine that took water from El Marchalico down towards the river and went to 'La Huerta del Taral' opposite La Herrería was known as the Barranco de la Fuente. However, this water was no good for drinking because of its gypsum content. For drinking water, they had to go with pitchers and animals to a spring at La Umbría, an hour's walk away, or to Cortijo de los Yesares, which was nearer and where there was an *aljibe* (cistern) that stored rainwater. There was no water storage in El Marchalico itself. Having to get water from springs was common to all the villages. "We were slaves to water," said María.

Water supply is a big issue nowadays. Streams that always had water are now dry. The local gypsum quarries are so deep that they have disrupted and destroyed the aquifers. Private boreholes have also negatively affected the water-table. The old people also remember that in the old days, although there were droughts in some years, there were floods in others. On 20th October 1921, for example, there was flooding that destroyed several mills and houses, then in 1943, recalls Gabriel, during stormy Easter weather, it rained for 60 hours and "took away the mill", though it's not clear just which mill he is referring to.

The villagers followed various trades. Although everyone built their own house, there were specialist builders, plasterers and woodworkers who could be asked for help or advice. A *matanza*, when the pigs would be killed and processed, was a regular feature in each family every year. It was a way of preserving meat to last from one year to the next. María's father was a pig-slaughterer, though this wouldn't have been a full-time job, of course. As well as these specialities, many people worked at least part-time as farmers and/or shepherds. The women brought up the children, did all the housework, worked in the gardens, looked after the old people and went to get water either on foot or with a donkey. The men used to go out with the goats on to the plateau, thresh grain on the *era* (threshing circle) and work the land.

In El Marchalico there were six *eras*. One was communal and it was there that all sorts of events were celebrated. Antonio describes La Piñata: "We gave someone a stick, bound his eyes and turned him round a few times. Between two *pitacos* (agave stems) was a pot fixed to a strong rope. Inside it were frogs collected from the ravine..." The modern version of this is less cruel. It involves blindfolded children trying to smash the pot to release a shower of sweets rather than amphibians.

The inhabitants of El Marchalico lived, without knowing it, among a range of unique geological formations. Antonio recounts that the gypsum tumuli were called *bochas* (bowls). Before geologists discovered them the villagers knew about them because rabbits used them as refuges and were hunted by the villagers with ferrets. He remembered specific place names too. There was La Cueva del Roble, where livestock could shelter and be shut in; the nearby Sima del Roble, thought to be the deepest pothole in the area; and a giant tumulus called the Cueva de José Ramón. An area of big fallen boulders, *'un caos be bloques'*, was known as El Torcal del Marchalico and there, by an ancient spring, is La Cueva de las Pistoles, where militiamen hid their weapons after the Civil War and which children found by chance years later. Smaller and nearer the village was the Cueva de los Trancos, a shelter behind the spring where courting couples would meet.

The period from the late 19th century was one of great social, political and environmental changes. In government it included the Second Republic, the Civil War, the Francoist dictatorship and then the restoration of the monarchy and the transition to democracy. During the dictatorship no political parties were allowed. I've been told that the people in Sorbas itself were very pro-Franco but out in the countryside sympathies varied much more.

At the time of the Civil War and afterwards, under the *dictadura franquista*, it was risky to talk politics. Nevertheless it seems that, at that time, a number of leftists in El Marchalico were determined to make their point. There was one episode when several youngsters went to set fire to the wooden statue of San Diego, the patron saint of Gacía Bajo, a village a few kilometres away in the

Sierra Cabrera. Those that were caught were shot in Sorbas, in *zahurdas* (pig-sties) at the side of the Venta de la Viuda (which is on the edge of the town, not far from the cemetery). Others who were suspected of involvement spent up to three years in jail. Everyone remembers the war as a horrible time: fear, plundering, people who disappeared and never came back. Many went to the war and the majority didn't return.

This was a key factor in the village being abandoned. Plundering of the village's resources was a common occurrence. It's never precisely voiced but 'they' came to the houses and requisitioned part of the harvest. This created severe hunger. It was during the dictatorship that the village was finally abandoned. That was the period of industrial expansion in the Basque Country and Cataluña. The great majority of people from El Marchalico emigrated to Cataluña or France, with all the sorrow of leaving behind their houses, gardens and half their families on their native soil. Things were changing. Money was needed for a better life.

Those who didn't migrate beyond Andalucía went to nearby places like Turre, La Huelga, La Herrería or Los Gallardos where they had family and where there was more chance of paid work. This process started at the beginning of the '50s and by the end of the '60s the village was completely abandoned. The last family to go was the married couple Gabriel Requena Padilla and Isabel Muños Galera, both now deceased, who went to La Huelga in about 1969.

In El Marchalico there are still over 20 houses standing. All have been ransacked even though they still technically have owners. Many of the ceramic flagstones that covered the *solanas*, the window grilles and the roof tiles have been re-used. Some can be identified in nearby villages but, because people no longer live in El Marchalico, no-one seems bothered about preserving the place. Time seems to have stood still at El Marchalico but, as more time passes, its houses will gradually crumble back into the gypsum slopes. Decades hence, when we are gone too, they'll just be mysterious and forgotten piles of rubble, perches for black wheatears amongst the tough old carob trees.

23. Threshing circles and pigeon lofts
'The great casualties of modernism are nature, the diversity of human tradition, and the particularities of place.'
(Barry Lopez)

An Annual Ritual

Scattered throughout eastern Almería province are hundreds of threshing circles (called *eras* in Castellano), distinctive elements of the rural drystone architecture of the province. It was on these *eras* that the locally-grown cereals, mainly wheat and barley, were processed after harvesting. The *eras* were made in prominent places, clear of houses or trees that might hinder the action of the wind but necessarily close to the farmhouses or villages which they served. As the cultivation of cereals has steadily declined over the past half century many of the threshing circles have fallen into disuse. Despite their abandonment, many *eras* are in a good state of repair and they remain impressive and attractive features of the landscape.

Within living memory, and again recently in one or two places, the annual summer use of the *eras* brings a reminder of traditional ways. The period from June to August would see the culmination of the year's work for the wheat and barley growers. There was a division of labour whereby the women would harvest the crop and the men would see to the processing that followed. The women, with wide-brimmed hats or headscarves, long sleeves and long skirts, would get up at the crack of dawn to begin reaping before the full heat of the sun scorched down. The harvesting was done by hand with sickles. For protection against cuts from the sharp ends of the stalks, the reapers wore leather finger-stalls.

As for the work, a big team would be involved; there would be several reapers, with someone in charge and someone else tying the crop into sheaves for loading onto a cart. This was pulled, by horses or mules, to the stacker at the threshing circle. Meanwhile, others would bring plenty of water for those working in the punishing temperatures and someone else would be making food for them all. It was a time when the community worked together, a show of mutual support that came round each summer with the natural cycle of the seasons.

As the cereals were harvested the centre of attention passed to the sheaves stacked on the *era*. The next phase was the threshing, the separation of the ears of grain from the straw. The sheaves would be spread out and a team of horses, usually up to four, guided by a man in the centre of the *era*, would drag a thresher behind them. One of the farmers would get up on the thresher to add his weight to the process and to guide the horses more effectively. The horses walked in a circle, their precise line being controlled to make sure they covered the whole crop. Depending on the size of the threshing circle, several teams might operate at the same time, being guided so as not to collide.

The key feature of this process was the *trillo de pedernal*, the flint thresher. A *trillo de pedernal* is the size and shape of a large door and is made of four big planks of wood, usually pine, set parallel, between a metre and a half and two metres long. The planks are fixed together with crosspieces and nails to make a single hefty board. On their lower surface about 1500 slits are made, in rows, with a hammer and chisel. In each slit a sharp piece of flint is set, parallel to the long sides of the planks. Four small iron wheels would keep the threshing board sufficiently far above the stone surface of the *era* to prevent damage to the flints. The front part of the thresher would curve upwards and have a strong ring set in it. Onto this was tied the rope that was linked, via a rocker arm, to the mules, horses or cattle that pulled the thresher. These *trillos de pedernal* can occasionally still be seen in antique shops where they fetch a high price. Turned over to display the flints, they have been made into glass-topped tables at the Bar Restaurant Los Molinos in Lubrín.

Men with pitchforks would ensure the thick layer of wheat or barley on the *era* was turned so that the stalks at the bottom came to the top to be threshed. These pitchforks were traditionally made from a single piece of wood with three, four or five curved tines which allowed for the easy tossing of the straw. Such pitchforks were usually made in the mountainous areas, preferably from ash or holly, with the branches of the trees being trained to grow into the correct forked shape before being cut and finished. As time passed more modern metal forks tended to be used instead, with the older wooden ones, each a distinctively individual tool, as often as not consigned to become an ornament, a dislocated moment of history, on the wall of a bar somewhere, though you can still buy them for their original purpose.

After several hours of co-ordinated hard work the accumulated crop, now a big flattened circle of golden straw, would be totally crushed. Next the grain had to be separated from the straw. In *South From Granada*, Gerald Brenan set the scene: 'As darkness fell, preparations for the winnowing would begin. A group of men and women would assemble on the threshing-floor, a lantern would be lit, someone would strum on a guitar.'

For winnowing, a favourable wind was essential and this usually happened during the night. The children and women would sleep out in the open air, having made little shelters from the saddles of the mules. As soon as they felt a gentle breeze from the right direction, work would begin. It was simple. They would throw the mix of grain and straw into the air. Brenan again, describing the activity towards dawn: '...the shadows would turn violet, then lavender, would become thin and float away, while, as I approached the threshing-floor, I would see the chaff streaming out like a white cloak in the breeze and the heavy grain falling, as the gold coins fell on Danaë, on to the heap below.'

Finally, a shovel would be used to throw up the last of the mix, including the smallest bits of straw. The grain would be swept into a big pile in the centre of the *era*, where it could be bagged into canvas sacks and hauled off, the final task, to the granaries or haylofts in the upper storeys of the local houses. The *eras* were used not only for wheat and barley but also less frequently for oats, and legumes such as chickpeas, peas and lentils.

Threshing circles

The most impressive threshing circles are the paved ones, the *eras empedradas*, found in areas such as the Sierra de los Filabres, the Sierra Alhamilla, Tabernas and Sorbas. Because the sites where they were built were rarely totally flat, they would tend to be cut into a slope at one side and built up with a retaining wall of masonry at the other. Some *eras* of this type had a low perimeter wall, typically 30 cm high, to keep the grain and straw on the *era* but also with a gap to allow entry for the working animals. Their construction was relatively complex and costly but the compensation for this was that they would last for many years, especially those that had been made by experts. One such was José Ramón Peña Martinez (1870 – 1938), a meticulous builder whose work can still be seen three kilometres from Uleila del Campo by the road to Cantoria at the Cortijo de Zofre, in the neat stonework of the Restaurante Casa Elisardo in Uleila and in the *era* at Las Palmeras. One of his lasting achievements, made in 1920, was the *era* of 'Pepe Higinio', named after his son-in-law, a beautifully-laid threshing circle on the edge of Uleila town.

In the Barranco de la Abuela at El Fonte north of Sorbas are three very distinctive stone *eras*. Two have the dates 1862 and 1899 etched into slates and the third has quartzite stones forming a white centre a metre in diameter that contrasts with the darker flagstones of the rest of the circle. At Los Herreras in Cariatiz an *era* was made in 1909 by the master builder from Lubrín, José Codina López, using gneiss quarried in Los Castaños. A pattern of radii divides the circle into twelve segments. Nearer Sorbas, at Cortijo Urrá, the *era* has neat stonework dividing the circle into segments and the carved date 1884.

Alcudia de Monteagud has two communal circles made from flagstones of metamorphic rock, the Era Grande in the Calle Era and the Era de Abajo in the Calle Tercia. The Era Grande, the largest stone threshing circle in the province, was constructed in 1894, has a diameter of 45 metres and a surface area of 1400 m², and is divided into 96 sections.

Simpler *eras*, *eras de tierra*, were made by clearing a suitable site of vegetation and stones, damping it with water and rolling it to compact the earth. This type of threshing circle was more common in the Almanzora valley and the Sierra de las Estancias. Sometimes the rollers of stone or iron would be conical to make it easier for the animals to pull them in a circle. These earth *eras* had their particular uses; at Cariatiz, for example, the villagers took their chickpeas for threshing to the earth circle at Los Mónicos because processing them on the stone *eras* caused too many to chip and split.

In recent years various attempts have been made to revitalize the use of some of the old *eras*, a much better idea than simply listing them as important but dusty old relics in the hope that they will be revered or, as happens frequently, just using them as convenient car parks. Amongst places where these initiatives have occurred are several of those mentioned above: the Era Grande at Alcudia de Monteagud; several *eras* in Cariatiz, including the one at Los Martinez which is used for music, dancing, skipping, eating and drinking in connection with the recently revived *romería* (procession) of San Gonzalo de Amaranto; and the *era* of 'Pepe Higinio' in Uleila del Campo. Juan Ramos Peña tells me that the Threshing Feast at Uleila, revived in 2012, has been so successful that it is now continuing as an annual event each July. Such efforts should mean that all is not lost for these fine old paved circles.

Pigeon lofts

At about Km 491 on the Autovía del Mediterráneo you pass the crumbling ruins of the Cortijo de los Arejos. This group of evocative buildings, set among scattered palms and sandwiched between the motorway and the old road that it replaced, the A1101 between Peñas Negras and Venta del Pobre, can easily be accessed from the latter. I scrambled up among the ruins in late 2011, clambering over tumbled rubble to have a closer look at the inside of one of the half-standing buildings. Because the building is gaping open at one end, the inside is visible from the motorway if you happen to be looking at just the right moment but it's difficult to see exactly what it is from a distance; you need to have a close-up view.

Teetering up on the piled remnants of fallen walls and roofs, you can see that the remaining walls do not simply have flat surfaces but are covered in vaulted niches, each one level at the base and curved at the top. This is a *palomar*, a pigeon loft. The base of each niche is tilted slightly upwards at the outer edge to protect the eggs from rolling out. It is clear that, when fully intact, this building would have housed a vast number of birds.

Rearing pigeons was an important part of the rural economy. The meat, especially of the young birds, the squabs, was a significant element in the protein supply of local people and pigeon droppings were a hugely valuable fertiliser in the times before chemical fertilisers swamped the market.

In many places the pigeon lofts were above the livestock quarters but it was not uncommon for them to occupy the upper storey of houses, a fact easily detected by the usually triangular sets of holes in the walls. Via these the pigeons could leave to fly around the countryside and feed themselves, then return to the loft for shelter and breeding. And there lay the double advantage of keeping pigeons: they went off to feed themselves so they didn't need much looking after and they always provided a steady surplus for the pot.

In some parts of the region pigeons produced such a good economic return in free meat and free manure that lofts were constructed as separate buildings, some of which housed thousands of birds. Such a building would tend to be near the *cortijo* but also near the highest local point so it would be visible to the returning birds. Certain builders specialised in the construction of such pigeon lofts. The demise of the lofts has meant that this unique trade has also died out.

Local geology

Invariably these *palomares* were built of the materials that were available nearby and therefore local variations arose both in their external appearance as well as their interior design. The local geology was obviously the key factor, so for example the sub-desert of Tabernas, the slate mountains of the Filabres and the gypsum karst area near Sorbas all had very different styles of pigeon loft.

Some of the most interesting lofts are in the rugged and distinctive landscapes of the Campo de Tabernas. This area is characterised by aridity and high insolation, surrounded by the *sierras* of Nevada, Gádor and Filabres, all reaching over 2,000 metres in altitude. In addition, the Sierra de Alhamilla cuts the Campo de Tabernas off from the sea. These natural barriers limit the amount of humidity reaching the area yet, despite its apparent lack of possibilities for human survival, man has made the most of the natural resources, especially in the flattest areas near to Tabernas along the margins of the *ramblas*.

Just north of Tabernas for example, in the area known as the Pago de Gergal, there lies the abandoned castle-like ruin of the *cortijo* of the Góngora family. The upper part of the building has several triangular sets of ten holes, suggesting the entire top floor was a pigeon loft. Not far away, the function of another building the size of a house, but with no windows, is given away by the holes just below the roof spelling out the initials JAD. This was the *palomar* of Juan Alarcón. I haven't managed to track down his second *apellido* (surname) represented by the D. In this context, where a farming culture developed to make use of the occasional torrential rains and other scarce resources, pigeon droppings were an essential way of enriching the poor soils so they could hold more moisture.

Outside our friend Lindy Walsh's house at Cortijo Urrá is a pile of tubular ceramic pots; 'pigeon pots', Lindy calls them. At the time I didn't think to ask but, knowing a bit more now, I realise these are what are called *arcaduces*, cylindrical pots about 20 cm in diameter and 30 cm deep. In the *palomares* they would be laid horizontally and built into a wall, with the open ends facing inwards. Sometimes they are partially closed at the inward-facing end, as mentioned above, to prevent eggs and squabs from falling out. These *nidales cerámicos* (ceramic nests) were traditionally made by local potters in Tabernas.

Juan Antonio Muñoz, in a survey of *palomares* in the journal *El Afa*, argues strongly that the best of them should be listed immediately for conservation: the group on the low hill at Cortijo del Pastor, for example, for its visibility and aesthetic appearance; the one at Cortijo de Madolell for its striking interior; and the one at Venta del Compadre for its size and distinguished appearance. He mentions another distinctive group of *palomares*, in the *barriada* (neighbourhood) of Espeliz just south of the N-340a in the northern foothills of the Sierra Alhamilla, about four kilometres from the junction with the Turrillas road. This is a group of 17 structures lined up around a central 'street'. They are obvious because they are tall and brightly coloured, he says, to make them more visible to the birds. The colours also act as a brand, a trade mark, of the different properties that own the lofts. However, a friend suggested to me that as birds don't see in colour, different bright colours would be pointless in terms of identifying the different *palomares* to the birds. Or do these translate into varying shades of grey that the birds can recognise?

To return to the local geology, the Sierra de Filabres is characterised by slate which determines the traditional constructions of the area. This has come to be called 'black architecture' (*arquitectura negra*). In effect the buildings are made from slate, clay, tree-trunks, skill and little else. The clay is a form of mortar and the tree-trunks, from the banks of the *ramblas*, are used for supporting the heavy slate roofs. Such buildings seem to emanate organically from the mountains. A fine concentration of *palomares* of this type can be found in the higher stretch of the Arroyo de Verdelecho near Olula de Castro. The main function of these lofts was to provide a supply of pigeon manure for the small vegetable plots in the valleys.

These lofts were rectangular, typically 12 or 15 by 6 or 8 metres in floor area, with the entire inside wall area covered by square, slate-built niches. There would be just a single small door at ground level. The access holes for the birds were set high up, usually just below the roof, to make entry difficult for vermin. Although originally these *palomares* were not white-washed, in time they did come to be treated with lime, making them landmarks against the uniform darkness of the slate landscape. Annual maintenance was important to ensure that there were no gaps in the slate walls to allow passage to rodents or other enemies of the pigeons.

In the gypsum karst area near Sorbas, the gypsum was used as the major material in the construction of the local *palomares*. Occasionally there would be a particularly fine and unusual pigeon loft; at the Cortijo del Pilarico, for example. Here there was a loft with a circular base roughly seven metres in diameter, forming a tower some eight metres high. The niches, covering the inner wall in a dense mathematical pattern, could house about 5,000 birds. In terms of height and volume, this *palomar* was bigger than the *cortijo* to which it belonged, proving clearly that the raising of pigeons and the sale of their manure were major activities. This distinctive building is now in a state of collapse, rather like the one at Cortijo de los Arejos with which this brief survey began.

In many villages and scattered *cortijos* pigeon lofts still exist but they rarely continue to perform their original role. In most cases they have simply been abandoned and, like the ones mentioned above, left to crumble but at Los Baños near Lucainena the *palomar*, with its mixture of circular and vaulted niches, has been renovated for use as a classroom/activities room. The exception proves the rule though, and with a lack of funds and lack of will to list and renovate some of the best examples of this unique aspect of vernacular architecture, the *palomares* will continue to deteriorate and the heritage of those specialised local builders will gradually disappear.

24. The road of 100 bends

'How I had longed for a bend in the road - even just a bit of a kink - for some relief from the relentless efficiency of travelling in a continual bee-line.'

(Roger Deakin, writing about the M1)

Counting the curves

We live 25 minutes drive-time away from Sorbas, much of which is along a twisting mountain road, the AL 1102 (still marked as the AL-140 on some maps). This road is best shown on the 1:25,000 maps, sheet 1031-I Sorbas and sheet 1031-III Polopos. For part of its route it bisects the Paraje Natural Karst en Yesos de Sorbas. One day it occurred to us, just for fun, to count the bends from our house along this route, as far as where it reaches a junction with the N-340a (A370 on some maps) just a kilometre or so outside Sorbas. The total turned out to be exactly 100, though of course this depends on your personal judgement as to where one bend ends and the next begins.

First you have to twist down past La Herradura, then make a ridiculously sharp left turn, and drop further to an almost insignificant bridge over the *rambla*, then climb steeply up to Los Rellanos. At least, this is what the maps call the small ridge-top hamlet, though a home-made sign has appeared within recent years announcing it as La Rellana. From there, twist down again to Gafarillos. Here there's a left turn and the road, relatively new and designed for a steady 70 kph, makes a series of flowing downhill curves for almost three kilometres to Peñas Negras.

A right turn at the T-junction at Peñas Negras takes you on to the AL 1102 in the direction of Sorbas, soon passes under the motorway, the Autovía del Mediterráneo, then climbs steadily, reaching almost 450 metres above sea level on the flank of Cerro Molatas.

A stunning panorama

Just beyond here, by a sharp left-hand bend at grid reference 58311046, there's a pull-off on the right with a complex and wonderful view. It's not an official *mirador* but it is a stunning

220

viewpoint, certainly one of the best in the region for those who like to reach their views by car.

In the foreground the AL 1102 loses height then falls in a steeper series of turns to the houses of Los Molinos del Río de Aguas, which are clustered on the slopes above the true right bank of the river. The name is often shortened to Los Molinos or even Los Mol by incomers, though the old Spanish residents always called it simply El Río. (You may already have read much more about this village in the chapter 'Río de Aguas: *acequias* and mills'.)

We are looking north-westwards at this point. Above the village is the prominent rocky snout known to those who would care to anglicise it as the Eagle's Head. Immediately behind this and much further away is the pale splash of the small town of Uleila del Campo. Behind Los Molinos are the huge cliffs and chaotic rockfalls that constrict the Río de Aguas. Sorbas, which is actually much closer than Uleila, is invisible from this point, hidden by the folds of the landscape. The far horizon is formed by the crest of the Sierra de los Filabres with, just a touch further round the compass, north north-west, the gleaming white buildings of the Sanctuary of the Virgen de la Cabeza on the conical peak of Monteagud, about 26 kilometres away as the kestrel flies.

Moving clockwise, due north lie the cream slopes leading up to the gypsum plateau, the Karst en Yesos de Sorbas. Closer at hand in this direction you look steeply down on the abandoned watermill buildings of Carrasco but the eye is inevitably drawn further right, to the deep rocky cleft of the Barranco del Tesoro. This wonder of nature is eclipsed by a huge curve of the motorway, slicing across the once wild landscape on vast concrete supports.

The cognitive dissonance this entails, the uncomfortable feeling of holding clashing ideas in our minds, is touched on by Joe Moran in *On Roads*: 'Perhaps this explains why we can't for the moment hold these two seemingly antithetical impulses in our heads simultaneously - to acknowledge the environmental destruction and human alienation wrought by roads but also the physical achievement of all those smooth lines of asphalt carved out of unforgiving earth.' That is spot-on for this situation, and the *barranco,* the once mysterious Ravine of the Treaure, seems to magnify the traffic noise and throw it upwards, exaggerating the visual violation of this spectacular landscape.

Back to the view from the bend on the AL 1102; as we sweep round a bit further, to the north-east there is a view all the way to Garrucha and the Mediterranean Sea, 24 kilometres away. Round again, eastwards, the slopes rise to Cerro de la Matica, 549 m high and just three kilometres away, and then, virtually due south, the asymmetrical profile of El Cerron at 602 m. Higher still (658 m) and slightly more distant, El Cerron de Hueli just peeks over the intervening ridge. East south-east, Peñon Diaz stands above a line of sheer crags with, behind it, Cerro Quemado, the Burnt Hill, though why it has this name is a mystery. Anyone know?

Behind this listing of hill names and heights is the sheer delight of seeing the slopes and ridges, one after another, hazing away into the distance, so that between the Filabres and the Mediterranean, through 180°, you can span a view across some 70 kilometres of superb terrain.

Clockwise, beyond the many undulations of intermediate ground, we come round to the far horizon of the Sierra de los Filabres again. Its high point is at the astronomical observatory of Calar Alto, 2,168 m above sea level and 46 kilometres from this viewpoint, its white spheres gleaming even against the dusting of snow on the Filabres crest as we look towards it on a late January day. A further 25 degrees round the compass a distinctive snowy peak pokes up beyond the general line of the Filabres. Is this the mystical 'marble mountain' that we were once told about? Will we ever know?

Down to Los Molinos and up again

Harvey 'Hogan' Appel from Los Molinos tells me that he has the following information from 'old Diego' of the Venta Alegre bar in Sorbas: when Diego was employed on making the A 1102 road in 1966, he was paid 17 pesetas per day. At that time the exchange rate was 168 pesetas to the £1. By contrast, locals employed as extras on the film *Lawrence of Arabia* in 1962 were earning 150 pesetas per day.

The road swoops on down to Los Molinos. Its surface is good because the lorries from the vast quarry below Peñon Diaz use it constantly to access the motorway and the quarry company funds its maintenance, or so I have been led to believe. At its lowest point, as it hairpins across the Barranco los Barrancones, a track leads off to the lower end of the village. A few metres along this track lies a well-tended memorial recording that Francisco Saez Hernandez and Juan Cayuela García *'fallecieron en esta lugar'* (died in this place) on 2nd November 1988. It's a poignant feature, the more so because there is no clue as to how they died or how old they were.

I've always assumed, though I'm not sure why, that it was two young guys who came off a motorbike but, suspecting Lindy Walsh might know, I rang her and was astonished to be told that she was actually at Los Molinos when the accident happened. It was late one night, after rain, so the road may have been greasy. There was a terrible noise made by a car coming off the road and crashing steeply down into the *barranco*. And so two young men met their deaths here in a tragic incident one winter's night over 20 years ago.

Most of the village lies below the road as it sweeps up under the glowering crags of the 'Eagle's Head'. Once it reaches the plateau and levels out, it's possible to park and take the easy 10-minute walk to the right, up to the top of this outcrop. The final stretch of this short walk is steep but for a minimal outlay of energy the reward is yet another riveting panorama.

Back at the road, a few metres further in the Sorbas direction, a road branches off left. This leads to the gypsum quarry and is used by a steady stream of heavy lorries. It's also the way to reach the deserted village of Hueli, well worth some exploration. Beyond Hueli a path leads up to the mountainous watershed and the summit of Cantona, an airy top at 755 m from where there is a great view due east, down into the deeply scooped valley of Mizala.

Soon after the quarry turning, where the A 1102 makes yet another of its many curves, is the Mirador de Urrá. This was created on land given to the Sorbas *ayuntamiento* by Lindy and Bill Walsh. There's an *aljibe*, a Moorish water tank which, when you open the small door and look through the grille, is of a surprising depth. Its location looks suspect though, on a high point. How would it fill in such a position? And indeed we discover that it is no longer a working water supply but was rebuilt here by the authorities as a feature of the *mirador*. Adjacent, beneath swaying eucalyptuses, are information boards with a map showing the Paraje Natural Karst en

223

Yesos de Sorbas and its own botanical jewels (*'joyas botánicas'*). These endemic plants of the karst steppes include Sorbas rosemary, Sorbas narcissus and Jarilla de Sorbas. There's a panel too, but only in *castellano*, explaining the origin of the Sorbas Basin (the *Cuenca de Sorbas*) and the formation of the gypsum plateau. Some time before the *mirador* was here, I am reliably informed, there was on this site a *casilla de camineros*, a house where two families lived, their menfolk being responsible for the upkeep of the local stretch of this road.

Less than a kilometre after the *mirador* the road twists across a major south-bank tributary of the Río de Aguas; this is the Barranco de Hueli o del Peral (it has alternative names). Quite dramatic in its central reaches, though fairly choked with vegetation and consequently difficult to negotiate on foot, it is usually, like most of the river channels in these parts, dry.

The buildings of the Urrá Field Centre are now visible in the direction of Sorbas and after a couple more bends the track on the right, leading off to Urrá, is passed. Soon there's a long downhill stretch leading to the Cuevas de Sorbas (Sorbas Caves). Just beyond but alongside these buildings another tributary *rambla* comes in from the south. This is the Barranco del Infierno, the Ravine of Hell. I vividly remember a day spent, on foot of course, with the Amigos de Sorbas exploring the remarkable twists and turns of this dramatic, steep-sided valley.

Immediately after this there's a sharp kink over the Río Aguas bridge and another brief climb to reach the N340-a, still known as the 'new road' but built in the 1890s to link Almería and Puerto Lumbreras. This is the end of the A 1102, our 'road of 100 bends'. A left turn soon enough brings you to Sorbas, with the road curving under the *casas colgantes*, the 'hanging houses' perched right on the sheer edge of El Afa gorge.

Camouflaged cars and bikers

We drive the A 1102 often and frequently see small convoys of cars, covered in fabric to disguise their precise outlines and with their rear wheels hooked up to on-board computers, curving smartly round the bends. They are from the Michelin research facility down at Cabo de Gata. Likewise files of bikers, their knees almost grazing the tarmac, sweeping round the scenic curves, often with one of their number strategically placed by a bend with a camera to capture the moment.

If there is a book called *Europe's 100 Best Bikers' Roads* catering for this niche market, this road will definitely be in it. Or so I thought until I thought to google 'best motorbike roads in Andalucía' and discovered that it isn't listed. The AL-P 117 (a recent road atlas suggests this is now known as the AL 6109) Los Gallardos - Bedar - El Marchal is mentioned though. This latter has 'hardly any traffic to speak of and spectacular views to the coast and surrounding valleys' and is given five stars. Perhaps the presence of lorries from the quarries is the reason for our twisty road, the A 1102, finding disfavour. Then there is the wonderful AL-P 115 from Sorbas north to Lubrín, and no doubt many another fine unlisted road whose delights I have yet to discover. Professional cycling teams including, recently, Garmin Cervelo and Rabobank, have given a further thumbs-up to these twisty mountain roads by choosing this area for their pre-season training.

If you have to drive half an hour to reach your local town, to visit the nearest bank or post office, or to buy flour at the baker's, you couldn't ask for a more spectacular road than 'our' A 1102 on which to spend that time.

25. Field notes from the hills

'Anything goes in a novel, so long as it's told with common sense; but in geography, naturally, it's not the same, and one must always tell the truth because geography is like a science.'
(Camilo José Cela)

In the heart of the Cabrera

Roads snake south-west from Turre up into the Sierra Cabrera, to the almost exclusively expat communities of Cortijo Grande and Cortijo Cabrera. Beyond these settlements the roads join and continue upwards, climbing just south of the ridge of Loma del Colorado, where a further road turns off to twist steeply up to the south. Beyond a series of tight hairpins, this road reaches a tiny white chapel dating from 1889 and a cluster of buildings perched spectacularly on the northern side of Cerro de la Mezquita (Hill of the Mosque). This is La Carrasca, a hamlet once virtually abandoned but now undergoing a renaissance.

This is where we have come one late October day in 2011 for a walk organised by the Asociación de Vecinos La Carrasca and the Club de Montaña Amigos de Sierra Cabrera. Gradually people appear on foot and in vehicles until around 40 folk and a handful of dogs have assembled. After the obligatory speech which is so typical of Spanish events, we set off.

Opposite the chapel a narrow path bears off to the right, soon reaching the Fuente de Abajo, the Lower Spring. This was traditionally used by the village women for washing clothes and both the main water tank and the adjacent washing troughs are in good repair. The path leads on, past small vegetable plots, back into the tiny village. Some of the tightly-packed buildings have been recently renovated. Others are still needing attention but it's obvious there is steady upgrading going on.

The narrow tarmac road by which we arrived continues above the village. As we look back over the tiny settlement I ask Pedro, a local with many years etched into his smiling face, how many people now live in La Carrasca full-time. "Well," he says, "there's one of my brothers and his wife, and a son and daughter. And I'm retired but I'm there five days a week, then I go to Almería for a couple of days." Soon enough we reach the Fuente de Arriba, the Upper Spring. This is also in good repair and is the drinking water supply. "Fill your bottles," announces Eduardo Sánchez, one of the walk leaders, "there aren't any more springs after this."

Trying to work out later exactly where we went on the 1:25,000 maps (sheets 1031-II Turre and 1031-IV El Llano de Don Antonio) proves surprisingly difficult, partly because the locals have names for every bit of their surroundings and these don't correspond to what appears on the maps. So we climb to Pozo Pablo (not on the map) before taking a faint path across the head of a steep valley to go via La Trocha (not on the map) and Cruce de la Manga (not on the map).

Pedro, the old boy I'd been talking to earlier, is telling us about the place. People came out here when they wanted to hunt, to avoid the *guardia*, he says, gesturing towards Faína. He points at a distant building which he calls the Cortijo de Faína and launches into a story about a woman from Carboneras who was there for forty days, or maybe not. His accent is thick and the details are hazy. And there is no Cortijo de Faína on the map. There are various other *cortijos* and *caseríos* and *corrales*, but nothing answering to that particular name.

We pass a circular drystone hunter's hide with a narrow entrance. It's about a metre high and draped with sprigs of vegetation to make it seem part of the landscape. Fifteen metres away is a small cairn of rocks. Pedro explains: the hunters would put a caged female partridge by the cairn and its calls would attract males who would perch on the adjacent cairn. Easy pickings for the hunters and, Pedro adds, illegal nowadays. It may be illegal but I've seen plenty of these in the Sierra Cabrera that are quite obviously still in use.

We drop briefly into the head of the Barranco de Faína and aim towards two sets of impressive crags. There used to be vultures on the far cliffs, says Pedro. A brief discussion concludes that the law that no longer allows dead livestock to be left out in the countryside is the reason for their demise. But there are still *aguilas reales* (golden eagles), he says. I'm surprised by this. I would have thought there's too much disturbance nowadays for golden eagles. They're not always here but I'm sure they're around, he adds. The difference, he points out, is that the vultures feed on carrion and the eagles catch live prey such as rabbits, pigeons and partridges. A few months later

I'm party to a conversation between our Spanish neighbour José and a Romanian friend of ours, Calin, where mention is made of the fact that the law has recently been changed. It has reverted so that it is again legal to leave carcasses out on the hills, the aim being to encourage vultures to return to some of their former haunts.

Back on the walk, we are now close to the crags, and we are on a watershed. Rain falling this side goes to Carboneras, says Pedro, pointing south to a hazy sea, and this side, pointing north, it goes to Garrucha. By now we've stopped for lunch and I finally get my map out. I identify where I think we are and stroll over to Javi, the President of the Club de Montaña. Are we here, I ask, the Collado de Faína? He confirms that we are. But later, when I check the written route description on the email that had arrived a few days earlier, announcing the walk, there is no mention of the Collado de Faína. Instead it seems to be referred to as the Collado del Portillo which, in turn, does not appear on the map. So we seem to have pinpointed where we are, a pass at 705 m above sea level, but as to what it's called, we seem to have another 'official map/local knowledge' contradiction.

We stop for a brief lunch during which our friend Jackie pulls small bottles of beer out of her bag. This is a double surprise: we don't normally have beer on a walk like this and, if there's beer about, it's usually Jackie's husband Charlie who's carrying it. A third surprise was the bag of mini *pains au chocolat* that Jackie had produced earlier while we waited for everyone to arrive at the beginning of the walk. But I digress.

We head east, pulling steadily up what is the upper part of the Barranco de Faína but what is known here as the Rambla de Los Jarales. This brings us to a small flat area, also unnamed on the map, which we are told is the Era de Los Borrachos (The Threshing Circle of the Drunkards). They don't make place-names like that anymore. From here, we veer north on an obvious track that rises to a pass on the flank of Cerro de La Mezquita, from where we soon rejoin our outward route for the descent back to La Carrasca. The views are huge, way over to Uleila del Campo and Bédar in the Sierra Filabres, and out over Garrucha to the Mediterranean. Despite the haze it's stunningly beautiful.

Looming over the hamlet of La Carrasca, at 962 metres, Cerro de La Mezquita is the highest point of the Cabrera range. Its summit, or rather its two almost equally high tops (962 m and 960 m) about two hundred metres apart, which I've been to on an earlier occasion, are airy places of quirkily eroded limestone pavement and low vegetation. One has a trig point and a small mast, the other has a tiny shed-like building and also a mast. So they are not pristine places but they nevertheless have a wild feel and are superb viewpoints. However, as Eduardo adds in a postscript to a couple of photos he emails the day after our walk, '... *es la que el ejercito piensa destruir proximamente, para construir un radar'*, '... it's this that the army is thinking of destroying in the near future by building a radar installation'.

What he is referring to is the intention of the Ministry of Defence to build a radar station at the top of the mountain. This 'intelligent communications' project, costing €850,000, will see the erection of a warehouse and sophisticated Scatar Levante radar equipment in a compound covering at least 2,500 square metres of the summit.

In July 2013 I finally go back to see what has happened to the summit of Cerro de la Mezquita. A wide black tarmac ribbon now veers up from the narrow road a kilometre or so above La Carrasca and goes right up to the new installation on the 962 m top. From the other top, the one with the trig point, at 960 m, what you now see on the 962 m summit is indeed a low warehouse inside a large enclosure, defended partly by a tall wire fence and partly by a tall concrete wall. It's ugly and intrusive, entirely destroying the natural feel of the highest point in the Sierra Cabrera. Yet I'm surprised and rather shocked to find that I'm relieved; somehow it's not as bad as I had been expecting. At least you can still stand by the trig point and, looking south, get some sense of how this mountain used to be.

Hunting for garnets

We've been told about a place where you can find garnets. A couple of friends and their five-year old son are staying with us. He's interested in everything. What better than to go searching for treasure? We drive west along the Autovía del Mediterráneo to Km 481, the first exit to Níjar if you are coming from the east. At the end of the slip road, we immediately turn back on a dusty track that parallels the motorway, heading for a point where the skyline consists of two steep outcrops facing each other across a symmetrical scoop. An inclined path is clearly visible leading up to the lowest point of the scoop. It's no more than a kilometre from where we have left the motorway.

Leaving the car, we reach the base of the path and begin the climb. In just a few minutes, at the crest of the path, we find ourselves looking into a huge circular depression. This is the Hoyazo de Níjar, the crater of a volcano which emerged from the shallow sea that covered this area about six million years ago. The obvious outcrops that tower up to either side are the remnants of coral reefs that developed in the warm waters around the volcano and the breach between them, the scoop in which we are standing, is where later erosion has broken through the crater rim.

This cut through the crater rim is known as the Rambla de la Granatilla and it was in the alluvial fan deposited by the waters of this *rambla* just to the south of the crater that garnets, very resistant to erosion, were first found.

At the crest of the path we spread out and begin to scour the surface of the ground, looking at the sandy matrix between the scrubby plants. Almost at once we start to see small dark red nodules. These are the garnets. The word garnet comes either from the Middle English 'gernet' meaning dark red, or the Latin 'granatus' meaning grain, possibly a reference to Punica granatum, the pomegranate, a tree whose seeds, with a little imagination, are similar in shape, size and colour to some garnet crystals.

The majority of the garnets are between two and four millimetres across, some slightly larger. They are mostly euhedral, which means they have sharp, clearly-recognised faces, though some are more rounded. Our friends' son Archie is intrigued but maybe not more so than we adults. After an hour we've collected quite a haul. I have since been told that, strictly speaking, it is illegal to remove garnets from this site. Under the louring sky and cool wind, we've had enough for one day. It's time to head into Níjar to celebrate the successful treasure hunt with coffee and tapas, and maybe an ice-cream for Archie.

The garnets, I learn, make up almost 1% of the volcanic rock. They were present in schists deep below the volcano which were carried upwards during the period of volcanic activity. There are many types of garnets in the world. The ones at the Hoyazo de Níjar are of the almandine variety, with the composition (for any chemists reading this) $Fe_3Al_2(SiO_4)_3$. When garnets form well-shaped crystals they are used as semi-precious jewels. That is not the case here, though some are faceted and attractive, but the almandine garnets have a high resistance to erosion and a hardness on Mohs scale of 7.0 to 7.5, making them ideal for industrial uses in sandpaper, abrasive wheels, and so on. Apparently cabinet makers also favour garnet paper for finishing bare wood.

In the early 20th century garnet exploitation was important here, peaking in 1933 before declining. Then in 1996, for a few years, before it finally proved uneconomic, a private company called Garnetkao S.L. restarted exploitation. The process involved collecting the garnet-rich sand, screening it, separating it magnetically, then washing and crushing the garnets to produce an abrasive powder.

My source for this information is a paper by three Spanish geologists on the internet which says: 'The end product is an 80-mesh garnet-rich powder, and the average yield was estimated at 6t/day.' From this I gather that they are saying that about 6 tonnes of garnets were processed each day. Now, the garnets are heavy but very small, so I weighed 100 gm of the garnets we collected then counted them: there were 550 individual stones. On this basis 6 tonnes would comprise thirty three million garnets. This seems an astronomical haul *per day* but I think my maths is correct. It indicates how prolific the garnet deposit is at Hoyazo de Níjar.

As a final note my friend Joe Evans tells me he has also found clear white crystals at the same location. He described them as looking just like shards of broken windscreen but a collector has told him they are white sapphires. As far as I know he hasn't cashed them in yet.

Ruta Teresa

Another walk, again in the heart of the Sierra Cabrera. From the appointed meeting place, Turre's main square, after the usual amount of hanging around whilst people turn up, Javi roars off in his

4WD. We are ready and follow him, along with a couple of other vehicles. He takes the old road west out of the town, roars through El Cortijo Grande taking no prisoners, and continues, climbing the twisty mountain road into the Sierra Cabrera for another three kilometres. He seems oblivious to the sparse nature of the convoy behind him, despite the fact that thirty walkers had assembled in the square.

We finally stop by a recently-erected information board announcing the Ruta Teresa. Javi is the man who has been way-marking walking routes in the Sierra Cabrera, devising the routes and carrying and installing the wooden posts that mark them. After some time, more vehicles arrive, helped by the fact that one of them is driven by Eduardo Sánchez, another of the locals who knows these mountains inside out. Meanwhile I'm looking on map 1031-II Turre to establish exactly where we are.

By 10 o'clock we are at last ready to roll. Actually, we have already come a couple of hundred metres along a track, curving round a hillock, and we're looking down on a large, isolated ruined building. Its roof has gone but its walls remain tall and solid. A black wheatear flits around the nearby rocks as Eduardo launches into a detailed explanation.

This is La Ermita de Teresa, built by Christians in 1505 on the site of a mosque. There had been a major Muslim settlement here. Above where the chapel is there are caves and fragments of old walls dotting the slopes, but there is little left to see now. There was far more water here in those times, says Eduardo, and the Muslims focussed on the rearing of silkworms.

By the time he has finished, the final stragglers are with us. We follow the track down into the *rambla* and find another information board just below the chapel ruin which towers dramatically above it. This board says that the villages at Teresa and Cabrera may have been settled as long ago as the eighth century and certainly pre-date the founding of Turre. Teresa is now totally depopulated and Cabrera, about three kilometres away, is now a high-end 'Moorish-style' settlement occupied primarily by British incomers. The villages were founded here because at that time they had reliable sources of water and the mountains afforded protection from marauding pirates.

Today, we don't even walk the few metres up the slope to have a close look at the ruin. A few of the party stroll the short distance to the waterfall, currently dry. Beautifully sculpted rocks, polished by water and just a few metres high, gleam in the sun and show where a cascade forms after heavy rain. No sign of water now, though. Back in the other direction along the *rambla*, Javi's off. Pink-flowering oleanders add a dash of colour to the grey gravel of the dry riverbed, which curves round below a huge craggy face. The path squeezes through a rocky cleft, twisting steeply down. A few steps take us across the notch and we gain the almost level line of an old Moorish irrigation channel. It too is dry but provides easy going, albeit rather narrow in places, with a steep drop-off to the left. The valley below the rocky notch we have negotiated is widening out. The continuation of the *rambla* lies some way below, fringed on one side by tall pines.

Shortly we clamber down another sharp slope and regain the *rambla*. This is the Rambla de las Chosas. About three kilometres downstream, if there can be a downstream in a dry riverbed, it decants into the Río de Aguas at Llano del Pino. It's easier going again now, virtually level. Among the pines lining the left side of the *rambla*, odd ones are burnt. How could some have caught fire and not others? On the right side are pomegranate trees, with vivid waxy scarlet flowers. Somewhere nearby, a golden oriole's song comes across the air, a delicate fluting. Corn buntings are singing too, a noise frequently likened to the rattling of a bunch of keys. Various ruins dot the sides of the increasingly wide valley. This was also part of the settlement of Teresa, once the largest village in the Sierra Cabrera.

As the *rambla* opens out, we climb up across the left side of the valley, passing close to the extensive ruins of Cortijo Teresa, a farm thought to date from about 1840. There's no obvious path. We just more or less follow those who are ahead of us. High on the south side of the valley a line of cliffs forms the horizon. The map has these as Loma del Colorado, the Red Hill. We've forgotten our binoculars but we can just make out two large raptors playing in the air currents, landing and taking off, swooping around each other. Bonelli's eagles, I suspect.

We continue to angle up the slope then begin to curve round to the left. By now we can see that half of our party has been following an obvious vehicle track that mirrors our route but is considerably lower and easier. This, I think, is the signposted route. On the other hand, it's longer. After a while we veer down and intercept the others. By now, a general murmuring and chuntering among the crowd is indicating hunger. It's midday, after all. The word goes out that we are heading for the *algarrobos*, the carob trees. That's where we'll have *desayuno*, breakfast.

Breakfast? We had ours at half past eight. Now we want lunch. The carefully constructed egg and tomato sandwiches we're carrying eagerly await our attention. The group is now reunited on an easy track and sets off again at a brisk pace. In fact the whole walk has been at a brisk pace. Apart from a spoken contribution each from Eduardo and Javi at the beginning there have been no stops to rest, explore, rehydrate or ask questions. The track weaves on, with extensive views north-west across an undulating landscape. At last we see a couple of carobs ahead and soon we're able to sink into their welcome shade. We've been towards the back of the straggling file though, so before we've really finished our 'snap', the group is up and setting off again.

We pass above the buildings of the Cortijo Ortiz, with goat pens nearby under tall trees in the Barranco del Azogador. Shortly our track drops into this same *rambla* and continues in the dry riverbed, heading pretty much due south. Apart from the heat, this provides easy going for a further one and a half kilometres, where we come on the leaders waiting in the shade again for the scattered walkers to regroup.

A further track, with clear red and white flashes on a waymark post, begins to climb, twisting up in an easterly direction. The occasional tiny patch of shade is thrown by an adjacent tree but it's a gruelling climb under this sun, one bend following another in a seemingly endless upward progression. Eduardo's medium-sized dog, which he rescued 14 years ago, is struggling. He picks it up and puts it like a scarf around his neck. The dog has enough energy to celebrate this by wagging its tail enthusiastically, batting Eduardo round the ears in the process.

At the top of the climb the group again gradually gathers, in the shade of pines this time. We are now back very close to the road. How much further, someone asks. The usual answer comes back from

Javi, about a kilometre. In fact, a few metres away by the road, a newish signpost, quite possibly erected by Javi himself, indicates with remarkable precision that Teresa is 2,352 metres away. Fortunately it is almost all downhill, this final stretch on tarmac, during which, typically for this remote mountain road, virtually no vehicles pass us. A prominent notice announces that €1,361,672, of which 70% has come from the EU, has been spent to restore the environments damaged in the fires of 2009. Given the lack of rain for weeks now and the tinder-dry nature of the vegetation again, it's a sobering thought as we plod these final kilometres.

26. Exploring the maps

'To conclude, some, for one purpose and some for another, liketh, loveth, getteth and useth Mappes.'
(John Dee, 1570)

Spanish maps

As mentioned in the introduction, the Spanish equivalent of the British Ordnance Survey map is the Mapa Topográfico Nacional de España at a scale of 1:25,000. To an eye raised on OS maps, Spanish maps take some getting used to. The nature of the land on my local sheet, 1031-IV, El Llano de Don Antonio, which is primarily the strongly dissected terrain of the Sierra Cabrera mountain range, means that the map is an endlessly complex scribble of contour patterns with twisting brown lines stacked up at ten metre vertical intervals towards the peaks. The highest summit of the Sierra Cabrera, Cerro de la Mezquita, 962 m, just makes it onto this map, less than a centimetre from the top, with close contours showing a slope falling away steeply to the south. Contours don't change over time but many other features do and the sheet in question, reprinted in a second edition in 2002, is based on photogrammetric flights in 1998, so the data is already a decade and a half old. Generally, it seems, Spanish maps are not updated with great frequency.

A feature of Spanish maps that is alien to British map-readers is the presence of shading and symbols to indicate a wide variety of land-use. The map key for *Usos del Suelo* (Land-use) has thirty separate categories, so careful study of the map will reveal if an area is *bosque frondoso* (broadleaf woodland), *arrozales* (ricefields, of which there are none round here), *viña con frutales* (vineyards with fruit trees), *lava* (lava, listed amongst the *terrenos incultivables* - uncultivable land) and so on. Each Mapa Topográfico is small and manageable. Perusing one, if you were to invest the modest purchase price (€4.50 at the time of writing), is instructive and entertaining.

These maps are available in Almería city and also, sometimes and rather unpredictably, in some other shops in the province. The official source in Almería is the Instituto Geográfico Nacional, Camino de la Sismológica 26, 04008 Almería. This branch of the IGN is actually in the building of the Laboratorio Geofisico y Sismológico. Its phone number is 950 759 210 and it is open between 08.30 and 14.30 on ordinary working days.

As regards tracking down particular maps, the easiest way to do this is online, as follows. Go to www.ign.es then choose *Información de Compra* from the menu at the top of the page. Click on this and then choose *Catálogo de Productos* from the drop-down list. You will now see a menu on the left-hand side. Click on *Series Cartográficos.* This produces another drop-down menu, from which you should choose *Serie 25 y Serie 50* (this is referring to the 1:25,000 and 1:50,000 scale maps). A map of Spain then appears. On this map, click on Andalucía. This brings up a more detailed map, overlain with all the sheet numbers of the maps. You can navigate with the arrows at the edge of this map. Then if, for example, you live in Lubrín and you want to find your local map, click on that location. You will see that map number 1014 is shown. This is the number of the 1:50,000 sheet and its four component 1:25,000 scale sheets are shown as follows: 1014-1 Albanchez, 1014-2 Cuevas del Almanzora, 1014-3 Lubrín and 1014-4 Vera. In this way it is relatively simple to track down your local map. Incidentally, it seems that the IGN has been updating its numbering system, moving on from Roman numerals so that what, for example, was formerly sheet 1030-III Tabernas is now sheet 1030-3 Tabernas and so on. It is also possible to buy maps online by going back to *Información de Compra*, choosing *Como Comprar?* from the drop-down list and following the process indicated.

For several years I've had a few of the local maps in this series but recently I splashed out another fifty euros or so to extend my coverage. Since then I've had many a happy hour simply looking at the dozen new maps, scanning areas I don't know very well to see what I might learn. Random scrutiny, you could call it. This always produces curiosities such as those below.

Just inland from the coastal village of San Miguel de Cabo de Gata lies a strange pattern of circles and wriggling snake-like roads. The 1:25,000 map 1059-II Cabo de Gata provides the clue: Centro de Experimentación de Neumáticos. The whole complex, established by Michelin in 1973, now covers an area of 4,500 hectares, equivalent to about 17 square miles. Here all manner of tyres, from bicycle tyres weighing a couple of hundred grams to huge dumper tyres weighing five tonnes each, are tested on a 100 km long maze of tracks. Michelin chose the location for this, the largest tyre testing facility in the world, because of the minimal rainfall and predictable temperatures. Its official entrance is on the road running west from Ruescas and though it is used for various long-running scientific projects by, for example, biologists, it is off-limits to the general public.

Another striking road pattern occurs north of Velefique (sheet 1013-III Velefique) in the Sierra de los Filabres. The ALP-405, heading ultimately for Bacares, performs a series of astonishing contortions. This is the Alto de Velefique where the road climbs more than one vertical kilometre, from 820 to 1860 metres, in just 13 kilometres. The average gradient is almost 8% with a maximum slope of 11%. White-painted names and slogans on the road indicate that this climb is a favourite with the organisers of cycle races, though the map alone would of course not tell you this.

A quite different but equally strange feature stretches in a wide swathe for several kilometres south south-east from the small town of Macael. The woodland that covers most of this map (1013-II Macael) is noticeably absent from this part and the contours swirl and writhe in chaotic patterns. The clue is there in the words Canteras de Macael; these are the marble quarries for which the town is renowned. The area can be seen close-up from the A-349 that climbs south from Macael, up past the quarries into the Sierra de los Filabres.

Back on the coast or rather, just inland, a left turn from the road between El Pozo de los Frailes and La Isleta del Moro leads to the small hamlet of Presillas Bajas. Just over one kilometre north of Presillas Bajas the 1:25,000 map (1060-I El Pozo de los Frailes) shows a distinctly circular arrangement of contours, like a steep-sided bowl, broken only on the west side where an intermittent stream beginning in the bowl appears to have eroded its way out. This is the extinct volcanic cone of Majada Redonda, which can be accessed by an easy signposted walk, the *Sendero de la Caldera de Majada Redonda*, via the *rambla* from Presillas Bajas. This is a very worthwhile stroll into the heart of the Natural Park during which you are unlikely to meet anyone else.

One final observation on the 1:25,000 maps: if you are a resident of Mojácar, your local sheet, 1032-I Mojácar, represents very poor value. This is simply because both the old village, the *pueblo*, and the newer development along the *playa* are at the far left edge of the map; all the remainder, well over 80%, is occupied by the uniform pale blue shading of the Mediterranean Sea.

A map of the Cabo De Gata-Níjar Parque Natural

Some specialised maps of specific areas, such as those produced by the Junta de Andalucía of the Natural Parks in its care, are excellent. Specifically for eastern Almería, there is the 1:45,000 scale map of the Cabo de Gata-Níjar Parque Natural, two-sided, on tough, waterproof paper. Published in 2005, it's a gem, with a rich array of detail. North of the Centro Experimental de Michelin begins a sprawling rash of mauve blocks, spreading as you go further north until they almost entirely surround the towns of San Isidro de Níjar and Campohermoso. These are the *invernaderos*, the industrial greenhouses which have brought enormous wealth to some people in the area. Other symbols, such as those for petrol stations, *aljibes* (water tanks), old quarries, and even the vivid red for settlements of all sizes, make the map very clear and easy to read. The colour-shading for different types of land-use helps sharpen the patterns too.

Coming back to those old quarries, they are scattered across the map but one thing we are not told is what specifically was being quarried at each one. Many different minerals have been dug out of the ground in eastern Almería over the centuries. The stories of iron ore at Lucainena and gold at Rodalquilar are told elsewhere in these pages. Generally, the product of many of these old quarries remains unclear but on another map, which came with one of the small Cabo de Gata guidebooks, where only some quarries are marked and most of them are simply noted as *abandonada*, there are a few quarries labelled 'Mina de Bentonita *(a cielo abierto)'*. These are opencast (*'a cielo abierto'*) bentonite mines.

One that is still operating is the Cantera de Los Trancos between Agua Amarga and Fernán Pérez. There's never seemed to be much activity at the quarry when I've passed but many low piles of white clay with just a tinge of pale green flank the road. When I first saw these I'd never heard of bentonite but the internet can be a wonderful thing and I now know it's basically a type of clay formed by the alteration of volcanic rocks. Greasy to the touch and very plastic, bentonite has the useful property of being able to absorb a quantity of water several times greater than its own volume. As a result it is an integral part of drilling mud, it's added to cement for certain purposes, it is used to prepare moulds in smelting and it's even used as a clarifier of wines and oils. My friend Pete Adeline, a talented potter, read this section and sent me this additional information: 'Bentonite is also an essential additive to almost all ceramic glazes. A tiny amount added reduces settling of glaze particles and has other benefits. Incidentally, some people ingest bentonite to give their bowels a special clear-out.' Thanks, Pete; almost too much information there.

The Junta de Andalucía Natural Park map has something I've rarely seen on a general-use map before: four different colour codes for offshore areas of submarine Praderas de Fanerógamas y Algas Marinas (Grasslands of Seed-bearing Plants and Seaweeds). One of these colour codes shows that the Cabo de Gata coast is particularly important for Neptune grass, a sea grass species endemic to the Mediterranean which forms large underwater meadows. Its presence indicates a lack of pollution and it is part of a rich habitat important as a rearing ground for young fish.

This 1:45,000 map is superb in terms of presentation, durability and user-friendliness, by far the best type of map I've come across in Spain. What a pity such fine maps aren't available for the whole country.

Place names

One key to interpreting Spanish maps is to know the meaning of the basic place name elements. In the mountains you will very frequently find *cerro* (hill), as well as *loma* (hill or hillside), *peña* or *peñon* (rocky outcrop or pinnacle), *puerto* (pass), *rincón* (corner), *rellana* (flat area on a slope or on high ground), *cuesta* (slope leading up a hill), *alto* (high ground), *risco* (crag), *cueva* (cave) and *fuente* (spring). *Collado* can mean hill but more usually refers to a pass between hills or mountains. *Pago* means place or something like 'neck of the woods'. *Cañada* means gully or ravine but can also refer

240

to a track for livestock. To know which meaning is appropriate, other clues on the map should make it clear which applies in a particular place. In less hilly areas you may find *llano* (a plain or flat ground) and *prado* (meadow). On the coast the best known place name element, which even casual foreign tourists know, is *playa* (beach). Then there are *punta* (point or headland), *cala* (cove) and *ensenada* (inlet or, again, cove).

The hand of man gives us a few more terms such as *huerta* (vegetable or market garden), *puente* (bridge), *cortijo* (not directly translatable but more or less 'farmstead'), *cortijada* (more or less 'farming hamlet') and *molino* (mill). Once you know a few of these basics, and with the aid of a good dictionary, Spanish maps begin to give up their secrets.

Many place-names are straightforward but still carry information, about trees and past and present human activities, for example. Names are often simply descriptive of the landscape and there are plenty of these on the maps of eastern Almería. To avoid breaking up the text too much I won't give grid references in this section. There's a Rambla Honda, a name that always sounds quite exotic to me, near Lucainena and there's another near Lubrín. It has nothing to do with Japanese cars but simply means Deep Dry Riverbed. Confusion may arise, as these examples show, because a name is not necessarily exclusive to one place. In contrast to Rambla Honda, between Moras and El Fonte there is a Rambla Ancha (Wide Dry Riverbed). Lots of other names are equally straightforward: Cerro de la Piedra Blanca (Hill of the White Stone), north-east of Cariatiz; Las Cuevas Frías (The Cold Caves), west of Mizala; and La Huerta Nueva (The New Vegetable Garden) and Cerro Redondo (Round Hill), just south of Los Gallardos. La Herrería (The Smithy) is clear enough, but La Herradura (The Horseshoe) refers not always to the same line of work but sometimes to the shape of the landscape. Hidden away in the folds of the Sierra Alhamilla, west of Níjar, is a place that pulls no punches, a hamlet called La Matanza (The Slaughter), the name used throughout rural Spain for the traditional annual pig-killing.

There is simple description of the vegetation too, such as El Chaparral and Los Chaparrales (scrub or thicket), a few kilometres south of Tahal. In the Sorbas area are Las Avellanas (Hazelnuts), Los Castaños (Chestnut Trees) and Los Algarrobos (The Carob Trees), the former two harking back to when the climate in this area was less harsh.

Other names are more puzzling: Cortijo de la Cueva Ahumada (Farm of the Smoky Cave); Cortijo de Boqueras (Farm of the Warders or Cold Sores...). And what about Cruz del Rojo (Cross of the Red... maybe something political such as Crossroads Where the Lefties used to Meet)? And, five kilometres west south-west of Níjar, Alto de Narices (High Ground of Noses). The coastline provides plenty of quirks too, with Punta de la Media Naranja (Half Orange Point), Playa de los Muertos (Beach of the Dead), Cala los Toros (Cove of the Bulls) and Arrecife de las Sirenas (Mermaid's Reef).

Then there are people whose names have passed on to the maps. Just south of Turre, in the Sierra Cabrera are Cerro del Judío (The Jew's Hill), Risco del Moro (The Moor's - as in North African's - Crag) and Diente de la Vieja (Old Woman's Tooth). Also near Turre is Llano del Gitano (Gypsy's Plain). North Africans appear again five km north-west of Níjar at Umbría del Moro (Shady Place of the Moor). The name Los Zurdos (The Left-handed People) appears on a mountainous part of the Sierra Cabrera to the north-east of Peñas Negras, though not apparently linked to any kind of settlement. We have friends who live at Los Guapos (The Good-looking People) near Lubrín, whereas we've never met the folk who live at Cortijada los Feos (Hamlet of the Ugly People) near Venta del Pobre. Down along the coast lies the celebrated Playa de los Genoveses (Beach of the Genoese, referred to elsewhere). Further west and inland, just alongside the old drove-road, the Vereda de Lubrín, lies the Corral de Juan Cipriano (Juan Cipriano's Livestock Pen). Among my favourites are, just outside Sorbas, the Cortijo de Paco el Americano (the Farm of Frank the American) and, a few kilometres south-west of Níjar, the Camino de la Cuesta de Juan Grande (the Path of Big John's Slope).

Maps record wildlife too. Loma de la Vibora (Hill of the Viper) is not far from Sorbas. Just south of the old film-set Parque Oasys, near Tabernas, is Barranco del Grillo (Ravine of the Cricket) and how about Cerro del Piojo (Hill of the Louse), two kilometres north-east of El Real near Vera? Rabbits feature at Rincón del Conejo (Rabbit's Corner) in the hilly wilds on the Arroyo de Verdelecho map, at Rincón de los Conejos near Mojácar and again, three km west of Níjar, at Cerro de los Conejos. Two km north of this Hill of the Rabbits is Cerro de la Fuente de Pavón (Hill of the Spring of the Peacock, more likely the butterfly than the bird, I suspect). Immediately above the village of Bayarque in the Filabres is Alto de la Peña de la Zorra, (something like the High Crag of the Vixen). *Zorra* can also mean whore but that is presumably not the meaning here.

As mentioned in another chapter the nearest wild wolves are now 200 kilometres away in the Sierra Morena but there is plenty of map evidence to suggest that they were once widespread here. Barranco de los Lobos (Ravine of the Wolves) is near Sorbas. The twin-topped hill south of Gafarillos is Cerro de los Lobos (Hill of the Wolves). Just to the east of that hill is the once abandoned village of Los Loberos (The Wolf-hunters) and a few kilometres south of Los Loberos is El Salto del Lobo (The Wolf's Leap). Finally, as far as wolves are concerned, ten kilometres west of Níjar is Cerro de la Fuente del Lobo (Hill of the Spring of the Wolf).

As mentioned in another chapter (Coasting: Beyond the Amethyst), when *lobo* appears at the coast, as at Torre de los Lobos, the reference is to *lobos marinos*, monk seals. This no doubt is also the case at Mojácar, where Playa Cueva del Lobo will be Beach of the Monk Seal's Cave.

Birds, especially the bigger and more obvious species, are represented too. Eagles are a favourite. There's the straightforward El Aguila (The Eagle), a kilometre south of Alfaix; Cerro (Hill) del Aguila and Alto (High Ground) de Aguila on the Verdelecho map; Risco (Crag) del Aguila six km west north-west of Carboneras and so on. Just south of Uleila del Campo is Vereda de los Aguileras (District of the Eyries). A hill called El Búho (Eagle Owl) lies three km north-west of Tabernas, with the Fuente (Spring) del Búho and Rambla del Búho nearby, whilst three km south-west of Macael is Piedra del Halcón (The Falcon's Stone). Down on the coast is Cala del Cuervo (Cove of the Raven).

Smaller birds do get a look in occasionally. On the Lucainena map there is Piedra de las Golondrinas (Stone of the Swallows). Just south-east of Tabernas is Los Abejarucos (The Bee-eaters). Two km north-east of El Pozo de los Frailes lies Cerro del Mochuelo (Hill of the Little Owl) and six km west of Agua Amarga El Mochuelo appears again. Hoya de la Perdiz (The Partridge's Hollow) is on the Uleila sheet. Pigeons inevitably show up too. Four kilometres south of Turre is Majada de las Palomas (Flock of Pigeons) and a similar distance south-west of Antas lies the Cañada de las Palomas (Gully of the Pigeons).

On the move

Striking south-westwards from the north-eastern corner of the Los Yesos map (Sheet 1030-II) and roughly parallel to the AL-3325 road is a double-pecked line labelled *Cordel de Ganados* (literally 'Rope of Livestock'), accompanied by the symbol used for a *vía pecuaria*, a traditional drove-road. It has clearly come from Uleila, which is a couple of kilometres beyond the edge of the map. Where the *cordel* reaches the AL-3325 it crosses and continues in the same direction, labelled now as the Camino Viejo de Uleila ('The Old Way From Uleila'). Then, just to the north of this camino is a whole network of others, the Camino del Vicario (The Vicar's Way), Camino del Pastor (Way of the Shepherd), ...de las Majadas (...of the Flocks) and so on.

Another Cordel de Ganados threads its way right across the Arroyo de Verdelecho map, joining Gergal, just off the map's western edge, cutting across the grain of the Sierra de los Filabres and strangely seeming to take little account of the difficult terrain, to pass the modern Central Solar de Almería, the solar research centre a few kilometres north of Tabernas. Here it seems to simply disappear from the map but a glance at the adjacent sheet suggests that, from its general direction, it would link up with the Camino Viejo de Uleila.

The Níjar map (sheet 1045-II) is another that is laced with old routeways. In the top left corner of the map the Camino de Turrillas threads along the crest of the Sierra Alhamilla. Many of the others, such as the Camino de Terrones (Path of the Lumps), the Camino del Cortijo de Acosta and the Camino de Talva are clearly leading down from the heights of the Sierra Alhamilla to the lower ground of the Campo de Níjar to the south. These would have been transhumance routes, used to move livestock between winter grazing on the lowlands and summer pastures in the mountains. Moving animals on foot was big business in the past. (For more on this see the chapters 'A historical perspective' and 'Lines on the landscape'.)

Alongside the older roads there used to be many wayside inns or *ventas*. Take the N340-a linking Almería to Puerto Lumbreras via Tabernas, for example. Far-sighted planners back in about 1890, when this road was made, planted many pines along it. As well as trees for shade, such roads once had many wayside stopping-places. If we follow the stretch from Los Gallardos westwards past Sorbas, we pass first the oddly-named Venta del Chocolate (Wayside Inn of the Chocolate) at Almocaizar, then the Venta los Castaños, at the eponymous hamlet. Next came the Venta de la Tencia (no obvious translation) which appears just south of the Cortijo el Aguarico on older maps but has vanished from the modern ones. Just before Sorbas was the Venta de la Viuda (Wayside Inn of the Widow); its name is still painted across the building but it has long been closed for business. On again beyond Sorbas there is the Venta Llana (...on the Plain), the Venta de la Mojonera (...of the Female Fibber?), the Venta del Viso (...of the Petticoat?), Venta de los Yesos (...Gypsum) and the Venta del Compadre (...Mate or Buddy). This latter is still going strong, a favourite with hunters. Its walls are liberally covered with the heads of slaughtered beasts. It seems to be in thrall to meat, this place; among its range of *tapas* (snacks), you will struggle to find many vegetarian options. There may be other *ventas* that have disappeared from maps and memories but already I've listed nine and, as we drive west, we haven't even reached Tabernas yet.

And not on the map...

Alongside the N-340a Sorbas-Tabernas road is a prominent race track, the Circuito de Almería. The circuit, 4.025 km long, with 13 turns and a back straight 900 metres in length, has become popular as a test facility with several major F1 and Moto GP (motorcycle) teams.

It puzzled me for some time that the circuit does not appear on the local 1:25,000 map. It used to be the case that military installations didn't appear on Ordnance Survey maps in the UK in the quaint belief that if they weren't shown on the map the enemy wouldn't know they were there. Maybe something similar occurs in Spain, I thought, but surely a racing circuit isn't a strategic target.

My mind was entertaining such bizarre possibilities when I stumbled on the solution to the mystery and it was simple. The Circuito de Almería opened only in 2001 and the most recent edition of the 1:25,000 map was published before that, in 2000, and would have been based on surveys from earlier still.

Atlas Almería

Maps of quite a different kind, lots of them, can be found in the Atlas Geográfico de la Provincia de Almería. I first saw this at a friend's house and couldn't believe it was only €30. Not exactly cheap, admittedly, but considering the fact that books in Spain are very expensive in general, this is astonishing value. With a combination of text, photos (including superb aerial imagery) and a huge variety of maps, this absorbing volume covers a wonderfully enlightening range of subjects: the first topographical map of Almería province in 1855; the night sky as seen from the Spanish/German observatory at Calar Alto; the coastline 6,000 years ago; the pattern of wind direction in the province; the threat of desertification; population distribution at different dates; the whereabouts of foreigners; the legacy of mining; esparto grass; grapes; intensive agriculture; the numbers of goats and pigs; marble production; the numbers of hotel beds; the different types of soil; Almería city from the air...

The Atlas Almería is a hefty, large-format hardback that also comes with a transparent overlay map with all 102 of Almería's *municipios* (administrative districts) marked, so you can easily check out exactly where your local area is on all of the major maps in the atlas, and a CD-Rom that contains all of the book's contents. In addition it includes a separate, full-colour 70 cm x 90 cm map of the province. The colour shading for height on this gives a superbly crisp visual sense of the shape of Almería's landscape and the way in which this determines the lines the main roads have had to take. Colour shading also shows the submarine contours, the blues deepening out from the coast as the floor of the Mediterranean falls away beyond the 1,000 metre mark. All in all an impressive package, and no, I am not on commission.

27. Lines on the landscape

'Humans and animals, seeking a route, are guided by the pre-configured habits of the terrain. These pedestrians create preferential pathways, which in turn attract the flow of subsequent pedestrians, all of whom etch the track of their passage with their feet as they go.'
(Robert Macfarlane)

Royal Roads

This chapter looks at how different types of routes have evolved to thread their way across the local landscape, particularly in the Sorbas area. The first parts will possibly be of interest mainly to social historians and map addicts. If this does not include you, feel free to skip ahead to the 'Autovía' section.

Eastern Almería has never been heavily populated but wherever there have been people there have been animals and this meant that a network of routes linked to farming, transport and commerce developed across the complex landscape of the area. Now though, this network of old routes is abandoned and at serious risk of disappearing.

Caminos reales were the most important of the pre-modern routes. The term 'royal road' is perhaps the closest we can get to a translation of *camino real,* which refers to any 'road' under the direct jurisdiction of the Spanish crown.

Often dry riverbeds such as that of the Río de Aguas near Sorbas provided the most convenient routes. However, the narrow and steep passages at El Tesoro and at Los Molinos, with ravines, huge tumbled blocks obstructing the streambed, flooded areas, glutinous mud and dense stands of *caña*, meant that the most important paths, including the *caminos reales*, sometimes had to find other ways.

The routes played a crucial role in commerce, for example by allowing distribution of wares from the Sorbas potters' quarter, by serving to transport processed gypsum from the kilns to its destination and by allowing farmworkers to get to the weekly market to sell surplus produce from their vegetable plots. Horses went with grain from the gypsum plateau down to the mills along the course of the Río de Aguas, then back with their consignments of flour.

Livestock also used these paths as part of the longer transhumance network between the summer grazing in highlands like the Sierra de Segura and the coastal wintering quarters of the Campo de Níjar. The routes were also used by the dealers and pedlars of Sorbas and Lubrín who periodically travelled to the Campo de Níjar.

Caminos reales linked the larger towns and were passable in carriages. Two of them, one linking Vera and Almería and the other connecting Vera and Sorbas, cut through the area that now forms the Paraje Natural de Karst en Yesos de Sorbas. Early information about them comes from Tomás López's Diccionario Geográfico of 1774.

Vera to Almería

An interesting section of the Vera-Almería camino real can be followed on the 1:25,000 maps 1031-II Turre, 1031-I Sorbas and 1031-III Polopos. The route came via La Huelga (in square 587108 on the Turre sheet), of which López says 'to its north, a rifle shot away, is the bed of the Río de Aguas'. The camino real followed the riverbed to La Herrería and on to Los Perales (square 584105 on the Sorbas sheet). Just by the mill at Los Perales the road left the riverbed, passed in front of the Venta de Honor and climbed the Cuesta de Honor, described by López as 'a very bad slope for carriages' and so reached Campico de Honor (square 585102 on the Polopos sheet).

The modern map shows that this slope climbs from 210m above sea level at Los Perales to 340m at the top of the Cuesta de Honor. The straight line distance between the two points is much less than a kilometre. The modern minor road that takes the same line only manages the climb by making a very twisting, convoluted ascent.

Folk-memory has it that Queen Isabella La Católica travelled via the camino real towards the end of the 15th century. The queen is said to have spent a night at the venta (wayside inn) near Los Perales. This has now been rather over-enthusiastically turned into a modern house. Whilst the queen was at the inn the women of the district gathered to present her with a bouquet of flowers to show how honoured they were by her presence. From then onwards the Venta, the Cuesta and El Campico (that is the inn, the steep slope up from Los Perales, and the small hamlet) were allowed to add 'de Honor' to their names in recognition of the episode.

The *camino real* passed alongside the *aljibe viejo* (the old water cistern), which disappeared during the construction of the motorway in the early 1990s. The only clue to this now is the name Llano del Aljibe adjacent to the motorway (584104), a kilometre and a half north north-west of Campico. From there the *camino* went via Peñas Negras (585101), also known as Los Ventorrillos according to the old folk. In fact this name, Los Ventorrillos, appears on the map midway between Campico and Peñas Negras, attached to an undulating area of fruit trees and scrub. In reality the wayside inn was at Peñas Negras itself, as López makes reference to a hostelry at this point. The name Peñas Negras, meaning Black Crags, refers to the dark ferruginous stone formerly quarried there.

From there the route dropped into the *rambla* again, as far as the Cortijo de Los Arejos (585098). Lopez calls this place Los Hanejo, a name now lost from the map, and mentions that there was also an inn here. Today the intriguing complex of buildings at Los Arejos, with arches and a fetching triangular dovecot window (see the chapter 'Threshing circles and pigeon lofts'), all set off by the sway of nearby palms, is abandoned and crumbling, trapped between the motorway and the old main road. A little beyond Los Arejos, at Collado de Almería, the *camino real* passed into the adjacent municipality of Lucainena, heading on for Venta del Pobre and Almería.

This route lost much of its traffic with the construction of the 'new' road from Almería to Puerto Lumbreras in 1890 (now the N-340a), which diverted traffic via Tabernas and Sorbas. The final abandonment of the old *camino real* came when the road from Sorbas to Venta del Pobre (the A-1102) was finished in 1960, thus improving access to the Campo de Níjar from the east. In part, the natural line of the *camino real* was later re-used by the Autovía del Mediterráneo which cuts almost parallel to, and in places just a few metres away from, the old *camino* across the Campo de Níjar.

Vera to Sorbas

The second *camino real* in the area linked Vera and Sorbas. The first mention of this route is in the Libro de Apeo de Sorbas in 1573 but again, more detailed information comes from Tomás López's Diccionario Geográfico two centuries later. Tracing this route east to west, the Vera-Sorbas royal road coincided in its eastern section with the Vera-Almería route, diverging from it just after La Huelga.

At that point it climbed steeply out from the bed of the Río de Aguas up onto the Los Yesares plateau close to the now deserted village of Marchalico-Viñicas (square 585107 on the Sorbas sheet). From there it went across the gypsum plateau, crossing the vertical notch of the Barranco del Tesoro on the Puente de la Mora.

The Puente de la Mora is a cultural gem, still impressive even though now sadly degraded. What remains is an elegant stone arch with tall straight sides and the remains of higher buttresses on either side of the ravine. The buttresses are all that remain of the original second tier with three arches, all now gone. In its original form the bridge was 26.4 metres long, 3.3 metres wide and over 13 metres above the bed of the *barranco* (ravine). It must have been very impressive. Astonishingly, despite being one of the finest fragments of history in the area, the bridge is not marked or named on the 1:25,000 map. Of the surrounding area, López says it: 'is composed entirely of stones of gypsum' in which are 'various potholes of incalculable depth and of no small danger to passers-by who ignore them.' He is referring here to dolines (see the chapter 'Sorbas and the Gypsum Karst' for more on this).

Beyond the Puente de la Mora the *camino* passed very close to the now ruinous Cortijo los Yesares (583107) and then near the Cortijo del Hoyo (581107) it rejoined the Río de Aguas riverbed and continued along this to reach the pottery quarter in Sorbas. This route also was no longer used after the Almería-Puerto Lumbreras road, the N-340a, was completed in the late 19th century.

Bridleways

As well as the *caminos reales*, the 'A' roads of their time, there were numerous bridleways threading through eastern Almería province, passable only by pedestrians, horses and mules. They linked smaller villages and hamlets or led out to areas of cultivated land. Many of these lesser paths have been virtually forgotten, with only the faintest traces remaining. What follows focusses again on the Sorbas district; even in that small area there was a complex web of minor routes, of which I'm mentioning just a few.

A bridleway from Cariatiz to El Tesoro coincided closely with the Via Pecuaría Vereda de Lubrin, 'the Drove Road from Lubrin'. Close attention to sheet 1031-1 makes it easy to follow the route, which went south-east from Los Alias (580111) via the Cortijo de los Yepes (582111). This substantial farmhouse once belonged to the Soler family who owned silver and lead mines in the Sierra Almagrera. From los Yepes the path continued south south-east by Cruz del Rojo (582109), crossing the line of the modern N-340a to pass the Corral de Juan Cipriano en route to the Cortijo Los Yesares (583107), then south and down the Cuesta del Gato to El Tesoro (583105).

From Cariatiz to Marchalico Viñicas and La Herrería, another bridleway initially coincided with the one described above, before following the line of the modern tarmac road south-east to cross the N-340a at grid reference 58331104. It then skirted the southern boundary of the enormous gypsum quarry along what nowadays is a very drivable track across the heart of Los Yesares plateau to the abandoned houses at Marchalico-Viñicas. From there the way plunges down to cross the motorway and so reach La Herrería. This latter part is not always drivable, as a friend of ours found out when his jeep grounded in a particularly vicious gully that runoff had incised into the surface.

One of the longer links was the ancient *camino* between Carboneras and Sorbas. Coming from Carboneras the path entered Sorbas district via Los Alamillos on the Río Alías then ascended past Cortijada Los Feos (in square 586097 on sheet 1031-III) to Los Arejos. This stretch, now a vehicle-width road, was resurfaced in 2009, thus becoming much more easily passable. At Los Arejos it joined the Vera-Almería *camino real* as far as Peñas Negras. From there it went to the east of Los Alpañeces (582101), mounted the *cuesta* (slope) of Mizala to the west of El Cerrón which, incidentally, at 602 m is a superb viewpoint, accessed without much difficulty via a track from the A-1102. It then passed to the west of the Cortijo del Peral (580104) in the direction of the Barranco del Infierno where it linked to the Hueli-Sorbas path. Near the Fuente del Peral constant wear by horses has scored the line of this path into the bedrock. After crossing the Río de Aguas it passed the gates of the cemetery on the last leg of its way into Sorbas.

Hannah Geetsema and Maarten van Lier have a house in Los Molinos adjacent to one of the old bridleways. Maarten showed me, with some pride, how he keeps his stretch of this sunken routeway clear of vegetation for the occasional passer-by. Hanna meanwhile said: "Diego told me that, when he was young - he's 88 or 89 now - he used to sit by this track. They called it the *camino major* or the *camino Campico* and he recalls seeing, every Sunday, *'más de cien caballerías para ir al mercado in Sorbas'*." I think this is the same Diego who appears in the chapter 'The road of 100 bends'. So, to translate, he used to see over a hundred people on horseback or with donkeys, going to the Sunday market in Sorbas; back then these old tracks were so important.

Despite efforts by local enthusiasts such as Andrés Pérez Pérez, who has organised many walks for the Amigos de Sorbas along these old bridleways and *caminos*, there is a gradual leaching away of knowledge about them as they drift quietly back into history. In a generation or two the precise lines of many of these old ways will almost certainly be lost.

Drove-roads

Andrés Pérez Pérez and Ana María Rodríguez Agüero record in *El Afa* that the older people of the Sorbas area still recall numerous routes used to move livestock. Despite this, in an inventory compiled by the Ministry of Agriculture in the 1960s, the only local livestock route recognised was the Vereda de Lubrín. Its function was to allow the movement of livestock that came to winter on the coast of Almería from the far uplands of Baza, Huéscar, Galera and the Sierra de Segura. For centuries the plains of Almería were leased to stockbreeders for feeding their animals during the winter when, in the colder conditions, there was not enough grazing in the hills.

On sheet 1013-I an intermittent parallel pecked symbol makes the line of this old drove-road, the Vereda de Lubrín, easy to follow. It came through La Mela (579113), down the Rambla de Castaños to Cariatiz (580111) then, as described above, on to the Cortijo de Los Yepes, the Cruz del Rojo, the Cortijo Los Yesares and down the Cuesta del Gato to El Tesoro. From there it went to Los Perales and climbed the Cuesta de Honor to the Aljibe Viejo, which provided a watering-place for the animals. On again, it went via Peñas Negras and Los Arejos to the Campo de Níjar.

Associated with this drove-road there was a whole infrastructure of watering-places that used the water from the Covadura underground system. There were protective shelters too, which were usually caves. For example, in the late 18th century, Tomás López described the Cueva del Tesoro thus: 'Its capacity is admirable, they assure me that when it rains 400 head of livestock, with their shepherds, can get into it, without a single one getting wet.'

In the late 1990s, in an attempt to breathe new life into some of these old routes and boost the depleted local economy, Andrés Pérez Pérez, who was at that time a councillor, succeeded, with collaboration from Sorbas town hall, in way-marking the path from Los Molinos del Río de Aguas along the *acequia*, the Moorish water channel, to El Nacimiento. This path formed part of what was christened the Sendero de la Mora, a 38 km long circular route starting from the Centro de Visitantes Los Yesares in Sorbas and covering much of the Sorbas and Karst en Yesos district.

Autovía

In an early issue of the journal *El Afa*, the Amigos de Sorbas published 'before and after' photos of the Barranco del Tesoro. In a 1990 photo, an incised meander of the Río de Aguas has chiselled deep into the gypsum, carving vertical bare cliffs above which perches a cluster of still solid-looking ruins among the shrub-clad slopes. Humans have made their mark - the old houses and a hint of terracing on the shadowed slopes behind - but it's clearly nature that has the upper hand. In those days, Lindy Walsh tells us, when she first came to live at Urrá, just a few kilometres away, a pair of Bonelli's eagles nested in the canyon. Then the motorway came.

From the same viewpoint in 2002 the mountainous horizon in the far distance is identical. A green scrubby ridge with a bare patch angles in from the top left, just as it did twelve years earlier. But the ridge to the right of the picture has been cut back and dominating the whole photo is a huge, sweeping motorway, the Autovía del Mediterráneo, hefty concrete legs carrying it high above the ravine. The old ruins are still there, just visible beyond, and now below, the new road. The place is utterly transformed; it's no longer nature that holds sway. And the nesting Bonelli's are long gone.

Will The AVE Ever Run?

The latest major element in the continuing story of 'lines on the landscape' is the 184.4 km long Murcia-Almería section of the AVE (Alta Velocidad Española), Spain's high-speed train network. Work began on this in 2009 after several years of planning, discussion and wrangling about the precise route it would take. Inevitably it is imposing itself ruthlessly, crossing, slicing through, and obliterating sections of the ancient, more organic *caminos* and tracks. A date of 2014 was originally mentioned for the completion of the Murcia-Almería railway but there seems to be no chance of the entire section being ready any time soon.

The whole history of the AVE network has been controversial. In the early 1980s there was a widespread feeling that the first AVE line should connect Madrid and Barcelona but when the plans were revealed they were for a Madrid-Seville link. Barcelona is much more significant than Seville, both industrially and financially, so many thought that the choice of Seville for the first AVE might be not unconnected with the fact that Felipe González, the then Prime Minister, was from Seville, and that this was a decision more related to local prestige than hard-headed economics. The AVE too has often been criticised for proving extremely costly, at the expense of the existing rail infrastructure which those in the know say is crying out for investment in basic maintenance and improvement.

On the Murcia-Almería section, one of the main centres of activity has for some years been clearly visible from near junction 510 of the Autovía del Mediterráneo, close to the small village of La Herrería. Here the Sorbas Tunnel (it is in the municipality of Sorbas though some distance from the town) has burrowed through the Sierra Cabrera. It has been an impressive engineering feat. Two parallel tunnels, 7.63 km long and 26 metres apart, have been bored. The tunnels are almost straight, with an average downhill slope towards Almería of 12.5%. 19 transverse tunnels, one every 400 metres, have also been built for maintenance and emergencies.

The machine used to bore the tunnel (the TBM), a German-built S-373 Herrenknecht Double Shield owned by the Spanish government, is reputedly the fastest in the world. 'Double Shield' means that it can excavate and line the tunnel at the same time. The TBM had come down from its previous project in Asturias in 500 lorries to be reassembled at La Herrería and, to facilitate this, the formerly narrow road linking the village and the motorway was widened out of all proportion to its normal importance.

In effect the TBM is a series of separate but linked machines working together. Its 9.63 metre diameter cutter revolves at high speed, and behind this a 'lining segment erector' repeatedly fits together seven segments to form reinforced concrete rings. Each segment weighs nearly nine tonnes and the concrete rings, each linked to the next to form a watertight seal, are 1.6 metres wide and 50 cm thick.

Adjacent to the motorway near La Herrería a specially-built electricity sub-station provided the power for the TBM. At each end of the tunnel a factory was put up to produce the concrete ring segments. One was at La Herrería and the other was on high ground about 500 metres north-east of Venta del Pobre, and very visible from the A-7/E-15 motorway. The endless ranks of stacked concrete segments, now gone, were used at a rate of up to 60 per day. The 'factory' sites remain at the time of writing though and it will be interesting to see what ultimately happens there.

Most of the tunnel goes through conglomerate, marl and sand, although the final kilometre towards the southern end is through gypsum, anhydrites and dolomites with fault lines. At the southern mouth of the tunnel are black shales. This southern part of the tunnel was dug without the TBM due to the unstable nature of the geology. In late 2012 the tunnel was finished and soon afterwards, in December of that year, a 432 metre viaduct immediately south of the main tunnel was completed. Tests to check its structural soundness were carried out by a squadron of heavy trucks and were declared a total success.

As the rock was quarried by the circular cutter it was passed onto a conveyor belt, part of the overall TBM, which took it up to a nearby gantry from where lorries took it to various dumps. One is close to where the Polopos road branches off the Peñas Negras-Venta del Pobre road, the A-1103. Another is near the Gafares turn-off from the Venta del Pobre-Carboneras road, the N-341. A notice, visible for a while at least, by the former suggested these would be temporary features. Will they be smoothed and landscaped, producing new hills where none existed before? When a major gas pipeline was put through the same area a few years ago the subsequent landscaping was of exceptional quality and the vegetation, superficially at least, recovered quickly. If it were not for a series of small yellow markers, the innocent eye would not realise the ground had ever been disturbed.

Immediately north of the Sorbas Tunnel, the 8 km stretch of line to Los Gallardos also runs through an area with virtually no flat land, so it is an almost continuous sequence of bridges, embankments and cuttings. This includes six viaducts of which the one over the Río Jauto, 120 m long and carried on a single arch, is the most dramatic. The longest viaduct, at 534 m, is near the Rambla Almocaizar. These works, impressive on one level, have nevertheless carved a wide swathe across the countryside.

In the Sierra Cabrera constructing the tunnel entrances has involved slicing the sides off mountains and facing them with what appears to be concrete; bleak and ugly intrusions, though some will say it's an area that has already been sullied by the passage of the motorway which in most places is close to the line of the railway. This challenging feat of civil engineering has certainly blighted the lives of nearby residents over a period of several years, as attested to vehemently by people in La Herrería.

Despite the fact that work on some sections of the line was proceeding, in June 2012 the mayor of Almería city, Luis Rogelio Comendador, dropped something of a bombshell at a conference in Seville, saying that he was convinced that the AVE in Almería would not be completed during his legislature or the next, which means not until at least 2019. He said Almería council was "in no fit state" to invest the €300 million needed to build the underground AVE terminal in the city. At this stage, of the 13 separate stretches on the Murcia-Almería part of the AVE route, only four were under construction.

Soon after this, in August 2012, in an appendix to his translation of the book *A Todo Tren,* Don Gaunt, an authority on the railways of southern Spain, took a similar line. He explained that the world financial crisis has had a critical impact on Spain's AVE plans, with the 'Corredor Mediterráneo', which is designed to link France to Andalucía, having effectively run out of funds.

One suggestion has been that the final part of this route, towards Almería city, should follow the 'existing line' rather than carving out a new one. However, there *is* no existing railway line between Murcia and Almería, and anyway, the standard Spanish gauge is 1,668 mm or 5' 5⅔", whereas the AVE is being built to the international standard gauge, 1,435 mm or 4' 8½", so an extra rail would have to be installed to accommodate both systems. The plot thickens!

In October 2013 €100 million of state funding was announced for the AVE in 2014 but this would be solely for awarding contracts and obtaining licences. Thus that money will not see the AVE advance even a single centimetre and furthermore, no date has been set for re-starting the works, much less for completing the project. It remains eligible for EU funding during the period 2014-2020 but this is in the form of 'co-funding', which means that complementary funding must come from Spanish sources. In effect, the future of the AVE hinges on the Spanish government stumping up 80% of the cost of future engineering works in order to release the linked funds from Europe.

Whilst this information was being absorbed, further shocks came towards the end of 2013. A suggestion was floated that between Murcia and Almería there should be just a single AVE track. A feasibility study indicated that this would save 40% of the construction costs. It appeared to conveniently forget that the twin tunnels in Sorbas municipality had already been completed at a cost of €291 million and that the new plan would render one of them redundant. And quite how would timetabling work for trains running in both directions on a single track?

A further bombshell related to the promised intermediate station at Vera. Engineers from ADIF, the Spanish rail authority, claimed that the contract for the station (which had been placed in 2011 at a cost of €320,000) would be cancelled. An official spokesperson merely said the plans were being revised. Some people cheekily point out that the Vera station was sanctioned by the PSOE government of then Prime Minister Zapatero who just happened to own a house at Vera Playa. He has since sold it at a loss. One key aspect of the original rationale for an AVE station at Vera linked it to well-publicised plans a decade ago for a massive residential development, complete with hotels, golf courses and other facilities, between Garrucha, Los Gallardos and Vera. Since the economic downturn, no-one realistically expects this development to come to fruition.

As things stand, 2018 is now the very earliest predicted date for completion of the Murcia-Almería section and there are those, not surprisingly, who question whether the Murcia-Almería AVE will ever run.

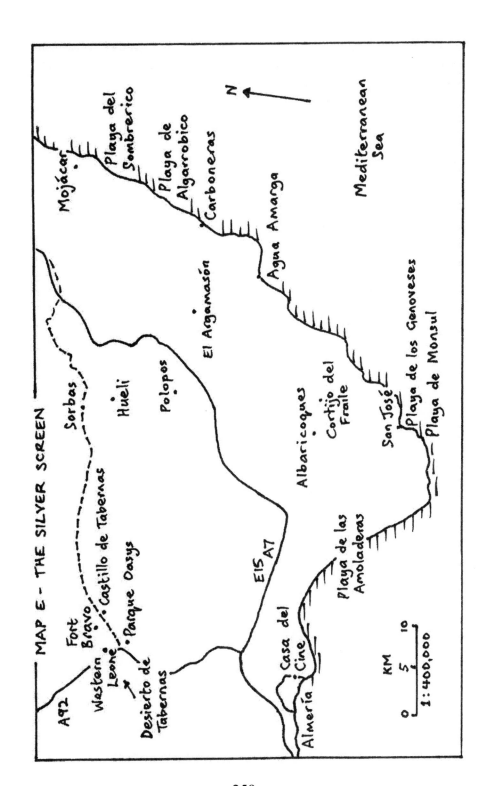

MAP E – THE SILVER SCREEN

28. Behind the silver screen

'Decidí pasar el resto de mis días en Almería. He viajado mucho, pero aquí encontré mi rincón en el mundo.' (I decided to spend my remaining days in Almería. I have travelled a lot, but here I found my corner in the world.)

(Eduardo Fajardo, actor)

Beginnings

In the mid-1950s the French film director André Cayatte had a good script and was looking for a desert that would fit the storyline of the film he wanted to make, *Oeil Pour Oeil (An Eye For An Eye)*. He had already been searching in Lebanon, Syria, Jordan and Egypt when someone in a Paris agency told him there was a desert in south-east Spain. His search ended when he found the dry *ramblas* of Alfaro, Indalecio, Benavides and Lanújar in the Desierto de Tabernas. *Oeil Pour Oeil*, released in 1957, was the first foreign film produced in Almería. Since then over 420 films have been at least partly shot in the province, along with innumerable commercials and music videos.

Incidentally, I won't say much in this chapter about films that are mentioned in detail elsewhere in this book, such as *Lawrence of Arabia* for which, see the chapters 'Coasting: Flatlands' and 'Coasting: Carboneras and Algarrobico'.

Sergio Leone

I'm scanning the Junta de Andalucia's 1:45,000 map of the Cabo de Gata-Níjar Parque Natural to find the Cortijada Higo Seco, a semi-abandoned hamlet where Sergio Leone shot a sequence for *The Good, The Bad and the Ugly*, released in 1966. The dates I give, incidentally, refer to the year when the film was released rather than when filming occurred.

Yes, there's the Cortijada Higo Seco, just north of the minor road that runs south-west from Fernán Pérez to Albaricoques. Leone had been in Spain searching for locations for *The Colossus Of Rhodes*, his directorial debut, in 1960. Although he didn't use Almería in that film, he remembered the area and came back to make his most famous films, the spaghetti western trilogy, between 1964 and 1966. The first was *For A Fistful Of Dollars* in 1964. Leone took as his model the film *Yojimbo*, about the samurai, by the Japanese director Akira Kurosawa. His adaptation was so faithful that Kurosawa sued him for plagiarism and negotiated a percentage of the global takings for Leone's film. The great (okay, that's just my opinion) Californian singer-songwriter Jackson Browne has this line in the track *Sergio Leone* on his 2002 album *The Naked Ride Home*: 'What he stole from Kurosawa he bequeathed to Peckinpah'. Almería gets a name-check too, not a common occurrence in the works of major songwriters. But yet again, I digress. Much of *For A Fistful Of Dollars* was shot in Madrid but Leone also used locations in the Tabernas desert and at Albaricoques.

Albaricoques is a dusty backwater of a village in the hinterland of the Natural Park. Approaching from the Almería direction, the road is flanked by scruffy and off-putting *plasticos*. You wouldn't have a reason for going there but for the fact that a few years ago Albaricoques woke up to the potential of its cinematographic connections. Now a larger than life black metal cowboy stands at the edge of the village and information panels show where Leone shot some of the distinctive sequences in *For A Few Dollars More*. The threshing circle in the higher part of the village, where the conclusion of the story is played out, has been neatly refurbished. Most of the original street names in the village, which was called Aguascalientes in the film, have gone, to be replaced by carved wooden ones commemorating the famous names who came here, so we have Avenida Sergio Leone, Calle Eduardo Fajardo and Calle Ennio Morricone, for example.

I called in for a coffee at the Hostal Restaurante Alba in the village in September 2012 and spent a while perusing its walls, a focal point of the spaghetti western legacy, which display all manner of memorabilia. Clint Eastwood, *el hombre sin nombre*, was even up there on the TV (a DVD, presumably) high in the corner, though the Spanish families enjoying their *menu del día* were paying him scant attention.

As I drove to and from Albaricoques my eyes swivelled in mild surprise at several posters advertising, in capital letters, SEX MUSEUM. Closer inspection revealed that this was the name of a band due to play a forthcoming gig in the area rather than the name of the latest visitor attraction in this out-of-the-way village.

Going east north-east from Albaricoques, it's just a couple of kilometres to the Cortijo de Doña Francisca. Here is a *noria* (a waterwheel that would have been operated by a donkey plodding in endless circles) that features in the first part of *The Good, The Bad And The Ugly*. Part of *Patton* was filmed here too, in 1970. Two kilometres further on, we are at the Cortijo del Fraile, referred to elsewhere (see the chapter 'Gold and murder') but also featured in many films, not least *For A Few Dollars More* and *The Good, The Bad And The Ugly*. If you want to know more about the locations used in *The Good, The Bad And The Ugly*, try this link http://www.youtube.com/watch?v=q2tKfBOv9Xs

At much the same time as Leone was making his westerns, the Spanish director Joaquín Luis Romero Marchent was shooting films such as *El Sabor De La Venganza* (1963) and *Antes Llega La Muerte* (1964) in the same locations, the Tabernas area and Cabo de Gata. These were referred to, including by Romero Marchent himself, as '*paella* westerns'.

Sets and settings

At the end of May 1965 Leone started work on *For A Few Dollars More*. For this a huge set was built on 40,000 square metres of land at Cortijo Genaro, at the side of what was then the main Almería-Murcia road, now the N-340a (long before the A7 motorway was built), not far from Tabernas. The most precise details of an authentic western town, both interior and exterior, were painstakingly reproduced. Subsequently many films used this studio but by the late 1970s it was in a very dilapidated state. In 1980 it was totally remodelled, rebranded as Mini-Hollywood, and opened to visitors. Upgrading has continued, although the central part of the set remains faithful to that seen in *For A Few Dollars More*. Swimming pools, a cactus garden and a zoo have been added more recently as the place has morphed again into Parque Oasys where, for a substantial entry fee, visitors can see scenes from the Wild West recreated. Every day there's a shoot-out with dramatic falls from the balcony, and can-can dancers strutting their stuff in The Yellow Rose saloon. On the 1:25,000 map (sheet 1030-III Tabernas) this is easy to find in square 550097, still labelled Decorado (which means 'set') Mini-Hollywood.

Also in the mid-60s, a deal was struck to build a totally new set. Sergio Leone had an initial interest, as did the producer Alberto Grimaldi who soon pulled out. Juan García, who was responsible for the construction of the set, persevered and although, at a cost of five million pesetas, it had a shaky start, it struggled through. In a second phase a Mexican settlement was built close to the original American one; this was a definite attraction for film-makers. The studio was initially referred to as the *poblado* (settlement) of Juan García, then became Texas Hollywood and survives today as Fort Bravo. The flier for Fort Bravo gives endless lists of the films and actors who once came this way and tempts visitors with horse-riding. It too is easy to find on the map, in square 551100 where it still masquerades under its former name as Decorado Texas Hollywood.

Yet another major set was built in 1968 for another Leone film, *Once Upon a Time in the West,* with Claudia Cardinale, Henry Fonda and Charles Bronson. It was made south-east of Haza Blanca, just off the Gergal road. This still exists under the name Western Leone (in square 549098) and is clearly visible from the Almería-Granada motorway. Adjacent to Western Leone, a magnificent fort was built in 1969 for the film *El Condor,* starring Lee Van Cleef. This remarkable set remained in good shape for a long time and was used by many more films, including 1977's *March or Die* with Gene Hackman and Catherine Deneuve. It continued in use beyond the turn of the millennium and, although it has since fallen into a ruinous state, the map still marks it as a Decorado Cinematográfico.

One of the best places to get a sense of the landscapes of the Desierto de Tabernas is from the ruins of the Castillo de Tabernas which overlook the town. You can park below and walk up for free to enjoy superb views. Amongst the remains of the castle an information board decorated with photos of Lee Van Cleef, Eli Wallach, Clint Eastwood and Gian María Volonté celebrates the *Trilogía del Dólar* and indicates where sequences were filmed. Not too far north from the castle, following a track that passes under the N-340a, you can walk for a kilometre or so to La Cabeza del Aguila, The Eagle's Head, a very distinctive conical hill with a rocky snout at the top. Here yet another information board recalls the time in 1965 when *El Ultimo Mohicano (The Last Of The Mohicans)* was filmed here.

Why did Almería province become so favoured by film-makers? It would be for some of the same reasons that many northern Europeans have chosen to make their homes here: over 300 sunny days per year and very little rain. In addition, there is a huge variety of scenery that provides 'dramatic value' and, back in the 1960s at least, cheap production costs. The peak time of the westerns coincided with the decline of the Rodalquilar gold mines, described elsewhere. This meant there were plenty of potential local extras, keen for film work. Those who were taken on recalled later that their film work was much easier, much more enjoyable and much better paid than mining had ever been.

Another fillip was given to the local film industry by the opening of Almería airport on 6th February 1968. Prior to that, film teams would fly into Málaga and have to make the gruelling journey of many hours on poor roads over to Almería. That wasn't the end of it either, because regular journeys also had to be made to get the footage that had already been shot to where it could be developed quickly, Madrid or even London, so that the director could see what was 'in the can'.

Once Almería had been discovered as a film location, the floodgates opened. Film-makers flocked to the area. The Tabernas desert was a definite draw, but the qualities of the coast were appreciated too. The San José area quickly became a favourite. Shoots were made there for *Shalako* in 1968, starring Sean Connery and Brigitte Bardot; *Hannie Caulder* in 1971 with Raquel Welch and Ernest Borgnine; and *Travels With My Aunt* in 1972, featuring Maggie Smith.

In the extensive valley behind Genoveses beach lie the Cortijo El Romeral and its outliers, owned then by Doña Francisca Díaz Torres. Here were filmed scenes from *For A Few Dollars More* and *Catlow*, Sam Wanamaker's 1971 western starring Yul Brynner and Leonard Nimoy. The latter said he was particularly pleased to be involved because it gave him a break from being Spock in *Star Trek*. The similarity of the scenery and the houses to those found along Mexico's border with the USA ensured that many westerns were shot here.

Further north, the stretch of coast around Playa del Sombrerico south of Mojácar, between Macenas and the Rambla del

Granatilla, as well as the Carboneras area, were used as locations in 1972 for a version of *Treasure Island* with Orson Welles playing Long John Silver.

Michelangelo Antonioni, Jack Nicholson and Cojo Juan

Michelangelo Antoniono's *The Passenger*, starring Jack Nicholson and Maria Schneider was, says Karin S. De Boer, the Dutch film producer to whom I am indebted for these details: "The film with the greatest end-shot ever made. The whole end sequence in one long shot, going through doors and windows...". The cast and crew members had to sign a contract which included a clause that they would never tell the secret of how this was done. I followed Karin's lead and went to YouTube, discovering not only, as you can now, how the camera apparently passed by magic through a *reja* (a metal window grille) but also that the bullring featured in this shot, despite supposedly being the one in Osuna, in Seville province, is actually the one in Vera.

Other parts of the film were shot in Sorbas. At one point the *casas colgantes*, the 'hanging houses' are prominent; in another brief shot Jack Nicholson sits in the small white square with the orange tree, just round the corner from the main square. Shooting also took place in front of what was then Bar Fatima, run by Cojo Juan ('Lame John', that would be, in English). Cojo Juan, who died in the early '80s, appears as an extra in the film and, Karin adds: "I know some Sorbeños who still remember and recognise their uncles or passed-away grandfathers playing in this film."

Antonioni and his crew used Bar Fatima as their base camp while they were shooting in Sorbas but they were behaving as film crews used to behave in the 1980s and after a couple of days *Cojo* Juan had had enough of them and threw them out. Says Karin: "So funny that the great award-winning Antonioni was sent away by this old man with one leg."

Karin again: "I like this story so much because I knew *Cojo* Juan when I was around 23 years old. I was staying for six months in Los Molinos, my first time in Spain. I always passed by his bar with my bike to have a glass of wine and a *tapa: jamón* with broad beans. He always used to give me a plastic bottle of his undrinkable house wine for the road back to Los Molinos."

Strawberry Fields

Richard Lester's *How I Won The War* became famous not for the film itself, which was a box office failure, but for the fact that it brought John Lennon to Almería for the six weeks that shooting occupied between mid-September and early November 1966. And in fact, John Lennon himself created less of a stir than the Rolls Royce that he brought with him. This somewhat avant-garde movie, set in North Africa during the Second World War, was Lennon's first and last film; he didn't like all the hanging around between takes. Also featuring Michael Crawford and Roy Kinnear, shooting took place in Carboneras, amongst the Cabo de Gata dunes, and in the famous trio of *ramblas*: Viciana, Lanújar and Alfaro, near Tabernas. However, none of these locations became as associated with the film as the Casa Romero Balmas, a large house in the north-eastern part of Almería city. Part way through filming, on October 9th, John Lennon moved from the Hotel Costasol to the Casa Romero Balmas, and it was here that he finished writing *Strawberry Fields Forever*.

After his spell in the area the Beatle left, having decided to take off for good his trademark wire-rimmed glasses, a move initially dictated by the script. He also had what would become an iconic song in his suitcase and a new impetus towards pacifism. By the end of the 1970s the Casa Romero Balmas had become forgotten and remained so until it was acquired by Almería council in 1991. Eventually, after major refurbishment, it reopened in January 2011 as the Casa del Cine Almería, a museum celebrating the story of film in Almería and the part this building played in it. It's been skilfully done, with intriguing use of holograms, video clips and imaginative exhibits.

David Lean's dedicated maniac

Back eastwards along the coast, at Carboneras, David Lean's right-hand man Eddie Fowlie, bought a plot of land and built the El Dorado Hotel. Fowlie, who was referred to by Lean as his 'dedicated maniac' and who died in 2011 at the age of 89, was a special effects expert, location scout and much more, who worked with Lean on all his major films but who was so captivated by eastern Almería that he decided to stay. The El Dorado was featured in *Nicholas and Alexandra* in 1971 and nowadays its walls continue to be home to a collection of film memorabilia.

English speakers tend to know only the English language movies, even if they were made by Italians, but many Spanish films have been made in eastern Almería too. Inland, what are now entirely unremarkable villages were once hives of film activity because of their likeness to Mexican villages. El Argamasón, a few kilometres inland from Carboneras, saw action in *Tepapa* (1969) and *Los Compañeros* (1970) and further inland still, Polopos (a quieter place would now be hard to find) was the location for *Tú perdonas, yo no...*(1967), *Cabalgando al infierno* (1970) and the series *Curro Jimenez* (1990). The information board recalling those days still stands, somewhat weathered, in front of the evocative white church in Polopos but the information it once provided has been long gone.

Music, ads, war and immigrants

The 1960s and 1970s were the peak decades for film-making in Almería. Since then the old sets have had to start reaching out for the tourist dollar - or euro. However, the film industry has not vanished. It has evolved, focussing now mostly on commercials, music videos and shorts. In 2003, members of the Manchester United squad: Beckham, Solskjaer, Neville, Giggs et al, found themselves at Fort Bravo, fighting a football duel against various Real Madrid stars for a Pepsi advert. How are the mighty fallen!

From the 1980s onwards, a string of musicians and bands, among them Chris Rea, Depeche Mode, Sting, Ocean Colour Scene, Jamiroquai and Kylie Minogue, came here to make videos. The foreign musician most associated with the area though is the late Joe Strummer of The Clash. In the 1980s he discovered Granada and became intrigued by Federico García Lorca, a fascination that led to the song *Spanish Bombs*. Strummer subsequently bought a house near San José and spent long periods on the Cabo de Gata coast. It was here that he made *Straight To Hell*, a comedy spoof on spaghetti westerns, in 1986. Directed by Alex Cox, it starred Strummer and featured Dennis Hopper, The Pogues and Elvis Costello. More recently, singer David Bisbal has stayed true to his Almerían roots by making several videos at the Playa de Monsúl and around Tabernas.

The days of the spaghetti and *paella* westerns may lie in the past but since the millennium, North European film-makers have found Almería. The Finnish film *Colorado Avenue* was shot here in

2007 and in 2009 the first movie of the Millenium Trilogy, based on the thriller *The Girl With The Dragon Tattoo* by Swedish writer Stieg Larsson, included a short sequence filmed in one of the Tabernas *ramblas*.

Using the Almerián landscape as a lookalike for Afghanistan, *Brothers*, by the Danish director Susan Bier, was made here in 2004. In similar vein, the Dutch production *Stella's Oorlog (Stella's War)* in 2009 used the landscapes of the Sorbas area for the exterior filming of a story about a Dutch army combat group in the Uruzgan area of Afghanistan. The main storyline concerns traumatised soldiers coming back from the war. Director Diederik Van Rooijen worked with producer Karin S. De Boer who, having had a house in a small village near Sorbas for twenty years, knew the area would provide exactly the landscape required and used the deserted village of Hueli and the Tabernas desert *ramblas*.

The issue of the immigrant experience has also raised its head in several films that have recently been at least partly shot in Almería. The French film-maker Tony Gatlif made *Exils (Exiles)* in 2004, the story of two young bohemians, Zano and Naima, who travel down through France and Spain, working casually as fruit-pickers en route, to Algeria, where Naima's parents come from. Scenes were filmed in Cabo de Gata and in the port of Almería. Also using Almerían backdrops, particularly at the end of his movie, Alain Gomis made *Andalucía* in 2007, a tale of a thirtyish Frenchman of Algerian descent trying to find himself and his place in contemporary France.

A Spanish take on the immigrant issue came from Chus Gutierrez in 2002 in *Poniente* (usually 'West' but here translated, with an obvious connection, as *Sunset*). This film is set almost entirely in the *invernaderos*, the industrial greenhouses, exploring the plight of immigrants and the inherent racism common in the intensive agricultural hothouses of Almería.

In *Naufragio (Shipwreck)* in 2010, Pedro Aguilera follows the saga of Robinson, a black African shipwrecked off the southern Spanish coast who manages, after a major struggle, to get ashore. Finding himself an anonymous exile and an illegal immigrant, he finds work in an *invernadero* but is troubled by interior voices; the plot continues from there.

The local film industry got an unexpected boost in late 2013 when, for a month, shooting took place in the province for the epic *Exodus*, directed by Sir Ridley Scott. The film, starring Christian Bale, Sir Ben Kingsley, Sigourney Weaver and Aaron Paul, explores the relationship between the prophet Moses and the Egyptian Pharaoh Ramses I. The main set, an impressive desert camp, was located in a valley near Pechina in the Sierra Alhamilla.

In total the shooting of the film brought €43 million to Spain, of which the Andalucía Film Commission estimates 60% came to Almería. This was made up of spending on hotels and restaurants, transport, property rentals, set building and materials, drivers, caterers, security guards, and locals who were employed as extras. The scale of this film suggested that all is not lost for the movie industry in Almería.

Where's Walt from?

A final quirk connected to the film world. In October 1940 the front cover of the Spanish film magazine *Primer Plano ('Opening Shot')* asked the question, alongside the grinning visage of the man in question: Was Walt Disney Born in Spain? This is a story that has raised its head many times. All the main sources actually indicate that Disney was born in Hermosa, Chicago, on 5th December 1901 but this has not put a definitive end to persistent rumours that hint otherwise.

Walt Disney, so the tale goes, was reputedly born illegitamately as José Guirao Zamora in Mojácar, the son of the village's doctor, José Guirao, and Isabel Zamora who, to avoid the taint of immorality that this situation would attract, emigrated to the USA. There, in Chicago, Isabel gave her son up for adoption by the Disney family. There was even, long ago, a road sign outside Mojácar announcing 'Birthplace of Walt Disney'.

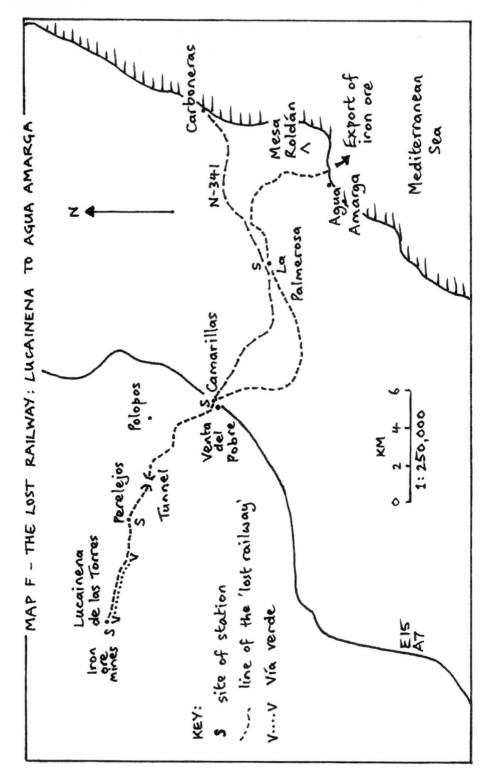

MAP F – THE LOST RAILWAY: LUCAINENA TO AGUA AMARGA

N

Iron
ore
mines
Lucainena
de las Torres

Perelejos

Polopos

Tunnel

Venta
del
Pobre

Canarillas

La
Palmerosa

N-341

Carboneras

Mesa
Roldán

Agua
Amarga

Export of
iron ore

Mediterranean
Sea

KM
0   2   4   6
1: 250,000

E15
A7

KEY:
S   site of station
---- line of the 'lost railway'
V....V Vía verde

29. Boom Town

'This was one of the more successful of the mining ventures in
Almería...'

(Don Gaunt)

The coming of the railway

In the late 19th century iron ore was found in the Sierra
Alhamilla mountains just west of the village of Lucainena de las
Torres. The Mining Company of the Sierra Alhamilla (CMSA), owned
50/50 by Ramon de la Sota and Eduardo Aznar, who had a strong
track record of successful operations in the Basque Country, was set
up to exploit this resource.

However, the only realistic way to transport bulky products
such as iron ore in the late 1800s was by water. Lucainena is only 30
km from the sea but the complex topography posed problems in
getting the ore to the coast. Various options, including an aerial
ropeway, were considered but rejected due to the challenging nature
of the landscape, with its hills and steep-sided *ramblas.* Finally a
railway was decided upon as the best method of transport. Agua
Amarga was selected as the coastal end of the route because its inlets
were sheltered from potential storms that might be brought by
easterly winds.

Plans for the route were finalised in March 1894. In
September of that year construction began and in October 63,000 oak
sleepers were ordered. This was a definite case of jumping the gun
because a Royal Order granting a concession for the construction of a
railway was required. This finally came in February 1895 and the
concession was given for 99 years. No time was lost and by March
1896 the works were completed.

The line was 35.5 km long, with an average downhill gradient
between Lucainena and Agua Amarga of 1.5% and a maximum of
2.5%. The outlay was 3,500,000 pesetas on the railway, 160,000
pesetas on the mineral storage works and 265,000 pesetas on the
loading facility. Two months after the works were completed, in May
1896, the first shipment of iron ore, which had already been
accumulating in the hoppers at the coast, was loaded into the
steamboat *Albia.*

Mining the iron ore at Lucainena

The Lucainena iron ore was initially worked on the mountain slopes high above the village by open-cast methods at the mines of El Visto, La Gracia and La Manuela. Soon, tunnels and galleries were needed to continue working the ore underground. Inside the mines, ore was taken in *esparto* baskets to the ore wagons, which were hauled by mules and men along narrow-gauge tracks. To move the ore from the mines, the Via Superior (High Road) was built along the mountainside to a small staging post called the Estación del Burrucho. From here it went down a huge inclined plane, the 604-metre long Plano Inclinado del Burrucho, still clearly visible today as a long straight line angling down the slopes above the village, to the railhead in Lucainena.

In 1900, as a result of newer exploitation lower down the mountain, a Lower Road was made, joining the Burrucho incline about halfway down its length. As the older, higher mines went out of production, the upper part of the inclined plane and the workings were abandoned. The ore wagons went down the lower part of the inclined plane to a hopper with a capacity of 1,500 tonnes near Lucainena station. Up to 1,000 tonnes of ore per day were passing through the station at this point. Photos from the time show the station took up a large area, with big engine sheds and sidings occupied by rows of full wagons.

By the early 1900s the mines were deeper and the ore-bearing rock was of lower quality so the ore needed to be concentrated somehow. However, there was also another issue. The ore was bound for England, where the steelworks of the time needed iron ore with a sulphur content of less than 0.05%. At Lucainena the ore contained more sulphur than this. The solution was to roast the ore to drive off the impurities in the form of sulphur dioxide. The key was to heat the ore sufficiently to drive off the impurities but not so much as to melt the iron.

To do this, a group of eight calcination ovens (kilns) was built on the mountainside. Their remains still form one of the most prominent reminders of the mining days. In 2011, to attract visitors and to highlight the wealth of the village's industrial archaeology, one of the kilns was fully restored, with a conical metal cap and a circular balcony from where you can look along the line of ovens and notice that their formerly crumbling walls have been capped with concrete to prevent further collapse.

Wagons brought the ore-bearing rock from the mines and tipped it into heaps near the kilns. The rock was hand-sorted and loaded into special side-opening wagons which went along narrow tracks to the top of the ovens. These were filled from the top with alternate layers of ore and charcoal. Each kiln could process 50 tonnes per day. After firing, they were unloaded from the bottom and the ore was again sorted by hand. The richest nuggets of ore were taken by wheelbarrow and loaded from small platforms into railway trucks. Close to the ovens, large spoil heaps of dark ferrous waste rock still remain.

Because the heat required was not great, local wood was used as the fuel. Two long ramps were made for the trucks to bring charcoal up to the ovens and wood to the mines, presumably to be used as pit-props. The trucks were raised by electric power generated at a diesel power station on the mountainside beyond the eight kilns. As the workings on the mountain expanded, more and more lines were built to service them. Eventually a network of narrow-gauge lines totalling 5 km in length, plus eight inclined planes, was used for moving the ore. Rather shockingly, there is barely a clue to any of this on the modern 1:25,000 map, sheet 1030-IV Lucainena de las Torres.

Boom town

The exploitation of iron ore and the presence of the railway changed life in Lucainena. As well as providing work, it supplied public and private electric light thanks to the surplus power from the mineral company's power station. The village reached its peak population of 2,455 in 1900. It had a telegraph office, a school, a court, a Guardia Civil post, a sub-post office, three banks and seven transport agencies, though I have yet to ascertain exactly what these agencies did. The mining company even installed a hospital in which, improbably, as well as scope for operations of some importance, there were four barbers, three tobacconists, two lemonade manufacturers, a watchmaker and a theatre called the 'Cervantes'.

From mineral line to *vía verde*

When production began in 1895, three engines were used on the Lucainena-Agua Amarga railway. Built by the British firm Nasmyth Wilson, they were of the 064 type, with large side water tanks and a coal bunker at the rear. They were called *Lucainena*, *Níjar* and *Agua Amarga*. In 1896 a further engine, of type 062T, from Hunslet, was delivered and began operating under the name *Carboneras*. They normally pulled 20 trucks, each of which weighed 2.9 tonnes empty and was loaded with up to 7.5 tonnes of ore. So with a full load an engine would be pulling about 200 tonnes.

In 1902 another 062 locomotive arrived. This had been built by Sharp-Stewart in Scotland and was initially called *Perelejos*, the name of the second station on the line, before being renamed *Rivas* after one of the company directors. This was the most powerful engine on the line and could pull 40 laden wagons. Because there was no turntable on the line the engines, painted in a distinctive red and black livery, always pointed in the same direction, towards Lucainena. In total, nine steam engines were used in connection with the iron-ore mining industry.

The wagons, over 150 of them altogether, were basic box shapes, taller than a standing man, painted red and with a CMSA emblem on the side. They opened at one end and, again due to the lack of a turntable, always had to face the same way for unloading at Agua Amarga. The gauge on the mining lines, in the loading bays, and on the main line was a consistent 750 mm, so the wagons could be used anywhere. In addition, the rolling stock included two passenger coaches; one was used for staff transport and the other, apparently, for going to bullfights. Quite where these bullfights were I have yet to discover; the notion of a passenger coach specifically used for going to bullfights sounds odd, so I wonder if it is true or whether it's a myth that has somehow crept into the history. Locals from Lucainena did, however, also use the trains to get to the beach at Agua Amarga, by all accounts.

The mineral railway closed in 1942, of which more shortly. In 2008 work began to renovate the first five kilometres of the old mineral line as a *vía verde*, a 'green way', for recreational use by walkers and cyclists and, according to Lucainena town hall, *patinadores* (skaters). No expense was spared: a major new bridge replaced the defunct one at Puente Rafaela. Wooden handrails, a well-designed picnic area with newly-planted shade trees, signage, and separate surfaces for boots and bikes were all installed, and by the start of 2010 the *vía verde* was open for business. At a launch in January 2010 a crowd of two to three hundred congregated to hear speeches, collect free tee-shirts and posters, eat a huge *paella* and consume free drinks. Between the speeches and the *paella*, quite a number actually walked the *vía verde* too.

The green way starts opposite a large solidly-square building, originally the offices of the mining company and now a primary school. Behind it, a clue to the past, stands a tall brick chimney. Across the road in an adjacent garden is a well-kept private chapel, the Ermita de Nuestra Señora del Rosario, built only a few years ago. A few yards along the *vía verde* is another small building that is also newer than you might imagine. It has the look of a refurbished station ticket office. No doubt that was the intention but it was newly built as an information point which is, however, more often closed than open. On one end wall, though, it has a fine ceramic tile tableau of the village and it's a good viewpoint up past the village and the 17th century church, the Iglesia de Nuestra Señora de Montesión to El Peñon, the rocky crag whose 827 m summit dominates the landscape.

As had the railway, the *vía verde* has a slight downhill incline, following the Rambla de Lucainena, a tributary of the Río Alías, in an easterly direction. By its nature this is easy walking, passing storage sheds built into the rock at one point, and its five kilometres can be covered on foot in little more than an hour. To the north lies a landscape of undulating esparto and thyme scrub, with scattered *cortijos*, and to the south, slopes leading up to the higher Alhamilla. Just before the end of the green way there's a view across to the remnants of a watermill near the Cortijo de las Tejas, with an aqueduct bringing the flow to a circular walled construction marked by a photogenic cluster of five palm trees. Close by is the Cortijo El Saltador. Run by Claudia Scholler, this centre offers courses, retreats, exhibitions, tranquillity and, occasionally, wonderful evenings of 'flamenco under the stars' in an unparalleled setting.

Keen to try to walk the whole length of the old line, I discovered that it is clearly shown on the excellent 1:45,000 scale Cabo de Gata-Níjar Parque Natural published by the Junta de

Andalucía. For a bit more local detail, the 1:25,000 sheets 1031-III Polopos, 1046-I Campohermoso and 1046-II Carboneras are also helpful.

At the end of the *vía verde* the surface debouches between neat stone walls onto a narrow tarmac road. This links Rambla Honda with Polopos and for the next seven kilometres eastwards the tarmac road more or less precisely uses the original line of the mineral railway. Optimistic signposts mark this as part of the *vía verde*, whilst in contrast the publicity literature points out that it isn't really a *vía verde* as there's the risk of traffic. In other words, it's a *vía* but it's not *verde*. In actual fact the road is not busy but obviously there is a conflict here with the stated intention that a medium-term objective is to extend the *vía verde* all the way to Agua Amarga. Quite how this might be resolved without enormous expense is a puzzle.

The original bridges were dismantled soon after the mineral line closed in 1942 and have not been rebuilt, so the narrow thread of tarmac that now links Rambla Honda and Polopos dips down to cross *ramblas* alongside the stark masonry piers of the old bridges near Cortijo los Olivillos and Cortijo la Boquera. Between these two locations the road passes through a roughly-hewn tunnel about 100 metres long, where you don't need much Spanish to understand the warning 'Tunel Sin Iluminación', in the lower slopes of Cerro del Molinillo. A few hundred metres before the tunnel, and north of the present road, lies the Cortijo de los Perelejos. This is the clue to the approximate whereabouts of the first of three intermediate stations on the former mineral line, though there are no obvious remains. The point of the intermediate stations was to allow trains going in opposite directions to pass and to provide watering points for the steam locomotives.

At the remains of a tall bridge called Puente Molinillo near Cortijo la Boquera, the modern road, after briefly taking to the *rambla*, veers off in a north-easterly direction towards the low-slung, quiet village of Polopos. At this point, by the Puente Molinillo, the mineral line veered away to the south-east.

30. The lost railway

'We must walk to see all this, and it is more difficult to walk along the railways...' (W.G.Hoskins)

Searching for the lost railway

It's the final day of May 2012. I've arranged to meet Frank Selkirk and Catherine Arthur to walk the next stretch of the old mineral line and we're incredibly lucky with the weather; it's cloudy after a run of blazing hot days. We're starting from the point where the Polopos road leaves the line of the old railway and tips down into the Rambla de Lucainena. While I'm waiting for them to arrive I clamber up on to the old line and walk out to where the arch of the bridge is missing. The neat masonry pillars are twenty metres high here and suddenly there's a gap, with no protection, where the top of the arch was removed long ago.

A movement catches my eye thirty metres away. A female ibex is coming up the slope followed by a kid. They cross the road and begin to climb the opposite slope, in no hurry. Then another doe with another kid. I hurriedly grab my camera, zoom in and take a few photos, average shots but clear enough to show the white patches around the tails of the adults. This is a highlight of the day before the walk has even started.

Once we set off, the old railway is obvious. Initially it runs, buttressed by revetments, high above the Rambla de Lucainena, before the occasional cutting varies the immediate scenery. The old bridge over the Barranco del Pino is down but easily by-passed. From near Cortijo Polopillos there's a more open view across to Polopos village. Catherine is pointing above it into the hills and telling me about a deserted village called Los Guardines that she once walked to. Later I find it on the map, about a kilometre and a half north-west of Polopos, obvious enough once you are searching for it, though I'd never heard mention of it before.

The old line is used as an unsurfaced road here, serving farm buildings. We chat about the notion of old railway lines being sacrosanct in that the line is not allowed to be obstructed. There seems to be no sense of that here. Industrial archaeology appears to have no value to the average *campesino* or the average local planner.

And the landscape is evolving; areas shown as *regadio* (irrigated land) on the most recent Polopos sheet (1031 – III) of the Mapa Topográfico Nacional de España, based on 1998 data, are now *invernaderos* (industrial greenhouses) and the old rail line across the scrubby area called La Camarilla is shown as a minor road on the same map.

As we head south, wind is swirling dust away from the active spoil heaps off to our left, where debris from the Sorbas Tunnel on the AVE high-speed train line is being dumped. In the final stretch to Venta del Pobre, the old line passes through low narrow cuttings choked with tall clumps of flowering esparto. Somewhere here was the second intermediate station, called Camarillas. I suspect it was little more than a siding and a platform, if that, and we are able to find no obvious clue to its whereabouts. However, a couple of hundred metres north-east, hard by the modern motorway, at Cortijo la Camarilla, the name recurs. As far as here, following the old line has made for an easy and worthwhile walk but things are about to change.

A tall gate blocks the old line where it enters the garden of a house close to the motorway and the adjacent parking area by the hotel at Venta del Pobre. These developments have totally obliterated all remains of the mineral line. We cross the motorway on the verge of the access roundabout then, behind a tyre dealership and various other industrial units, cast around for the continuation of the railway. We do manage to find the line, a clear trace, if you are looking for it, leading south south-east across almost level scrubby, stony ground. The level ground is a problem for amateur detectives like us. It means there are no cuttings or embankments to give definite clues. And, as we discover in a few hundred metres, that's not all.

The trace we are following fizzles out and ahead lie vast ploughed fields. Beyond them, on a low rise, partly buttressed by massive stones, is a huge *plastico*. We are in the land of agribusiness (there's a modern sign by the main road announcing it as Cortijo los Vergeles, though the map has the original hamlet here as Cortijada los Vergeles) and the traces of a narrow-gauge railway that came this way and was closed seventy years ago are bound to be hard to find. We guess the line might have angled across the lower ground to the

278

left of the rise, so we skirt bleak, bare fields on tracks of packed earth to reach that point.

Scouring the sloping scrubland to the northeast of the *invernadero* in search of the line, we put up a pair of stone curlews, a brief, enriching wildlife interlude in an agricultural desert. That said, there are lots of patches of disused ground among these industrial fields, so I suspect there is quite a population of stone curlews and other scrub specialists living here, well camouflaged until they are put to flight.

Within seconds we find what may have been the old line but again, soon, it peters out, so perhaps it wasn't. We know from the 1:45,000 map that we are in the right area and must be very close to the line though. Ahead lie ruined buildings on another low rise. There are actually two ruined farms but just the single name, Cortijo las Contraviejas. Signs here announce we are entering the Parque Natural. Once we reach the buildings we search the area just to the west of them, where the map indicates the railway once ran, perhaps a hundred metres away. We find no clues during our quick search. We've run out of time though. A call to Frank's mobile tells us that his wife Sheena is quartering the main road and wondering where we are. With some reluctance we abandon the search for another day, put our heads down into a surprisingly strong westerly wind, and flog out for a kilometre and a half back to the N341 and our chauffeuse, who takes us back to Venta del Pobre for coffee and *tostadas*.

Trying to pick up the trail

Four months later, towards the end of September and after a long hot summer, I'm back in the same area. It's depressing. The carelessly arrogant techniques of modern agribusiness have left huge fields of disc-harrowed and unprotected soil at the mercy of the frequent winds and sure enough, tan dust is being whipped up and blown away. What a crazy way to treat the soil in a semi-desert. Haven't any of them read *The Grapes of Wrath*? Someone is making short-term profits and that seems to be the over-riding consideration.

At the Cortijo de las Contraviesas, despite my best efforts, I can't find the line of the old *ferrocarril mineral*. I can see roughly where it is on the map, I have a compass pointing in the direction it should be going, but despite quartering the ground carefully, I can't find any definite sign of it. There are many more plastic greenhouses than the map shows though. If the professed ambition of eventually making the *vía verde* walkable, and enjoyable, all the way from Lucainena to Agua Amarga is ever to be realised, this stretch will present a major challenge.

I give up and try another tactic. I come in from the eastern side, checking backwards with the map, as it were. I do eventually pick up where the railway used to be but it proves dispiriting and it certainly doesn't make for good walking. Round about Collado de Albacete the old line took a virtually straight course east north-east for about four kilometres. You can follow it easily here but would you want to? What it amounts to is just a wide dirt track along the south side of a string of huge *invernaderos*. These huge greenhouses, worked largely by immigrant labour, have turned this into an industrial landscape. It's hardly inspirational.

In the distance I can see a few sub-Saharan Africans emerging from one of the *invernaderos*. At the beginning of his riveting book *Andalus*, Jason Webster, as part of his quest to investigate Spain's Moorish legacy, finds himself in a life-threatening situation with a young illegal immigrant from Morocco in just such an *invernadero*. As an aside, *Andalus*, and indeed Webster's other books about modern Spain, are well worth reading.

Finally, the track by the giant greenhouses makes a T-junction with another track that runs across it at right angles. The old railway can be made out continuing ahead as a low embankment overgrown with scrub. A few metres to the north, beyond a narrow belt of dusty, sickly-looking almond trees, is yet another greenhouse. The best tactic now is to walk south-east for 150 metres to the extensive tumbledown ruin of Cortijo El Jali. An arch and buttresses remain to show that this was almost certainly once an impressive building. Now it is crumbling to rubble among piles of green bottles, general detritus and scrappy banners of plastic flapping in the wind.

From El Jali a track goes north-east, staying parallel to the lost railway, to pass close to the Cortijo de los Balcanes. This house, deserted but still showing its elegant simplicity, its hefty wooden door locked against intruders, still has cast-iron balconies on the five upper-storey windows. As I approach, the current occupier, a kestrel, flies off quickly. Nearby is the long, low white-arched curve of an *aljibe* (water cistern). The imposing look of the place is slightly undermined by the roughly-painted warnings *PROHIBIDO EL PASO* and *PELIGRO* (DANGER) in large capitals splashed across the facade, but this was clearly once a house of some standing. The lost line can be seen just a few metres away but trying to follow it through the scrub and spines of the vegetation would be a trial and has no obvious merit; easier to continue along the parallel track for the next kilometre or so, to reach a minor road where things will soon begin to improve again. For all the insights into ancient and modern rural Almería that this stretch from Venta del Pobre furnishes, I can't, as will already be obvious, recommend it as a walk. Maybe when that pipe-dream full-length *vía verde* comes to pass, things will be different.

Back among the clues

Immediately on the right at the Agua Amarga/N-341 road junction, the line of the railway isn't obvious, but walk 100 metres towards Carboneras and you will see a 'Termino Municipal Carboneras' sign. Just beyond this on the right is another ruined *aljibe*. A few metres beyond this, and still only 30 metres from, and parallel to, the road, is a slightly raised embankment. This is the lost railway line.

It soon enters a low cutting just beyond which, on the right, is a flat area, its edge clearly shaped from the bedrock. Might this have been the last of the intermediate stations, La Palmerosa? As far as this, and for a little further, the old line is quite overgrown with esparto, but things soon get better. A higher embankment follows, with a loop of the old road visible just below and to the left. Halfway along the embankment the old bridge is down, an obstacle that can be by-passed by scrambling easily down on the right. Another cutting follows and none of them seem to show any signs of shot-holes, suggesting they were all cut by hand, a prodigious feat given that the whole line was built in just 18 months.

The old line soon opens out on to a modern gravelled track. Go to the right here; this is obvious on the ground. In 100 metres the line bears off again at a shallow angle to the right. An alternative is to stay on the gravelled track, which soon turns to tarmac. All three routes: the modern N-341, the old road, and the vanished railway, run parallel here and within a few metres of each other. The railway has the advantage of being in a low cutting which provides some cushioning against the traffic noise from the main road. If you choose to leave the railway here to follow the old road along this stretch, you can regain it where you see the 11 km marker on the N-341. The railway swings off to the right here, climbing slightly through further cuttings.

Beyond the cuttings, the flat, high profile of Mesa Roldán comes into view. Through this area, called Las Covaticas, the old line makes for easy and enjoyable walking. Apart from a few pylons and a wide track, crossed at an oblique angle, there are few modern intrusions. A couple of small bridges have gone and have to be by-passed; only a potential hazard if you are whizzing along on a mountain bike. By now the trend of the old line is south-eastwards, with Mesa Roldán looming ever larger directly ahead. At Cabeza de Cañada Blanca (which on older maps is given as Cabezada de Collada Blanca) there's a small wooden post with an arrow. You approach it from the back because it relates to a circular walk that loops north from Agua Amarga and it points off to the west, a red herring as far as our route is concerned. Should you be tempted though, it would take you past the venerable olive tree in the Rambla de las Viruegas (see the section *'Olivo Milenario'* in the chapter *'Acebuches* and olives').

From here the line begins to climb, steeply at first (well, steeply in railway terms, that is). As in several other places, on the left, a neat cave has been carved into a cutting here. One of them has an entrance area, two rooms and a recessed storage space. Were these just for storage of tools and maintenance materials or were they ever lived in?

The line continues to rise steadily until, after a long straight and almost at journey's end, it reaches Los Ventorrillos, where a house has been built partly across the line. The high ground here is known as the Meseta Alta. A large information board gives details of a circular walk of four or five kilometres, the Sendero: Vía Verde de Lucainena a Agua Amarga, as referred to in the previous paragraph. The name of this *sendero* is rather strange as this particular loop goes nowhere near Lucainena but that *is* what it's called.

Go to the left of the first couple of houses, then to the right of the next one and you will see the way out to the road. This is the road up from Agua Amarga and its construction cut straight through the remains of the old mineral line. Just across this road and a few metres to your right, you will see a low cutting that marks the final stretch of the line. Look ahead and you can see the remains of some of the buildings that marked the coastal terminus of the iron-ore operation.

The end of the line

The railway came across the high land of the Meseta Alta to the west side of the Barranco de Calareno, not named on most maps, at a height of 80 metres above sea level, and split into two. The main branch plunged straight ahead into the short but steep *barranco* (ravine) via a broad inclined plane that was 231 metres long and dropped 40 metres in height. Sets of six wagons worked on this incline, three going down laden with iron ore as three empty ones came back up. An information board by the ruins at the top of the inclined plane provides an explanation of what was happening here a century ago. This inclined plane also allows a relatively easy descent on foot to the lower complex. Chunks of dark brown iron-bearing rock and crushed piles and drifts of the same material contrast starkly with the pale cream of the local bedrock and buildings.

At the bottom of the inclined plane, lines branched out to feed the main hoppers, formed by building buttressed masonry walls, like dams, across the *barranco*. The extent to which the engineers used the natural shape of the *barranco* to create their storage capacity is very obvious from above and particularly from down below, among the towering stone remains of the buttressed walls.

There were no engines below the inclined plane, so if ore needed moving, it was done in wagons, each pushed by half a dozen men. At the base of the main hoppers, 600 mm gauge lines (narrower than everything on the main system) came out of access tunnels where wagons were filled and moved, by simple manpower, a distance of just over 150 metres along what seems to be a natural rocky shelf about 15 metres above sea level. Because these wagons were different from those on the main line, of narrower gauge and moved only by humans pushing them, they had handbrakes.

It is perfectly possible to find a way down on foot to the seaward side of these hoppers. Common sense is a good guide in telling you where to go and where not to, and there are lines through the vegetation made by the passage of previous inquisitive visitors. Do take care though; Don Gaunt tells me he nearly fell into a 15 metre-deep hole concealed by vegetation. From the base of the hoppers, looking at the access tunnels and the tilted angles and dramatic height of the stone walls, buttresses and towers, the sheer scale of the operation becomes very evident. The hoppers had a capacity of 45,000 tonnes. It was an impressive achievement.

As in many other locations, Spain's industrial archaeology quietly moulders into the ground, with just the odd information board to stand witness to past activities. For those interested, this allows a sense of genuine discovery with no entrance fee, no visitor centre interposed between the site and the enquiring eye, and no health and safety concerns preventing careful curiosity.

Once you are down, it's an easy walk out along the rock shelf to the site of the vanished cantilever bridge. The bridge itself, made of metal and built by Miravalles, extended 70 metres out to sea and 14 metres above sea level. It carried two lines out, and two back. At the end were chutes that discharged the iron ore directly into the ships' holds. The location of the landward end of the cantilever bridge is still obvious, with the squat rock stack that was used as a support for the bridge still visible a few metres offshore. A fuzzy black and white photo shows how far the open metal structure of the cantilever reached out over the sea.

Back at the Meseta Alta, a second branch from the main mineral line continued, virtually level, along the western rim of the Barranco de Calareno. This was used, if the main hoppers in the barranco were full, to fill auxiliary underground hoppers via small branch lines on its eastern side. It's a level walk along the old track-bed, part of which is obvious as a raised embankment leading out to a ruined building on a rocky headland. From here there are clear views down into the hoppers and to the site of the cantilever bridge. The western branch also connected with a different inclined plane. You can still stand at the top of this today and let your eye follow its line straight down to the eastern end of Agua Amarga's beach.

Supply ships came in as close as possible to Agua Amarga then unloaded onto smaller tenders that could reach the beach. In this way machinery, food and other supplies for the miners were brought up via the inclined plane from Agua Amarga's beach to the mineral line and so were taken to Lucainena.

At its height, the whole operation was spectacularly successful. Between 1896 and 1931 the railway carried a total of 3,795,569 tonnes of ore. However, by the second decade of the 20th century, some of the same factors: a collapse of market prices and rising salaries, that were affecting the gold mines at Rodalquilar were also upsetting the iron industry. Competition from iron mines in North Africa, where labour was cheaper, exacerbated the crisis. In 1919 and 1920 the storage silos at Agua Amarga were overflowing with a mineral for which there was no market. Operation of the railway was suspended and although it opened again under the auspices of its workforce during the Civil War, there was minimal activity. Rail transport began on a bigger scale again briefly in 1939 but time was running out and in 1942 the final consignment was loaded onto the single-funnelled steamboat *Bartolo*. Not long afterwards the rails and bridges were dismantled and, together with the rolling stock, taken off to Almería for sale to other railways or for scrap. The locomotive *Carboneras*, for example, was bought by the Hulleras de Riosa Society for use in the coal mines of Asturias in northern Spain.

Agua Amarga now makes its way in the world mainly as a small and attractive holiday resort (see the chapter 'Coasting: A coral reef in the sky'). I suspect most of its visitors, despite a few visual clues, have no idea of the thriving industrial activity that went on here a century ago. For three quarters of the year it's a very quiet place and this is when it's best to go and explore the remains of the old iron ore line. And so, for the moment at least, our story ends.

Afterword

There are a lot of facts in this book. In some cases they are part of an ongoing story such as the building of the AVE high-speed railway or the stalled white elephant that is the Algorrobico hotel. I have tried hard to ensure that the details are as accurate and up-to-date as possible but things inevitably move on and there may well have been changes even as this book is produced and distributed.

In our study is a raised relief map of Andalucía. The Sierra Nevada rises like a wall. I think they have the vertical scale somewhat exaggerated. The smaller mountain ranges: Gádor, Filabres, María, Cabrera, occupy only tiny patches of Andalucía. As for Almería province, on a global scale it barely registers and yet I realise there are so many parts of even this limited area about which I'm saying nothing.

The more you know, the more you realise you don't know. One pair of feet and one head can only go to so many places. Or, perhaps more realistically, can only fit so much into one book. There's so much more to discover that, if this book finds a receptive audience, perhaps I will work towards a follow-up.

I would be very happy to receive constructive comments, corrections and suggestions for further exploration by email at kevindborman@googlemail.com and if you missed it in the introduction, a reminder that you can email me at this address and I'll send you a link to a web album of photos that illustrate many of the places and features described here.

Kevin Borman
Sorbas
January 2014

About the author

Kevin Borman was born on the Lincolnshire coast in 1950. He moved to Sheffield in 1968 and from 1972 until 2004 taught Geography in comprehensive schools there. In the sixth form in 1967 he ran 10.1 seconds for the 100 yards. In 1989 he ran 'The Fellsman' in the Yorkshire Dales (61 miles and 11,000' of climb) in 16 hours. Now he just walks about a bit.

Between 1989 and 2004 he also worked as a writer, photographer, reviewer and news editor for *High* magazine. He has written several books and contributed well over 300 articles to a wide range of magazines and journals. In 2003 he received an Award for Excellence for his regular *Walking World* column in *High* from the Outdoor Writers' Guild. His interests include natural history, hillwalking, travel, music, writing, dark chocolate and the occasional glass of red wine. He has been exploring Almería since buying a house there with his wife Troy Roberts in 2005.

Other books by Kevin Borman

Poetry
Lovemapping (Rivelin Press 1974)
Dust & Jungle (Rivelin Press 1976)
Seasons in a Raw Landscape (Rivelin Press 1982)
Inside The New Map (Redbeck Press 1999)
Blue Is Rare (Redbeck Press 2005)

Guidebooks
Peak District Short Walks (Jarrold 2001)
The Derwent Valley Heritage Way (Jarrold 2003)
Peak District Walks: Pathfinder Guide (joint author, Jarrold 2003)

And contributions to these anthologies
Perspectives on Landscape (Arts Council of Great Britain 1978)
Speak to the Hills (Aberdeen University Press 1985)
Orogenic Zones (Bretton Hall 1994)
Kinder Scout, Portrait of a Mountain (Derbyshire County Council 2002)

Acknowledgements

"If you don't know where you are, you don't know who you are."
(Wendell Berry)

My sources for this book have been a mixture of personal experience and exploration, many conversations, assorted verbal leads, and a wealth of written material. One of my intentions has been to make available, in English, information about Almería which has previously only been available in Spanish, often in relatively obscure sources. All background reading is listed in the bibliography.

I have a lot of people to thank, all of whom, as Wendell Berry suggests above, in the context of Almería, know where they are and who they are. Authors always wax eloquent about how wonderful their editor is. I do likewise but only because I really mean it; Helen Evans, a huge thank you, not only for judicious and skilled editing and for many intriguing queries and links that kept me on my toes, but also for introducing me to the Atlas de Almería and for the rescue described in the chapter 'Río de Aguas: From the source...'.

Barbara Hart Appel and Harvey 'Hogan' Appel provided intriguing snippets about Los Molinos; Tim Bernhardt kindly clarified my occasional misapprehensions about agaves; Karin S. de Boer was a source of fascinating tales about films in the area; many days in the field with both Pete Brown and Dave Elliott-Binns significantly improved my understanding of local birds; Jesús Contreras Torre told me about Dupont's larks and white-headed ducks; Don Gaunt helped with all manner of details about the Lucainena-Agua Amarga mineral line; Hanna Geertsema took a lot of trouble to tell me at length about the old days in Los Molinos; Andy and Nadine Highfield put me straight on spur-thighed tortoises; Roy 'Alex' Alexander was a fine teacher who showed me the local wild flowers; Thomas Neukirch clued me in on the Vireugas *olivo* and a vibrant new way of seeing the local area; and Lindy Walsh has been a constant help these last years with information about the gypsum karst, the caves and cavers, local characters and much more besides.

Francisco Espinoza Crespo and his wife, the late Inés Reolid Martínez, welcomed Troy and I warmly as neighbours and shared their extensive local knowledge. As for Andrés Pérez Pérez and Ana María Rodríguez Agüero, their enthusiasm for, and sheer depth of knowledge of, the local area has been a key factor in my wanting to write this book.

I have checked many sections of the text with Spanish and English experts. In addition, I'm enormously grateful to my eagle-eyed proofreaders: Pete Adeline, Chris Borman and Carol Jepson checked the entire book in forensic detail and gave me enormous help; Cathy Borman, John Driskell and Dave Pearce did likewise for substantial sections of the text. If errors remain, though hopefully they will be few, they are my responsibility alone.

Christine Morgan Douglas, Tony Redston of Mellow Mountain Press and my old fellrunning mate Tim Mackey, a professional design-and-print man, all helped point me in the right direction during the final stages. Gary Lincoln's enviable design skills gave me a cover with which I am delighted.

Those above, strictly speaking, should appear in this paragraph too. In addition to them for, variously, entertaining and relevant conversation, being quirky neighbours, useful leads, clarification, answers to obscure requests, good company on walks, and general support and enthusiasm, my thanks to: Catherine Arthur, Linda Church, Jackie Bragg, Charlie Brown, Margaret Brown, Carmen and Juan, Shirley Cook, Harvey and Kathy Defriend, Margaret Dyson, Marcus Field, Terry Gifford, Enrique González Pérez, Pepe Guinea, Lynne Hall, Phil Hardy, Joe Evans, Susie James, Jon and Hazel Large, Maarten van Lier, Gabrielle Lincoln, Pete and Mary Loyndes, Archie Luckett, Rae Luckett, Sue Macdonald, Kath Menghetti, Bego de Miguel, Finn Campbell-Notman, Susanna Notman, Dan Osborn, Paco the goatman, Juan Ramos Peña, Robert Purland, Emma Randle, Alastair Reid, Ian Roberts, Luke Roberts, Francisco Javier Rodríguez Arias, Eduardo Sanchez, Calin Sandru, Claudia Scholler, Frank and Sheena Selkirk, Jacki Smart, Pete Thom, Alec and Margaret Thompson, Jyoti Tyler, 'Ponytail' John Wallis, Julie Widdowson and Andrew Wilson, with apologies to anyone I have inadvertently forgotten. In the text, incidentally, I have altered the names of some of our close neighbours in the interests of privacy.

On a local note, the Amigos de Sorbas is a vibrant organisation intent on highlighting the culture and history of the Sorbas area. They do a fantastic job in all sorts of ways, not least via their bi-annual journal *El Afa*. It is an astonishingly professional production, behind which is a team including the pivotal Ana María Rodriguez Agüero, Andrés Pérez Pérez and Pedro Soler Valero. *El Afa* is an ongoing cultural document that has, twice a year for almost a decade and a half, come out of a town numbering just a few thousand people. The 'Especial Número 20' in 2009, commemorating the twentieth anniversary of the Paraje Natural Karst en Yesos de Sorbas, was superb; 134 pages of the highest quality. Past copies of *El Afa* are available from the Centro de Visitantes in Sorbas at just €3 each. If you read some Spanish and have an interest in the area, check it out and support the *Amigos*.

In the spirit of community endeavour, *El Afa* allows the use of its articles, provided that the source is acknowledged. Consequently, my sincere thanks to all those Spanish authors, including Francisco José Contreras, Isa García Mañas, Juan García Sanchez, Juan Salvador López Galán, Diego Molina Simón, Juan Antonio Muñoz, Domingo Ortiz, Andrés Pérez Pérez, Rosa María Piqueras Valls, Juan Ramos Peña and Ana María Rodríguez Agüero, whose work in *El Afa* has helped me to understand many aspects of the local area.

In a wider context many people have led me to my fascination with landscapes and the way that human lives interact with them, so please indulge me for a paragraph. This fascination has been evolving for over half a century so it would be impossible for me to list all those who are implicated in the way I record and celebrate it. I have drawn inspiration from a wide sprinkling of writers, poets and walkers, mapmakers and artists, and un-pin-downable others. Among those who have been particularly important to me, and sooner rather than later I'll realise I have omitted some crucial names, are Edward Abbey, Kenneth Allsop, Wendell Berry, Hamish Brown, Sue Clifford, Mark Cocker, David Craig, Nick Crane, Roger Deakin, Tim Dee, Annie Dillard, Monty Don, Chris Drury, Bob Dylan, Andy Goldsworthy, Andrew Greig, John Hillaby, W.G. Hoskins, Kathleen Jamie, Angela King, Paul Kingsnorth, Barbara Kingsolver, Aldo Leopold, William Least Heat-Moon, Laurie Lee, Richard Long, Barry Lopez, John McPhee, Richard Mabey, Robert Macfarlane, Peter Mathiessen, Kathleen Dean Moore, Adam Nicolson, Jim Perrin, Jonathan Raban, Tim Robinson, Christopher Somerville, Gary Snyder and Kenneth White. If my book has just a few echoes, but not too many, of some of these people then I will be happy.

Finally, for all manner of support, for not complaining too much when I left her to do more than her share of the housework and particularly the gardening, and for being my partner in our continuing discovery of eastern Almería, my deep thanks go to Troy Roberts. To Troy and to the friends, both Spanish and *extranjeros*, who have helped me come to know part at least of this hidden corner of Andalucía, I dedicate this book.

Bibliography
The following list gives background reading and sources consulted:

Ajicara, N° 2 (dated Octubre 2009)

Allen, Betty Molesworth, *A Selection of Wildflowers of Southern Spain* (Fuengirola 1993)

Anadón, José Daniel, Andrés Giménez, Irene Pérez and Alicia Montesinos, *La Tortuga Mora en el Sureste Ibérico: Una Especie Amenazada*, El Afa N° 9 (Sorbas 2004)

Anderson, Miles, *The World Encyclopedia of Cacti and Succulents* (London 1998)

Balasch, Enric and Yolanda Ruiz, *Diccionario de Plantas Curativas de la Península Ibérica* (Madrid, no date)

Barkham, Patrick, *The Butterfly Isles* (London 2010)

Bernhardt, Tim, *Pita-Escuela del Río Aguas*, El Afa N° 28 (Sorbas 2013)

Berry, Wendell, *The Gift of Good Land* (Berkeley 1982)

Blamey, Marjorie and Christopher Grey-Wilson, *Wild Flowers of the Mediterranean* (London 2005)

Boloix, Igor, *1000 Plantas Medicinales, Aromáticas y Culinarias* (Madrid 1999)

Borman, Kevin, *A close call for the White-headed Duck*, Birds of Andalucía Vol 2, Issue 2 (Ronda 2013)

Borman, Kevin, *Birds on Spanish Maps*, Birds of Andalucía Vol 3, Issue 1 (Ronda 2014)

Boyd, Alastair, *The Sierras of the South* (London 1992)

Brenan, Gerald, *South From Granada*, (London 1957)

Brown, Pete, *A Patch In The Sun,* Birds of Andalucía Vol 2 Issue 2 (Ronda 2013)

Cavanagh, Lorraine, *Mediterranean Garden Plants* (Nerja, 2005)

Chinery, Michael, *Garden Wildlife of Britain & Europe* (London 2001)

Clifford, Sue and Angela King, *England In Particular* (London 2006)

Cocker, Mark and Richard Mabey, *Birds Britannica* (London 2005)

Contreras, Francisco José, *El Karst en Yesos en la economía de Sorbas*, El Afa N° 20 (Sorbas 2009)

Costa Pérez, Juan Carlos, *Restauración de Zonas Incendiadas en Andalucía (Manuales de Restauración Forestal N° 8)* (Andalucía, no date)

Crane, Nicholas, *Two Degrees West* (London 1999)

Davey, Vic, *Esparto Grass - Special & Historic*, Almeria Living N° 09 (Zurgena 2013)

De Stroumillo, Elisabeth, *Southern Spain* (London 1986)

Deakin, Roger, *Waterlog: A Swimmer's Journey* (London 1999)

Dillard, Annie, *Pilgrim at Tinker Creek* (London 1976)

Ellingham, Mark and John Fisher, *The Rough Guide To Spain* (Tenth Edition, London 2002)

Elliott, Tim, *Spain by the Horns* (Chichester 2007)

Ellis, Jerry, *Walking The Trail* (New York 1991)

Finlayson, Clive and David Tomlinson, *Birds of Iberia* (Fuengirola 2003)

Flores, Clemente, *No me toquéis las cabras (II parte)*, Actualidad Almanzora N° 367, (Feb 2010)

Fowlie, Eddie and Richard Torné, *David Lean's Dedicated Maniac: Memoirs Of A Film Specialist* (2010)

García, Ernest and Andrew Paterson, *Where to Watch Birds in Southern Spain* (London 1994)

García Lorca, Andrés (Director), *Atlas Geográfico de la Provincia de Almería* (Almeria, no date given but approx 2010)

García Mañas, Isa, *La Vida en El Marchalico de las Viñicas*, El Afa N° 25 (Sorbas 2012)

García Sánchez, Juan, *Cómo Pasa El Tiempo*, El Afa N° 20 (Sorbas 2009)

Garvey, Geoff and Mark Ellingham, *The Rough Guide to Andalucía* (London 2003)

Gibbings, Robert, *Coming Down The Wye* (London 1942)

Gil Albarracín, Antonio, *A Guide to the Cabo de Gata-Níjar Natural Park* (Almería - Barcelona 1999)

Gomez Martinez, José Antonio and José Vicente Coves Navarro, *Trenes, Cables y Minas de Almería* (Almería 1994)

Goytisolo, Juan, *Campos de Níjar* (Almería 2010; originally published in 1960)

Greeves, Tom, *The Parish Boundary* (London 1987)

Greig, Andrew, *Getting Higher* (Edinburgh 2011)

Hayman, Peter & Rob Hume, *Bird* (London 2007)

Jacobs, Michael, *Andalucía* (London 1998)

Least Heat-Moon, William, *Blue Highways* (London 1983)

Lopez, Barry, *Natural History: An Annotated Booklist* in *The Picador Nature Reader* edited by Daniel Halpern and Dan Frank (New Jersey 1996)

López Galán, Juan Salvador, *Las eras de Almería: comarca de Los Filabres y Sierra Alhamilla*, El Afa N° 26 (Sorbas 2012)

McEwan, Ian, *Black Dogs* (London 1992)

Mabey, Richard, *The Common Ground* (London 1980)

Macfarlane, Robert, *The Wild Places* (London 2007)

Map, *Cabo de Gata-Níjar Parque Natural,* 1:50,000 (Granollers 2001)

Map, *Parque Natural Cabo de Gata-Níjar*, 1:45,000 (Sevilla 2005)

Mapa Topográfico Nacional de España, 1:25,000, many sheets, but particularly *1031-I Sorbas* and *1031-II Turre* (Madrid, various dates)

Mather, A.E., J.M. Martin, A.M.Harvey and J.C. Braga, *A Field Guide to the Neogene Sedimentary Basins of the Almeria Province, South East Spain* (Oxford 2001)

Miralles García, Jose Manuel, *Espacios Naturales Almerienses* (Almería 1990)

Molina Simón, Diego, *La Parroquia de Gafarillos, los lugares del sureste del municipio*, El Afa N° 4 (Sorbas 2002).

Moore, Kathleen Dean, *Riverwalking: Reflections on Moving Water*, (New York 1995)

Morales, Marga, *Guide to the Nature Reserve Cabo de Gata Níjar* (Sant Lluís, Menoría 2001)

Moran, Joe, *On Roads - A Hidden History* (London 2009)

Morton, H.V, *In Search of England* (London 1927)

Mueller, Tom, *Extra Virginity: The Sublime and Scandalous World of Olive Oil* (New York 2012)

Muñoz, Juan Antonio, *Palomares tradicionales en la comarca de Filabres Alhamilla*, El Afa N° 23 (Sorbas 2011)

Muñoz-Espadas, María-Jesús, Rosario Lunar and Jesús Martínez-Frías, *The garnet placer deposit from S E Spain: industrial recovery and geochemical features.* (Online, found by googling 'garnets in Almería')

Neukirch, Thomas, with Marcus Field, *paintings 2006-2009* (Almería 2009)

Newspapers and journals: *Actualidad Almanzora, Costa Almería News, Diario de Almería, El Pais, Heraldo de Madrid, La Voz de Almería, The Almería Focus,* various dates

Nuevo Levante N° 48 (dated Julio 2010)

Ortiz, Domingo, *A Propósito de los Incendios Forestales*, El Afa N° 23 (Sorbas 2011). (This article was originally published in *Vera Al Día* on 18th July 2009)

Parker, Mike, *Map Addict* (London 2009)

Peña, Juan Ramos, *Artistas de obra en piedra vista*, El Afa N° 26 (Sorbas 2012)

Pérez Pérez, Andrés, *El Puente de la Mora*, El Afa N° 1 (Sorbas 2000)

Perrin, Jim, *River Map* (Llandysul 2001)

Piqueras Valls, Rosa María, *Apeo y repartimiento de la villa de Sorbas tras la expulsión de los moriscos*, El Afa N° 1 (Sorbas 2000)

Polunin, Oleg and Anthony Huxley, *Flowers of the Mediterranean* (London 1978)

Richardson, Paul, *Our Lady of the Sewers* (London 1998)

Robinson, Tim, *Connemara - The Last Pool of Darkness* (London 2009)

Rodríguez Agüero, Ana María, *Sorbas también es tierra de cine*, El Afa N° 19 (Sorbas 2009)

Rodríguez Agüero, Ana María, *Vida cotidiana en el Río de Aguas y los Yesares antes de 1989*, El Afa N° 20 (Sorbas 2009)

Rodríguez Agüero, Ana María and Andrés Pérez Pérez, *Caminos del Río de Aguas y Los Yesares*, El Afa N° 20 (Sorbas 2009)

Rodriguez Agüero, Ana María and Andrés Pérez Pérez, *Neorrurales en Los Molinos del Río de Aguas*, El Afa N° 20 (Sorbas 2009)

Rodriguez Agüero, Ana María and Andrés Pérez Pérez, *Ecoaldea de Los Molinos*, El Afa N° 20 (Sorbas 2009)

Rodriguez Agüero, Ana María and Andrés Pérez Pérez, *Vivencias de un molinero, Rafael Llorente Galera*, El Afa N° 20 (Sorbas 2009)

Ruiz García, Alfonso (Coordinador), *Guías de Almería, Territorio, Cultura y Arte: El Litoral Mediterráneo* (2ª edición, El Ejido 2006)

Ruiz García, Alfonso (Coordinador), *Guías de Almería, Territorio, Cultura y Arte: Naturaleza Almeriense: Espacios del Litoral* (El Ejido 2010)

Ruiz García, Alfonso (Coordinador), *Guías de Almería, Territorio, Cultura y Arte: Cine* (Roquetas de Mar 2011)

Sociedad de Amigos de Sorbas, *Conserva Tu Patrimonio, Las Fotos No Mienten*, El Afa, N° 5 (Sorbas 2002)

Snyder, Gary, *Back on the Fire: Essays* (Emeryville 2007)

Steinbeck, John, *The Grapes of Wrath* (New York 1939)

Stevenson, Robert Louis, *Travels with a Donkey* (London 1879)

Stewart, Chris, *The Almond Blossom Appreciation Society* (London 2006)

Tapia Garrido, J.A., *Historia General de Almería y su provincia* (Almeria 1990).

Tolman, Tom and Richard Lewington, *Collins Butterfly Guide* (London 2008)

Trutter, Marion, ed., *Culinaria Spain* (Königswinter 2004)

Villalobos Megía, Miguel, ed., *Geology of the Arid Zone of Almería* (Andalucia 2003)

Villalobos Megía, Miguel and Ana B. Pérez Muñoz, *Geodiversity and Geological Heritage of Andalusia* (Junta de Andalucía, no date)

Walker, Sandy, *Campo - A Guide to the Spanish Countryside* (Fuengirola 2005)

Walsh, Lindy, *Neo-rurales: Los Nuevos Repobladores*, El Afa N° 7 (Sorbas 2003)

Webster, Jason, *Andalus* (London 2004)

Whitwell, Ben, *Los Molinos, Village of Mills* (Sorbas 2004)

Websites:

The following websites, though this is by no means an exhaustive list, may be helpful to anyone looking for more information about some of the topics and places mentioned in this book:

www.amigosdesorbas.com The website of the 'Friends of Sorbas', including a link to the journal *El Afa*.

www.cabodegata.net The website of the Asociacion de Amigos del Parque Natural Cabo de Gata-Níjar, supporters and conservationists of the Natural Park.

www.costaalmeriatours A small family-run company offering bespoke tours and trips, concentrating on local 'hidden secrets' (English/Spanish speaking).

www.cuevasdesorbas.com The Sorbas Caves, offering underground visits in the Gypsum Karst area.

www.dgseturismoactivo.com Javi Rodriguez's small sustainable tourism and development company, including guided walks (Spanish speaking).

www.elsaltador.com Claudia Scholler's unique and inviting centre near Lucainena.

www.faydon.com Don Gaunt's site, very good on Almeria's old railways and industrial archaeology.

www.ign.es The site to visit to find out about Spanish maps.

www.indalodeoz.com Jesus Contreras's site, offering sustainable tourism, particularly relating to birds, wildlife and geography (Spanish/English speaking).

www.pitaescuela.org Timbe's site about Europe's only Agave School, based in Los Molinos.

www.sunseed.org.uk Giving much information about 'low impact living in southern Spain'.

www.unique-almeria.com A quirky guide to many aspects of 'Spain's best-kept secret'.

www.urra-enterprises.com The website for the university field centre and assocated cortijo at Urrá.

Index to selected people, places and subjects

watermills 86, 172-73, 178-83, 186, 196, 209, 221, 247, 275
Weaver, Sigourney 269
Webster, Jason 204, 280
Welch, Raquel 264
Welles, Orson 265
Western Leone 263
Whillans, Don 183
white-headed duck 23-25
wild boar 74, 77, 142, 182
wild stock 38, 185
wildcat 81
wildfires 92, 96-97, 138-41, 144-47, 154, 235
Wilson, Andrew 96

Winstone, Ray 56
wolves 49, 87-88, 243

Xarqui, Juan 91

yellow-legged gull 34
Yesares, Cortijo de los 209, 250, 252
Yesares, Los, plateau (see also gypsum) 250-51

Zapatero, José Luis Rodríguez 257
Zurgena 152, 154

Lightning Source UK Ltd.
Milton Keynes UK
UKOW03f0449170414

230128UK00002B/36/P